High Praise for

LEVITATING THE PENTAGON AND OTHER UPLIFTING STORIES

by Nancy Kurshan

NANCY KURSHAN'S MEMOIR will inspire you to do more and to do it better. To take risks, and also to reflect. To assume responsibility for what is being done in our names. To act up and speak out in these treacherous and urgent times. Buy or borrow or *Steal this Book*!
BERNARDINE DOHRN, Founder, The Children and Family Justice Center, School of Law, Northwestern University

IN HER CANDID, unvarnished and revealing memoir, Nancy Kurshan tells us what it was like to be an idealist of the '60s whose political activism shunned the drift into the mainstream and careerism. Beginning with the hijinks of the Yippies, as the partner of Jerry Rubin, she navigates the trial of the Chicago 7 and then, post Rubin, the movements against the Vietnam War and racism, a personal dawning of feminism, the radical call of the Weather Underground Organization and finally, with her husband, the fight for prison reform. It's a tale of sacrifice and squabbles, fulfillments and failures, and at the end the satisfaction of a lifetime of combating injustice.
JOHN DARNTON, Pulitzer Prize-winning journalist; author, *Neanderthal*

THIS BOOK IS a blueprint for today's activists, and a reminder that a life guided by conscience and action is a life well led. Just do it! READ THIS BOOK!
CLARA BINGHAM, author, *The Movement* and *Witness to the Revolution*

NANCY KURSHAN BELONGS in the pantheon of the American left along with Emma Goldman and Mother Jones. She is wrong when she writes, "I am not exceptional." You are exceptional, Nancy; your memoir is also exceptional and outstanding. . . . When I'm asked to recommend a book about the American left over the past 60 or so years, I will suggest readers turn to *Levitating the Pentagon*.
JONAH RASKIN, *The Rag Blog*

WITH PASSION, INSIGHT, and humor, Nancy's narrative invites us to think critically about the successes and failures of her generation's aspirations for liberation. Her feminist sensibility infuses her understanding of both systemic oppression as well as its reproduction within activist struggles for equality. For those who share her history as well as others for whom this is an introduction into American left political culture, this memoir is an essential and special treat.
NANCY CARO HOLLANDER, author, *Uprooted Minds: A Social Psychoanalysis for Precarious Times*

IF THE IDEA of levitating the Pentagon sounds absurd now, it wasn't nearly as insane as the mass slaughter of peasants in Vietnam, the generals inside that haunted building were orchestrating. Absurdity was, and remains, the weapon of choice against madness. Kurshan's provocative and spirited book is a reflection of how she has lived her radical life in the Sixties and ever since: humane, fearless and, even after all these perilous years, still charged with a luminous faith that a more just future is possible.

JEFFREY ST. CLAIR, editor *CounterPunch*; author, *Born Under a Bad Sky*

WHEN WE FIGHT, we win, at least some of the time. Other times, it seems like we might have lost—until we look back and realize that our actions were part of a crescendo that ultimately sparked change. Through an extraordinary combination of humor, reflection and political analysis, *Levitating the Pentagon* shows us both. Nancy Kurshan details the many David-vs-Goliath type movements battling injustices across six decades. At the same time, she also chronicles the quiet, unsexy, and often unrecognized work of herself and many other women in sustaining those struggles—and pushing towards victory.

VICTORIA LAW, journalist; author, *Corridors of Contagion*

LEVITATING THE PENTAGON is no manifesto. It's an unpretentious first-person account of American radical activism in the second half of the twentieth century. And in my view, we can always use more of that.

PETER RICHARDSON, author, *Savage Journey: Hunter S. Thompson and the Weird Road to Gonzo*

NANCY KURSHAN'S MEMOIR is a true gift. . . . Without succumbing to protagonism, Nancy tells us about her activism, her commitment to radical change for the liberation of humanity, to the building of a world where there are no oppressors and no oppressed and where the people themselves are the leaders of their own freedom.

JOSÉ E. LÓPEZ, Executive Director of the Puerto Rican Cultural Center, Chicago

LEVITATING THE PENTAGON

LEVITATING THE PENTAGON

AND OTHER UPLIFTING STORIES

A LIFE OF ACTIVISM

NANCY KURSHAN

THREE ROOMS PRESS
New York, NY

Levitating the Pentagon and Other Uplifting Stories: A Life of Activism
by Nancy Kurshan

ISBN 978-1-953103-71-0 (trade paperback original)
978-1-953103-70-3 (Epub)
Library of Congress Control Number: 2026930681

TRP-124

First edition

Publication Date: March 24, 2026

BISAC category code
BIO032000 BIOGRAPHY & AUTOBIOGRAPHY / Social Activists
BIO022000 BIOGRAPHY & AUTOBIOGRAPHY / Women
BIO026000 BIOGRAPHY & AUTOBIOGRAPHY / Personal Memoirs
BIO010000 BIOGRAPHY & AUTOBIOGRAPHY / Political

COVER PHOTO:
"We Are All Outlaws In The Eyes Of America"
Anita Hoffman, Nancy Kurshan, and Tasha Dellinger burning judicial robes during the Chicago 8 Trial; Photo courtesy of Nancy Kurshan

INTERIOR PHOTOS:
All interior photos: © The Archives of Nancy Kurshan. Photos on pages 24, 28, 29, 36, 42, 52, 81, and 82 were taken by Nancy's father, Norman Kurshan.

COVER AND INTERIOR DESIGN:
Darryl Norsen, D.Norsen Design

PROJECT EDITOR AND ASSOCIATE PUBLISHER:
Pat Thomas

DISTRIBUTED INTERNATIONALLY BY:
Publishers Group West: www.pgw.com
Ingram Content Group: www.ingramcontent.com

PUBLISHED BY:
Three Rooms Press
New York, NY
www.threeroomspress.com
info@threeroomspress.com

For Steve who fought by my side,
cheering me on and cheering me up for 30 years.

For Julian and Santi, our two new sprouts.
May they carry the banner in whatever ways they see fit.

"I could tell you my adventures beginning from this morning," said Alice a little timidly, "But it's no use going back to yesterday, because I was a different person then."

"Explain all that," said the Mock Turtle.

"No, no! The adventures first," said the Gryphon in an impatient tone: "Explanations take such a dreadful time."

LEWIS CARROLL,
ALICE'S ADVENTURES IN WONDERLAND / THROUGH THE LOOKING GLASS

TABLE OF CONTENTS

FOREWORD

Nancy Kurshan invented and lives a robust, creative, and riotous Movement life. From the early days of the Black Freedom Movement and the anti-war struggles against the U.S. invasion of Vietnam, through the Chicago 8 Conspiracy trial, radical solidarity with Puerto Rican independence and Palestinian liberation, and her feminist insistence on speaking up and being heard, Nancy Kurshan is a wise woman, and a gifted storyteller as well.

Nancy is a born internationalist—a Red Diaper baby, raised as a child of the Communist movement, a veteran of demonstrations for racial equality and against nuclear arms while still in high school. She expanded her internationalist perspective as she matured, always recognizing the U.S. as an exporter of violence and war, and the American people as a potentially potent ally in the effort to build a world at peace and in balance.

I first met Nancy, naturally, in the streets and confronting the war machine. It was October 1967 and the broad peace movement had mobilized a huge mass demonstration in Washington D.C. Nancy—always a militant who understood and embraced the power of direct action—was with the young radicals who crossed the bridge intending to actually shut down the Pentagon. Troops surrounded the headquarters of the warmakers, backs against the wall and bayonets fixed, and we surrounded the troops, lighting bonfires and planning to spend the night.

Nancy inspired me as she approached the young and anxious soldiers, one by one, put a flower in each gun barrel, and spoke quietly about the war, urging each to abandon their posts and join the Movement.

Nancy Kurshan—unlike some of us—melded her activism with humor to great effect, organizing with people who vowed to "levitate the Pentagon" that night. She was a founding member of the Yippies—the Youth International Party—engaged in wholesale disruption and widespread resistance as well as ridiculing the kings who had no clothes and dramatizing the hypocrisy of the warmongers, the rulers, and the captains of capitalism.

Nancy was and still is an outstanding organizer, bringing new people into the struggle for racial justice, Puerto Rican independence, and Palestinian freedom, and more recently recruiting older women into theatrical demonstrations for peace and justice in Oakland.

Nancy Kurshan's memoir will inspire you to do more and to do it better. To take risks, and also to reflect. To assume responsibility for what is being done in our names. To act up and speak out in these treacherous and urgent times.

Buy or borrow or *Steal this Book*!

SIGNED:
Bernardine Dohrn
Founder, The Children and Family Justice Center,
School of Law, Northwestern University

PREFACE

Nancy Kurshan's memoir is a true gift, especially to those who know her deeply. Intimate and inspiring, it spans her teenage years to her life now as a super adult (as our renowned artist Antonio Martorell refers to the third age). As I read the memoir, a passage from Julia de Burgos' poem, "A Julia de Burgos," repeatedly came to mind:

When the multitudes run rioting
Leaving behind ashes of burned injustices,
And with the torch of the seven virtues,
The multitudes run after the seven sins,
Against you and against everything unjust and inhuman,
I will be in their midst with the torch in my hand.

This is Nancy, not leading the multitudes but in their midst, carrying the torch of struggle. Without succumbing to protagonism, Nancy tells us about her activism, her commitment to radical change for the liberation of humanity, to the building of a world where there are no oppressors and no oppressed and where the people themselves are the leaders of their own freedom.

Nancy's memoir tells the story of a powerful woman with whom I have had the honor and privilege of sharing some of the best and most challenging moments in the struggle for the self-determination, self-actualization, and self-reliance of the Puerto Rican people in the Diaspora and Puerto Rico over the past four decades. Our friendship—and her principled solidarity for our cause—was forged in the heat of one of the most repressive periods, unleashed against the Puerto Rican independence movement. A little-known or understood aspect of the FBI's COINTELPRO activities, we experienced concerted attempts to disrupt, divide, and destroy our movement with the targeted use of the Federal Grand Jury as a political witch hunt, the infiltration of our movement by agent provocateurs, political incarceration, political assassinations, and raids on our homes and our political spaces. The repression that we endured also involved massive, indiscriminate political arrests by the Chicago Police, including detention without a lawyer or access to phones for more than 24 hours, the use of Control Units aimed at our captured political prisoners, and efforts to promote serious divisions, including among families. The list is long, but at every step of the way, Nancy and her beloved husband, Steve Whitman, were always there in solidarity.

I should note that Nancy and Steve's equally deep commitment to the Black Liberation struggle, the Mexican/Chicano liberation struggle, and the Puerto Rican liberation struggle still need to be written. It is this indomitable Nancy, who was there for us in the bleakest of times that I have known. In her poignant memoir, Nancy presents, through her personal story, an example of political ethics at the highest level. She can honestly say, "I fought the good fight and have no regrets."

For me, Nancy truly embodies an ancient Japanese practice that serves as a counter-narrative to the Western concept of happiness. This practice is known as "Ikigai." The writer Héctor García, who co-authored the book, *Ikigai: The Japanese Search to a Long and Happy Life* claims there is no word like it anywhere in the world. Ikigai is not an emotion, "it is more like something worth living for." In other words, it is living a life for—and with—others. Not looking inward, but outward, to see how effective one has been, or in the words of Saint Francis: "Master, Grant that I may not so much seek to be consoled as to console; to be understood as to understand; to be loved as to love." As Che Guevara once

Above: Xmas 1986 March in downtown Chicago. Left to right: Margaret Power, Doug Spalding, Nancy Kurshan with poster, Jose Lopez with umbrella.
Below: Nancy Kurshan and Jose Lopez, Humboldt Park, Chicago, 2018.

reminded us, "The true revolutionary is guided by great feelings of love." This is Nancy's life, a life of unswerving and steadfast devotion to selflessness and struggle; to a life that fully realizes the maxim of our great poet Consuelo Lee Corretjer: "Live and help to live."

José E. López
Executive Director of the Puerto Rican Cultural Center, Chicago

LEVITATING THE PENTAGON

INTRODUCTION

On the 35th anniversary of the 1969/70 Chicago Conspiracy Trial, I was interviewed by a public television reporter for a retrospective piece on the Chicago 8. As he and his cameraman entered my house, he quipped, "I just interviewed Richard Schultz (Assistant Prosecuting Attorney). He insists that you came to Chicago to overthrow the American government. He knows it sounds silly but that's what he believes to this day." Without missing a beat, I replied, "It doesn't sound silly at all. That was in fact what we wanted to do."

And then I added, "Why wouldn't we want to overthrow a government that murdered two to three million Vietnamese and sixty thousand U.S. troops? Why wouldn't we want to overthrow a government that launched a joint FBI/police force campaign to destroy the Black Panthers that left in its wake scores of dead revolutionaries and many others imprisoned for life?"

It still rings true—but somehow it doesn't. It sounds like the old me. We were good at sounding sure of ourselves, as well as at hiding how scared and unsure we felt. It leaves out a lot. So how did a 24-year-old white girl from Long Island end up running from cops through the streets of Chicago in a purple sundress and pigtails? And how did a Ph.D. student in psychology end up having tea with the FBI's Most Wanted? Did I know what I was doing? Yes and no. Much of the time I was improvising.

Chicago '68 was pivotal for me but it was just part of a longer road that led from summer camp singalongs with Pete Seeger to civil rights "shop-ins" at Sears Roebuck and civil disobedience on the steps of the Pentagon. It led on to North Vietnam, to the inside of America's courts and jails, and again and again back to Chicago. I traveled that road because it felt right and because much of the time it was fun.

My journey has also been about becoming a woman with a voice: from an affirming childhood but one in which "sexism" was a word unknown, through some difficult relationships with men, the male-dominated Movement, and the transformative yet anxiety-producing challenges that feminism presented to me.

This is my story but it's not only mine. It's the story of a whole generation set in motion by the Civil Rights movement and the Vietnam War. It's a story that's already been told, mostly by men. Now it's my turn.

ORIGIN STORY

To understand the Chicago 8 Conspiracy Trial and what motivated us Yippies, you have to know something about the extraordinary times that brought our "conspiracy" together. Our small circle of New York and Berkeley activists, later to be known as the Yippies, had come together around the first huge anti-war protest—250,000 strong!—that culminated at the Pentagon in October 1967.

My boyfriend Jerry Rubin had gone to New York ahead of me to help shape and organize this national anti-war march on Washington. I was the woman who stayed behind to do the grunt work of moving. Jerry called me to tell me how excited he was about his new friend Abbie Hoffman, and I knew from the conversation that he had met his match in the countercultural scene of New York's Lower East Side. Abbie and Jerry seemed a perfect fit. Jerry was already an effective and controversial anti-war leader on the West Coast, the "PT Barnum of the Left." Abbie was a counterculture celebrity of the East Coast, a Civil Rights activist who had brought theatricality and humor to the Movement.

When I arrived in New York weeks later I saw with my own eyes that even visually they resembled one another. Jerry stood at 5'4" to Abbie's 5'7". Both had brown eyes and curly brown hair that seemed to be growing longer and more unkempt by the minute. Jerry, who often wore a sports jacket when I met him two years previously, was now dressing in casual and sometimes tie-dyed t-shirts.

The next few months were spent devoted to this Pentagon protest, but the reader will hear much more about that down the road. For now, let me say that buoyed by the successful outcome of that protest, and excited by the explosive growth of the anti-war movement, Jerry and I left DC and returned to NY with our Lower East Side friends.

St. Marks Place was the main thoroughfare of the countercultural scene in New York. And the strip between Second and Third Avenue was the happening epicenter, vibrating with energy day and night. The Electric Circus was a music venue where Linda Ronstadt and the Stone Poneys would play a benefit for the Chicago '68 Yippie organizing efforts. On the Second Avenue corner was Gem Spa, a community gathering space masquerading as a tiny newspaper and candy store, famous for its egg creams. (Gem Spa shuttered up forever in 2020 much to the chagrin of all egg cream lovers and all those who hung out there). On Second Avenue was Ratner's Jewish vegetarian restaurant where you could get blintzes and potato pancakes in the middle of the night. The underground newspaper, the *East Village Other* (EVO)was a short walk away. And imagine being able to walk out your door, then take a quick stroll to Bill Graham's Fillmore East to catch a show with Big Brother & the Holding Company—Janis Joplin with purple and pink feathers, boas and ribbons interlaced with her long brown hair which seemed to have a force of its own when she belted out her powerful mezzo-soprano voice, singing the blues with incredible heart and passion. Yes, it was quite the neighborhood!

Between them, Jerry and Abbie seemed to know everybody: poet Allen Ginsberg, satirist Paul Krassner (*The Realist*), folksinger Phil Ochs, Ed Sanders of The Fugs, WBAI personality/host Bob Fass, artists Martin and Susan Carey, pacifists Keith and Judy Lampe and more.

Phil Ochs was one of my favorites. His *Talking Vietnam Blues* was probably the first explicitly anti-Vietnam war song. There was a gentleness, a kindness about Phil and also a perceivable vulnerability/sadness that was not common among movement men. His dress was more preppy than hippie. His hair stayed relatively short and he never smoked weed. His drug of choice was alcohol, which was later to do him in.

I loved being with this crowd—organizing and networking, but also just hanging out, toking, and talking non-stop, dreaming and scheming. It was during one of our late-night sessions (in fact New Year's Eve, the last night of 1967) that the Yippies were born. It was in Abbie and Anita's under-furnished Lower East Side apartment.

I had seen photos of the marriage of Abbie Hoffman and Anita Kushner splashed all over the New York media: HIPPY WEDDING IN CENTRAL PARK. Sitting smack on the ground, both dressed all in white from top to bottom, both striking with their short dark haircuts. Anita in a formfitting white dress, tastefully revealing her perfect hourglass figure, with white mesh stockings and white slippers. Abbie dressed in matching whites, and both with white flowers in their hair and beads around their necks. They were both beaming with what appeared to be genuine broad smiles.

Abbie Hoffman seemed born into comedy and charm. His short, tightly curled hair would grow into a long, bushy dark mane, completely chaotic, a Jewfro emblematic of his audacious character. It was hard to anticipate what he would come up with next, whether announcing to the media, in his characteristic Boston accent, that the water at the Chicago Democratic Convention would be laced with LSD; or standing on his head in the courtroom of the Chicago 8 trial; or carrying a toy bomb. Abbie was a frenetic and unpredictable ball of energy. A creative ball of energy that was committed to fighting for liberation for all, using humor and ridicule to expose the powers that be. But make no mistake, he had a deeply serious side. Joining the Student Nonviolent Coordinating Committee (SNCC), Abbie had cut his activist teeth helping Black folks register to vote in Mississippi. He then established Liberty House, a New York outlet for handmade products produced by people's cooperatives, mostly Black women, in the South: "Crafts for Freedom."

Anita was slender with straight dark hair, beautiful blue eyes and sculptured features. She and Abbie were a striking couple. Never the raggedy hippy, Anita always managed to express a natural beauty and aesthetic sense. She had a contemporary Cleopatra look.

QUICKSILVER TIMES

25¢

VOLUME II NUMBER 17 JULY 14-24 WASHINGTON, D.C.

Nancy on the cover of Quicksilver Times, circa 1969.

Two things were clear from the start with Anita. She was alienated from mainstream America, and she was head over heels in love with Abbie. She was so devoted to him that I wondered, is she an activist or is she essentially a groupie? I quickly learned that if she was not an activist in the past, she sure was now. Sharply intelligent, opinionated and adventurous, Anita always carved her own path. Yet it would become years before we'd become real friends.

In addition to the four of us, Paul Krassner was in the room. As a child Paul had been a prodigy violinist, the youngest to play at Carnegie Hall. As an adult he was a satirist extraordinaire who published *The Realist,* an iconoclastic, irreverent magazine of social and political commentary. A lesser known fact is that Paul helped many desperate women find ways to get safe abortions when there was no such thing as reproductive rights and abortion was criminalized.

All five of us were raised in Jewish families. While none of us were practicing Jews, I believe we all shared an identification with the underdog and a certain alienation from WASP America. There were other things we shared as well. Anita, Abbie and I had all studied psychology, although I don't remember ever talking about that or almost anything else related to our pasts. It barely registered that Abbie was a divorced father of two! We were so bombarded with current events, mostly out of our control but some of our own making, that the past seemed a universe away and unimportant. Retrospectively I'd say we had a lot in common with two-year-olds. Living in the moment exclusively offered rewards but also liabilities. For all of us but especially us women, our relationships could have been so much richer.

It was a very male scene. Anita and I were present much of the time but we were quieter. The balance of power was very skewed. Speaking for myself (because she and I didn't talk about any of this back then), I was 23 years old and six to ten years younger than most of the Yippie men. In addition, so many were celebrities or at least well-known personalities around the Big Apple and beyond. Great big roly-poly Bob Fass ran a daily radio show on WBAI. Allen Ginsberg was already a world renowned, if controversial, poet—author of "HOWL". Ed Sanders and Tuli

Kupferberg were members of The Fugs rock band. Phil Ochs was a fabulous songwriter musician. I had plenty of thoughts and opinions but found it hard to find my voice in that environment. At the same time I was awed by this collection of characters and impressed by the reach they had in terms of influencing thousands of other people.

Colorful characters all and now here I was in Abbie and Anita's St. Marks Place railroad flat. Just at the other end of the block from our fourth-floor walkup, their apartment was literally on the street, no steps up or down. You just opened the door and *Voila!* You were in a sparsely furnished living room with pillows on the floor along the walls. It was a clean-as-a-whistle one-bedroom apartment with a loft bed that Abbie had built.

Origin stories are usually mythic— exaggerated and romanticized. The Yippie story is no different. I've read it so many times, it may have replaced my own memories. What I do know is that it was New Year's Eve 1967. The five of us—Abbie, Anita, Jerry, Krassner and me—were sitting around smoking weed and enjoying each other's company on a snowy eve.

Ever since the October Pentagon demonstration, we had all been talking about the next Democratic Convention. Part of a larger coalition, our little band had been crucial in setting the stage for the Pentagon protest, crucial in getting our anti-war message around the globe, and now we wanted to break out on our own. We needed a vehicle for helping to unleash the creativity of the counterculture in order to strongly confront the Democratic Party's war-makers at their August convention. Now it was just eight months away.

Here's my mythic version of that New Year's Eve conversation—I have the last word as the only one left standing:

Imagine the standard "smoke-filled room" of politicians, only note that the smoke was weed and the politicos were long-haired hippies sprawled out on pillows and cushions.

Paul said, "The media created the hippies. Can we change the "H" to a "Y"? Then the five of us can create the Yippies!"

"Y not?" I called out. "Give me a Y!"

Abbie responded: "The Y is for youth. Give me an I!"

Jerry responded: "The I is for International. It's an international revolution. Give me a P! No, two Ps!"

Anita completed the cheer: "It's a party—people trying to have fun, meaning, ecstasy. Give me a Y! What d'ya got?"

All in unison we declared the solemnly faux-respectable title: YOUTH INTERNATIONAL PARTY!

Paul chimed in again: "Yeah, a Yippie is a hippy who's been hit over the head with a policeman's club. A flower child who's been arrested. A warrior of the Aquarian era."

"Okay," Abbie added pragmatically. "We can print up Yippie cards so that anyone can become a card-carrying Yippie."

Thus the Youth International Party was born. It was a joke but it was a perfect fit. It was what we were and wanted to be: serious activists with a sense of humor, freedom and fun. Forward! Our intention was resistance, not just protest. Our intention was to add wit, theatricality, and countercultural hippie elan to the growing militancy of the antiwar movement. We were ready for 1968. Or so we thought.

CHICAGO

I BECAME THE "MANAGER" OF our tiny one-room office on Union Square, coordinating the printing of thousands of buttons, posters, and leaflets calling people to our Festival of Life in Chicago. But most Yippie action took place on the streets, and I was often in charge of bailing everyone out.

As the Yippies we were developing a rep and a name. We tried it out by calling for a "yip-in" at Grand Central Station—a midnight party to celebrate the coming of spring in the center of midtown New York's transportation hub. Expecting as many as a hundred to respond, we were amazed when thousands of long-hairs jammed the terminal, thanks in no small part to Bob Fass and WBAI. So were the cops, who of course went nuts, arresting as many as they could grab and even throwing Abbie through a plate glass door. But like all of us, Abbie was more encouraged than injured. Our core group was tiny, and our "Youth International Party" was a joke. But everyone got the joke; there were no card-carrying Yippies. Anyone who declared themselves a Yippie, was. We were a multitude.

Meanwhile, 1968 was a rollercoaster year. The Vietnamese rang in the New Year by launching an enormous and completely undetected popular uprising in South Vietnam known as the Tet Offensive. The whole world was stunned by their ability to mobilize their entire nation right under the noses of the American military. A small country challenging Goliath, the most powerful military force in the world.

On March 31st of that year, LBJ effectively resigned, hounded out of the presidency by a war he couldn't win yet couldn't bear losing. Weeks later Martin Luther King, Jr. was assassinated and urban centers around the U.S. went up in flames. In May, French students triggered a national strike of students and workers. That summer Robert Kennedy came out against the war—and then was assassinated. In Mexico City a huge protest ended with the murder by police of hundreds of unarmed students. The world was in turmoil and it seemed like people were resisting everywhere. We were determined to join them. And where else but Chicago, where the Democrats would be nominating LBJ's successor?

So what was our original intent for the 1968 Democratic Convention? Resistance. Rebellion. And more. We knew there would be antiwar delegates inside the convention, and many more on the streets outside. We would add our special sauce. Our tiny Youth International Party (Yippie!) would organize an alternative—a Festival of Life, in order to expose, oppose and confront the Democrats' Festival of Death. There would be an extravaganza of musicians, poets, and guerrilla theater—a union of hippies and political activism. We would smoke dope, make love, not war, and dance in the streets. We would nominate a pig for President.

Yes, a Festival of Life would be great. But if that were not possible, if the boot came down—then a confrontation in the streets that would capture the attention of the whole world would also be great. If it could not be a Festival of Life, so be it. We were down for it either way. Any traces of pacifist thinking were disappearing.

As a white middle class American I nonetheless shared a yearning for a thorough ongoing revolution that would welcome in a better world, a better life for all. Not only were we waging an imperial war against a small Asian nation, but our country was built on conquest, a genocidal campaign against the indigenous peoples of the Americas. (I have always loved the T-shirt that shows the Bedonkohe Apache fighter Geronimo and three other resistance fighters, armed with rifles, under the banner "HOMELAND SECURITY: FIGHTING TERRORISM SINCE 1492"). I knew the kidnapping history of perhaps millions of Africans, forced to become chattel slaves.

But it wasn't just the history. I believed the contemporary leaders of our country as well as many just plain white folks were actively resisting any attempt to make America into the democracy it claimed to be. The denial by the 1964 Democratic Party Convention to seat the Mississippi Freedom Democratic Party deepened my disenchantment with both parties. Then there was Malcolm X's assassination, the Vietnam War. In my mind the disconnect between the myth and the cold reality was growing exponentially and fueled my desire for change.

So we got to work, organizing our Festival of Life in contrast to what we saw as the Festival of Death of the Democratic Party. We were down for whatever might happen. I'll spare you the details of the hundreds of phone calls, meetings, and negotiations that ate up our next few months.

In response to the Black rebellion in Chicago that followed the shocking assassination of Dr. Martin Luther King, Mayor Daley had earlier that year issued his infamous "Shoot to kill, maim or cripple" order, and those words were reiterated over and over again in the time leading up to the Convention. We had been negotiating for months for a permit to sleep in the park. We knew that young people would arrive from all over the country without money or resources and would need a place to stay. The city stalled and stalled. The Chicago Yippies, on the flower power end of the continuum, encouraged us to keep negotiating and assured us we'd get the permits in the end. They were wrong. Mayor Richard Daley refused to issue any permits to sleep in Lincoln Park and he waited until the last minute to let us know this with certainty.

Many movement people began to say it was crazy to go to Chicago. Eugene McCarthy, the peace candidate, warned people not to come. Even our fragile Yippie cabal was fracturing. The folks from *The Seed,* a Chicago-based alternative newspaper, were our local Yippie allies, but they became fearful of the consequences. They said, reasonably enough, that they would have to live with the aftermath of repression that Daley would rain down on the locals after the rest of us left for home. Up until the end, we were divided about whether we'd be allowed to sleep in the park. With or without permits, we thought that if enough of us arrived in Chicago, the city would relent, preferring us to sleep in the park, rather than be pushed into the streets and cause a major confrontation. At least each of us thought that some of the time. At other times we thought we might die in Chicago.

I am sure that thousands of Yippies and other antiwar people were frightened away. Of the scheduled Festival of Life performers, in the end only Phil Ochs and the MC5 (Motor City 5), a band out of the Ann Arbor/Detroit area associated with the White Panthers, actually made it to Chicago. It was rumored that Country Joe and the Fish showed up but that Joe had been threatened by some beefy Chicago cops in an elevator, and therefore headed out of town ASAP. Musicians were especially reluctant to bring all their expensive equipment to such an iffy scene.

But our small circle of friends knew we all had to go, no matter what. Otherwise we would be acquiescing in the implementation of a police state. It would have been a done deal and we were not ready to concede that kind of defeat.

On the opening days of the Democratic Convention, a few thousand stalwarts arrived at Lincoln Park. Jerry and I spent most of our time with Stew Albert and his new girlfriend, Judy Gumbo, who had arrived in NY just months before. Stew loomed over the three of us, a big, strong presence with a head full of curly blond hair, the Uncowardly Lion from the *Wizard of Oz*. I knew right away that Judy would be good for Stew. With brown eyes and curly brown shoulder-length hair, she stood at about 5 feet. Short like me, only thinner but very solid. There was no doubt that Judy was a spunky political activist and could easily give Stew a run for his money.

But there were problems already. I am not talking here of the police presence. Not yet. Although all us hardcore Yippies were there, we were barely on speaking terms. Jerry and Abbie were feuding, and although I can remember most political arguments for years afterwards, I can't for the life of me reconstruct what they were fighting over at that point.

When Jerry and Abbie were estranged, so were Anita and I. We "stood by our men" in those days. Other Yippies were pulled into the fight as well. No matter how hard people tried to remain neutral, it was generally Stew, Judy and Phil who ran with Jerry and me, with Krassner and Anita at Abbie's side. We tried to appear united. But we were a fractured bunch.

Already, there were police everywhere. Not just in uniform but also undercover. Everywhere we went we were followed by tails, cops whose job was to stick to us like glue. They made little attempt to camouflage their task. They followed us as we walked down the street. They followed us into restaurants. We entered a Lincoln Park cafe and three cops sat down at the counter. We waited for them to order, and when their meals arrived, we got up and walked out. They also got up and walked out, leaving all their food behind, uneaten. We got some satisfaction out of ruining their lunch.

A tall, burly, dark-haired biker presented himself to us shortly after we arrived in Lincoln Park. He said he knew that Jerry would be a target and offered his services as a Yippie bodyguard. "Why not?" we thought. We didn't feel we had anything to hide. We said pretty much what we believed and what we wanted to do. Anyway, it never occurred to us that he was a cop. Even though we were admirers of Che Guevara, we were still naïve in so many ways.

Lincoln Park had one character in the light of day and another at night. During the day, the weather was hot and humid, a typical Chicago summer. I wore a short sundress and two long pigtails to stay cool. The park was filled with a few thousand people doing their own things. Our friend Wolfe Lowenthal was teaching people tai chi. Jeff Shero, later known as Jeff Nightbyrd, the editor of *The Rat*, one of New York City's underground newspapers, brought a special Chicago convention issue to distribute in Chicago. Also, Thorne Dreyer came from Texas to produce an SDS-sponsored wall newspaper, *Handwriting On The Wall*, which was published daily with updates on what was going on and where." *Ramparts Magazine* also published some wall posters in Chicago.

Scores of activists from Students for a Democratic Society (SDS) were there as well. The major organization representing the burgeoning New Left, SDS had criticized us Yippies for various reasons—too frivolous, not really organizing on a local level, etc.—but were now full participants, even leaders, since the situation had changed. They were disenchanted with the standard civil disobedience of the peace movement and had formed small groups to engage in the newly popular "mobile tactics" that were springing up around the country. We were glad to see them there. They seemed more prepared than we were for the actual situation.

There were small groups of medics with white armbands—carrying first aid supplies—on the ready. They were associated with the Medical Committee for Human Rights. Attorneys and law students from the National Lawyers Guild wore legal observer armbands. Some people were learning how to monitor police radios. Others were riding around on bicycles bringing news from one place to the next. (Imagine that, no cell phones!) People were reading, sharing food, hanging out. Both the days and the nights were freeform in nature. If you couldn't "go with the flow," it would be rough.

I ran around with Jerry most of the time, not quite sure what to do with myself, moving at different moments from exhilaration to fear to occasional boredom. I can't remember why I decided to take THC, but one afternoon I did just that. It turned out to be a really bad idea. I became very jittery and felt off for a half day. My 82-year-old self wonders, "What was I thinking?" But hey, I was 24 years old!

Well-known cultural figures who understood the importance of this historical moment were arriving. Celebrities such as Norman Mailer, Jean Genet, Terry Southern, and William Burroughs could be spotted walking around, mingling with the crowd and sharing in the anxious anticipation.

Although no permit for sleeping in the park was granted, we thought a small concert could stay under the radar and they'd let that go. That turned out to be completely wrong. As the MC5 started playing, a conflict with the police ensued over the flatbed stage, and the performance ended in confusion as the cops cut the power. The concert was short-lived.

Also during the day there were various political forays out of the park. At the beginning of that week the Russian Army had marched into Prague. In a theater of solidarity, we marched on the Russian embassy with signs that proclaimed the commonality between Czechoslovakia and Czechago. Also in the prelude to the week, 17-year-old Dean

Johnson, a Native American youth, was killed while shoplifting in a food store. He had come from out of town and had drifted in to join us, and we felt an affinity with him.

The next blood to flow was that of Yippie Stew Albert. In broad daylight on Sunday, August 25th, in the midst of the crowd in Lincoln Park, Stew cried out. I turned around to see blood dripping through his curly blond hair and down his face. They had cracked open his head! He and Judy Gumbo took off for an emergency room. That night I learned about Stew and Judy's courage and commitment when six stitches and a couple of hours later they returned, ready to go another round!

On Tuesday the 27th, Bobby Seale, a national leader of the Black Panther Party, addressed the crowd in Lincoln Park. He had not been an organizer of the events but was an invited speaker. Despite all the potential violence and the actual repression the Panthers had been experiencing, Bobby showed up and spoke briefly. (He was to pay later with a federal indictment for exercising his right to free speech.)

It was at night that the real contest took place, from Sunday night, August 25th through Tuesday night, the 27th. As evening began to fall, people started to build barricades with whatever could be found—picnic tables, garbage cans, etc. Other people made bonfires and sat around them playing on drums and other instruments.

There were only a few thousand of us in Lincoln Park and we felt small and weak. Some people wanted to take a stand and resist the police if they tried to force us to leave the park. My circle of Yippies didn't really want to fight over sleeping in the park, but we wouldn't leave the park until the situation was resolved one way or another. We felt responsible for all the people who had come and we would remain with them if possible.

Once the 11 pm curfew came, the police stomped into the crowd and started clubbing people from behind. That first night it was as if the cops thought they could just come in and club a few of us and end this pathetic gathering. A good head-banging and it would all be over. If so, they seriously underestimated our determination.

As Norman Mailer reported in *Miami and the Siege of Chicago*: "Children, and youths, and middle-aged men were being pounded and gassed and beaten, hunted and driven by teams of policemen who had exploded out of their restraints like the bursting of a boil..."

In the midst of all the tear gas and police clubbing sat Allen Ginsberg, cross-legged with a circle of people around him, for hours at a time "omming" in deep sonorous tones, attempting to create calm and drive away the evil spirits.

Washington Post reporter Nicholas von Hoffman did a good job of capturing the nighttime scene:

> *The attack began with a police car smashing the barricade. The kids threw whatever they had had the foresight to arm themselves with, rocks and bottles mostly. Then there was a period of police action before the full charge.*
>
> *Shrieks and screams all over the wooded encampment area while the experienced militants kept calling out "Walk! Walk! For Chrissakes don't run." There is an adage among veteran kids that "panicky people incite cops to riot."*
>
> *Rivulets of running people came out of the woods across the lawn area, the parking lots toward Clark Street. Next, the cops burst out of the woods in selective pursuit of news photographers. Pictures are unanswerable evidence in court. They'd taken off their badges, their names plates, even the unit patches on their shoulders to become a mob of identical, unidentifiable club swingers.*
>
> *There is the scene at Henrotin Hospital with editors coming in to claim their wounded. Roy Fischer of the* Chicago Daily News, *Hal Bruno of* Newsweek. *Television guys who took a special clobbering waiting in the anteroom describing what happened and looking angry-eyed at the cops hanging around with the air of guys putting in a routine night.*

The nights were characterized by crowds of young people trying to figure out what to do, with continuous sporadic violence and tear gas. We streamed out of the park, and were pursued by police cars and cops on foot, along with the tear gas. Who could have imagined that tear gas could be delivered in so many different ways—from sanitation trucks, from flame-throwing devices, as well as from the usual canisters.

I tried Vaseline and wet handkerchiefs to deal with the gas. Tears were dribbling down my face as my eyes burned. I tried not to wipe them, afraid I would make it worse. It was difficult to see, and when the gas hit my nose and mouth, I began coughing. I feared being hit directly by the canisters themselves. But I also felt anger and a stubborn persistence, resistance to their lawless disrespect. Later on I would think about the Vietnamese and how they had had to deal with napalm—which made tear gas seem like confetti—as well as the children of Birmingham, when the police sent dogs to attack them. But at the time I was just frightened and angry. I was learning to defeat fear by allowing my righteous anger to flow. How else could I proceed?

Groups of young people roamed through the streets, and as a consequence, were blocking traffic. The whole area was in turmoil. There were helicopters flying close overhead and on the ground there were cops with gas masks using their rifle butts as clubs. Dragging. Chasing. Slamming.

We were out on the streets until late every night, one night making it all the way downtown to the Hilton, which was the center of the Democratic Party. The tear gas followed us and reportedly wafted into the hotel, spreading its ugly fumes toward the delegates lodged inside. Each night when things died down in the early morning hours and we were bone-tired, we would wend our way back to a Lincoln Park apartment and fall into bed to catch a few hours of sleep. But the tenaciousness and solidarity of our people was exhilarating, and that inspired us.

Wednesday, August 28th, held the promise of something different. After all, it was easy to marginalize the Yippies—a bunch of scruffy longhairs who needed showers. But this day was organized by the National Mobilization Committee to End the War in Vietnam, better known as "The Mobe," and The Mobe was a respectable peace organization.

The Mobe was the sponsor of the rally that day at the Grant Park bandshell but by now we were all in this together. Every Yippie who had come to Chicago was now part of the Mobe.

Daley had given us a permit to rally but not to march. I've read accounts of the rally but I don't remember a single speech. It was hard to concentrate and I felt totally on edge, steeling myself to deal with whatever would happen next. Fully armed police were arriving in flying wedges, shoving and pushing and clubbing people from behind. It felt like we were sitting ducks. This time it was Mobe organizer Rennie Davis, the All-American boy with blood dripping down his face. Somehow the rally continued despite the attacks, and then we tried to move into a line to march, to head toward the amphitheater where the Convention was taking place.

But Daley had no intention of letting us march and blocked us so that there was no way to move. The crowd was forced to disperse and spilled out of the park and over to Michigan Avenue and the Hilton Hotel, where all the delegates wined and dined. The Hilton was surrounded by a huge phalanx of cops and military personnel. But our people pressed forward and cops clubbed us back and lobbed tear gas into the crowd. As night began to fall, the crowd thickened. The police continued to beat and club people, demonstrators and reporters and "innocent" Chicagoans alike. The Battle of Michigan Avenue was on. But the crowd seemed to actually grow, or at least people held strong, chanting over and over: "The Whole World Is Watching!" At that point, we knew we were back on the world stage and it was exhilarating. So this was the Festival of Life after all. What had been happening for days in Lincoln Park was now being repeated in front of the Hilton; only this time it involved a broader swath of citizenry and THE WHOLE WORLD WAS WATCHING!

After a while Jerry and I, along with Stew, Judy and others, left the Hilton Hotel and began running around the Loop, Chicago's downtown area, blocking traffic and setting fires in garbage cans. That was the most militant action I'd ever engaged in. As we were turning the corner under the El, Jerry was surrounded by cops who dragged him off and arrested him. He later told us that they brought him into the station where he was confronted by Bob Pierson, the "biker bodyguard," who revealed himself to be an undercover cop, or a "pig," as we were fond of calling cops, always reminding ourselves that we were maligning real pigs in the process. (That was not the last we would see of Bob Pierson.

He would later appear as a mendacious key witness in the Chicago Conspiracy Trial.)

The journalist John Schultz reports that there were 668 arrests recorded that week. Half of the people were from the Windy City. The rest came from 36 states and five countries. 550 had never been arrested before and 75 percent were 25 years of age or younger.

The Chicago Corporation Counsel's *Walker Report* later concluded that there had indeed been a police riot in Chicago that week, suggesting cops had gone amok. But calling it a "police riot" is a whitewashing of the situation and underestimated the cold-blooded calculations of the establishment in this country. It is hard to imagine that Richard Daley, the shoot-to-maim-and-kill czar of Chicago, would have allowed such spontaneity from his officers. No, the Battle for Chicago was orchestrated from on high. The clubbings, beatings, and tear gassing were all conscious decisions from at least as high as the Daley administration. In fact, we later learned that there were about one thousand federal agents sent to work in Chicago that week, including FBI and military intelligence. One can only wonder what exactly was the role of the federal government in the events that ensued?

The problem for them was that they underestimated us. We were frightened but despite our fears we persisted. They may have thought their threats before the Convention would deter us. They were wrong. They may have thought the first round of tear gas would frighten us. They were wrong. They may have thought the first cracked head would stop us. They were wrong. We would not be turned back.

It was an amazing few days and a Yippie's delight in the sense that we were always out to capture the media's attention and in this case we did. The media reported the truth, the whole truth, and nothing but the truth, because they found themselves at the same end of the billy clubs and tear gas as we were. Even reporters as respectable as Dan Rather were attacked by the cops. They were not embedded journalists. For that moment in time there seemed to actually be a free press! One reporter is quoted as saying: "This whole thing has moved me so far left, I can see the back of my head."

The long-term impact of Chicago '68 has been much debated. There are many layers to such an analysis and that is not the subject of this piece. But there is no doubt that Chicago 1968 became an iconic moment in American history. And as fractured and unfocused as we were, we Yippies were proud to be part of it.

RED DIAPER BABY

I WASN'T BORN A YIPPIE of course. I was a Red Diaper Baby. If you were one, or knew one, you know what I mean. It meant summer camps with Peter Seeger, Paul Robeson records at home, maybe an old grandmother who spoke Yiddish. "Red Diaper Baby" was the term used to describe the children of people in the Communist movement of the 1930s, '40s and '50s.

My mother, Charlotte Tina Schwartz Kurshan, was part of a large extended Jewish family. Her parents, Clara and Louis Schwartz, and grandparents on all sides were immigrants who came to Brooklyn from the village of Stupcet in the Galician Province of the then Austrian-Hungarian Empire. It is somewhere around the Carpathian Mountains on the periphery of Ukraine near Kolymay. A Ukrainian dialect was spoken in daily life, along with Yiddish, and in the schools the language was German.

My maternal grandparents, Clara and Louis, had four children, two boys and two girls. My mother, Charlotte, born April 7, 1918, was the second in line after her older brother Miltie. The family was very poor and Louis worked many different low-paying jobs. All the children were born at home. Groceries were often bought on credit and the family moved frequently from one rented apartment to another.

All the members of our extended family lived in Brooklyn or on the Lower East Side. One day a relative, Sol, was sent to do some labor in the affluent suburb of White Plains. He returned home all excited and exclaimed to his aunt, "Tanta, Tanta, I found America! I found it! It's in White Plains!"

My grandfather Louis was a member of the Amalgamated Clothing Workers Union. He told his kids all about Sacco and Vanzetti, and one day he came home very depressed and upset. He said, "They killed them and they were innocent." He always voted for Labor, the American Labor Party. But my grandfather was considered "apolitical" because he never could understand defending the Soviet Union.

My grandparents' Brighton Beach apartment was often filled with famous stars of the Yiddish theater. Clara herself was a member of the Hebrew Actors Union and was actually rehearsing a part when my mother Charlotte took ill with scarlet fever and Clara had to quit.

As a young adult and oldest of the four children, my Uncle Miltie was exposed to all kinds of cultural events: plays by Eugene O'Neill, concerts in Carnegie Hall, long discussions about art, sex and politics, lectures by the socialist Norman Thomas.

It was my great aunt Francine, my grandmother's baby sister and the only one of her siblings born in America, who was primarily responsible for opening up this world to Miltie. Francine was colorful and exotic with deep olive skin, black hair, embroidered peasant blouses, and large gold hoop earrings. For many years she was married to Bill Albertson, one of the leaders of the Communist Party USA (CP). Years later he was accused of being an undercover FBI agent. By the time of the accusations, Aunt Francine was estranged from Bill. While everyone in the family agrees that Bill was a philanderer, nobody believes that he was an FBI agent. My Uncle Abby says: "An agent? That was a lot of shit. This guy was an organizer of the miners in Pittsburgh, then the hotel and restaurant workers. He risked his life defying Dutch Schultz and his mob. He was a leader of the CP and it was his whole identity. He was probably the only member of the Central Committee who was **not** on the FBI's payroll. That's probably why they were after him!" (Years later Bill sued the government with information received through the Freedom of Information Act (FOIA) and won a $75,000 settlement.)

Schwartz family women in kitchen. **Left to right:** My mom Charlotte, Clara's cousin Fanny Levine, my grandma Clara and my great aunt Francine; Brooklyn, NY, circa 1953.

Eventually Miltie, as well as my mom, joined the Communist Party or the Young Communist League. Miltie took a civil service exam, scored extremely high and became an apprentice at the Brooklyn Navy Yard sheet metal shop where he worked for the next 17 years. There was no union in the Navy Yard, so Miltie started agitating for one. Eventually the American Federation of Labor gave them a charter and Miltie was head of the grievance committee and then vice president of the local as well as the delegate to the Metal Trades Council.

Uncle Miltie was also the weekly open-air (soapbox) speaker on Graham Avenue and Cook Street as well as the English speaker at the Italian workers club. One time he was sent down to the Red Hook waterfront to speak, and anti-communists wrecked the platform. During the McCarthy period of the 1950s, subversion charges were brought against him. He was blacklisted and reduced to selling Fuller Brushes door-to-door, and eventually moved to a kibbutz in Israel.

My mom, a few years younger than her brother Miltie, was also politically engaged, but her activities have been more difficult to uncover. Everything Miltie did became legend in the family, whereas it was only after both of my parents died and I was cleaning out their basement that I came across my mother's yearbook picture with the telling caption: "She always shouts of what's right and fair / whenever she's in Union Square." Miltie had been, after all, the eldest son, and in a Jewish family this privileged position harkens back centuries to Jewish law dictating that the eldest son was entitled to the larger portion of the father's estate (Deuteronomy 21). Since there wasn't much of an estate in the Schwartz family, perhaps it was legend and esteem that was passed down instead. My mother was neither the eldest nor a son, and so her history had to be excavated rather than simply recorded.

In her last years, when Charlotte's memory was failing, my daughter Rosa and I tried to pump my mother for information. She told us she had been a Communist Party cell leader and was once arrested and jailed for raising money on the boardwalk in Coney Island. She recalled that several people were involved in the collection and none of them knew you needed a permit.

"We had been collecting contributions in a 'pishka' (Yiddish for a collection can) for the World Youth Conference of the American Youth Movement—a Communist 'front group.' The cops surrounded us and one of the other girls started crying and saying, *'Charlotte, what should I do?'* I whispered, *'Just calm down and do what I do, don't give your right name.'*

"We ended up in a miserable, filthy cell, a horrible place. Money was raised from people who had property and the three others were bailed out. But there wasn't enough for me so I spent the night in jail. When I got to the judge, he said, *'You were in jail all night?!' Case dismissed!'* I was 18 years old and working for a dentist. Luckily the dentist, Victor Hanover, was a progressive guy, a Party man and so it all worked out okay."

Charlotte was quick to point out that the World Youth Conference was endorsed by none other than Eleanor Roosevelt, for whom she held great respect. However, in later years my mother wistfully shared with me that when she was young, she had been an activist out of duty but had never really liked it. "But you," she told me, "You seem to enjoy it, to love that life."

Miltie was of course a star, but the true heroes for our family were those who had served in the Abraham Lincoln Brigade, trade unionists and communists who had fought on the side of the Spanish Republicans against the Fascists prior to World War II. My mother Charlotte spoke sadly of her friend Pinky, who had perished on the battlefield in Spain.

My biological father, Robert Kahn, was a Communist as well, but he came from a wealthier family. Bob Kahn and my mother had been married only briefly when he went off to the army during World War II. While he was overseas, I was born, and when he returned home after the war, my parents divorced. I saw my father from time to time over the years. He worked as a furrier and since he was a union member, he had access to the union's vacation resort in upstate New York. On one very memorable occasion, although I was only 7 at the time, I still vividly recall meeting Paul Robeson. He was very tall and big and dark, and extremely friendly. He seemed to smile all over and I got to shake his hand!

My mom remarried when I was three. It was love at first sight between my new Dad and me. Norman Kurshan became my father for the rest of my life. My experience with him convinced me that biology is not destiny. He loved and cared for me with the love of a father and I returned that love with the love of a daughter. Three years later Lulu was born; she was technically my half sister, but that distinction never mattered in our family. Although Lulu was my pesky little sister by birth, Louise is my dear friend for life.

Norman was in the Army Signal Corps during World War II as a photographer with General Patton's army. He too was involved with the progressive political movements of the times. In fact, he had met my mother at a meeting where she'd been fundraising for a radical activity. From those early years, I remember the electric excitement of marching in May Day parades, being pushed in a stroller alongside thousands of others. One of my earliest memories is of a smoke-filled room, that in retrospect, was probably campaign headquarters for the Progressive Party in Henry Wallace's 1948 presidential bid. As a family, we were very emotionally involved in the fight to save Julius and Ethel Rosenberg from being executed as Soviet spies. On June 19, 1953, the Rosenbergs, who had two young sons, both went to the electric chair and my family wept. By then I was nine years old.

I don't remember anyone in my immediate family ever attending synagogue or temple, except myself that is. As a child I went through a phase where I fasted on Yom Kippur and went to temple with friends. While my parents did not discourage me, neither did they come along. Neither of my parents believed in God. On the other hand, we were always proud to be Jewish. I was sent to Sholem Aleichem Schule, a progressive and secular Jewish school named after the renowned writer and humorist. I enjoyed learning Yiddish, singing Jewish songs and hearing about the long history of Jews struggling for freedom. My parents never tried to blend in with the dominant Christian culture. We looked forward to and celebrated all the Jewish holidays that had anything to do with food and family.

My Mom and Dad, Charlotte and Norman Kurshan, circa 1948.

Above and **below:** My Mom and me, circa 1949.

Most importantly, my Jewish family's attitude toward fascism profoundly shaped my worldview. In the face of genocide, in the face of oppression, to my mother there were no "Good Germans." In fact, I recall an incident where Dieter, a summer camp counselor from Germany, tried to shake hands with my mother and she recoiled and walked away. This was despite the fact that he had been probably 8 years old during World War II and was now a politically progressive adult. While I rejected my mother's reaction toward Dieter, I nonetheless embraced the general philosophy of personal responsibility. *"Never again"* in our part of the Jewish community meant that there could be no justification for turning one's back on injustice wherever it was encountered. There could be no excuses for inaction such as *"I didn't know what was happening."* or *"I was just doing my job."* This way of thinking laid the basis for my subsequent responsiveness to the civil rights movement, the struggle of the Vietnamese people and indeed, the plight of the Palestinian people.

The Communist movement affected me most deeply through my experiences at Camp Woodland in Phoenicia, New York. Located in the Catskill Mountains, Woodland was one of a number of summer camps for children who had some relationship to the radical movement. It was founded in 1938 and closed in 1962. Norman and Hannah Studer were the heart and soul of Woodland. The Studers were from the left wing of the Progressive Education movement. Woodland was not officially affiliated with any Communist organization, although Norman, a Mennonite, wrote for the *New Masses* and would often take his students to the May Day parades.

My parents sent me to Camp Woodland (an act of political courage during the McCarthy years) for seven summers up until the age of 17. As the years progressed, it became one of the strongest influences on my life and consciousness. Woodland was this strange and wonderful place where people of different backgrounds came together. It was first and foremost an interracial setting, where campers and counselors, both black and white, lived and ate and worked and socialized together. Angela Davis was once a counselor there and some of the students who were brave enough to attempt to integrate the schools in Little Rock were campers.

Woodland was internationalist, an affirmation of a world community and of the unity of humanity. Instead of "color wars," the usual athletic competitions at other camps, we had the World Olympics. The camp was divided up into four countries. Each group learned about the culture of their assigned country and there would be expressions of that culture in food, song, dance, as well as the usual athletic competitions. (Never mind that one country seemed always to be the Soviet Union and another was, with unusual frequency, Israel.) We had counselors from Cuba, Germany, Japan, and Ghana. There were staff members from the Communist Party and other smaller radical groups such as the Progressive Labor Party. Every Sunday we would all get together in an outside amphitheater for Sunday meeting. These Sunday gatherings were a cross between Quaker meetings and a raucous sing-along. We saw Charlie Chaplin movies and summer stock plays like *Inherit the Wind*, about the 1925 Tennessee trial that dealt with the teaching of evolution.

Equality for all and respect for human labor were underlying themes. Everybody worked. We took turns setting and clearing tables in the dining hall and were responsible for cleaning our bunks. The older the children, the more work there was. The adolescent part of the camp was called "Work Camp" and we spent half the day maintaining the roads, clearing woods, building and maintaining structures. This had a practical side that contributed to the maintenance of the camp, but it was also ideological, intended to build respect for manual labor. Consumerism was taboo. There was a very simple list of clothes and items that you were to bring from home, and that was it; nothing more was permitted. Campers were to have no money and if care packages came from home, they were shared by the entire group. And although this was communism in its purest form, every morning began with a trudge down to the flagpole where we would raise the Stars and Stripes and recite the Pledge of Allegiance!

Woodland was a folk-singing place and it was a folk-singing time. It seemed like every other person there played the guitar and we were constantly teaching each other new songs and ways to play: songs of struggle and songs of love, international songs, and Negro spirituals. "Dark As a Dungeon," a Kentucky coal miner's ballad, was one of my favorites. I learned a good deal of history through these folk songs. In part because of this experience, I have always seen culture and politics as intertwined. Anywhere you find a truly dynamic movement there will be a synergistic relationship with the arts.

One of the most exciting events of every summer at Camp Woodland was the arrival of folk singer Pete Seeger, often accompanied by his wife Toshi. Camp Woodland and Pete, as we called him, had a mutual love affair. We woke up every morning to the sound of music over the loudspeaker; Pete Seeger singing "Good Morning, Captain" was a big favorite. Pete wove together all the strands of inter-racialism, internationalism, respect for labor and equality, and we would have a rocking time with the whole camp singing along. We would sit on the stones in our outdoor amphitheater and sing our hearts out while Pete stomped his feet, his tall, lanky frame pointing to the sky, his Adam's apple working hard.

Of course, the House Un-American Activities Committee (HUAC) was listening as well. HUAC was a reincarnation of Joséph McCarthy's campaign to root out communism, and it wreaked havoc on peoples' lives by subpoenaing them to testify against individuals and organizations in the progressive movement. Many people associated with Woodland were targets of HUAC, and rather than cooperate with this witch-hunt, a popular strategy was to refuse to testify by invoking the Fifth Amendment.

In August of 1955 when I was 11 years old, Pete came to Camp Woodland a few days before he was due to testify before HUAC. He sang *Die Gedanken Sind Frei* to all of us as we gathered in the outdoor amphitheater. He also sang the children's song *Abiyoyo* about a giant. He told us that some stories have a moral and that the moral of this story was that one good song can beat a giant. He then explained that he would soon be questioned by some men who wanted him to stop singing.

Even at the tender age of eleven I understood that Woodland was a refuge, a place to come to renew energy, to gain sustenance in order to go out and do battle with the forces of reaction. I will never forget the thrill of watching Pete autograph my paper with his fast scrawl, encircling a drawing of a banjo. Years later, I got a card from Pete with a contribution to our prison work and the same distinctive autograph.

Not everyone felt the same way as I did about Woodland. There were problems in paradise. The summer of my 13th year, I fell in with a smart-mouthed bad boy. Eric was a year or two older than me, had curly blond hair, big lips, and a heavy Brooklyn accent. Campers were not allowed to smoke cigarettes, and Eric refused to go along with the program. I was a model camper, probably could have won a Young Pioneer medal if they were giving them out, but I sided with Eric and his bid for personal freedom. After all, no one had ever French kissed me before. Eric was kicked out of camp and I was really pissed off.

I'm sure there were other more serious issues that arose but for me it was a magical community and helped me to be able to "imagine all the people living a life of peace." I loved Woodland. Every summer I felt like I was in a Utopian oasis and even though I also loved returning to my family, I was incredibly sad to leave Woodland at the end of each season.

My dad was eventually able to start a business of his own, using the photographic processing and printing skills he had honed while in the Army. Then thanks in no small part to the GI Bill, when I was ten years of age, my family left Brooklyn for suburban life on Long Island. Goodbye, extended family of the immigrant community;hello, American nuclear family. Although it was a sea change for our family, nonetheless we did cling to some aspects of the extended family. My aunt's family lived across the street and various relatives came to stay for periods of time—my grandmother, my cousin Michael, my Israeli cousin Yona. But I was the only Jewish kid in all of the sixth grade! Well, apart from Joan Mahoney who was Irish and Jewish. She and I became fast friends for life, drawn to each other at first due to a common love of books.

On arrival I loved the suburbs: the wide, open spaces allowed me such freedom of movement. I rode bicycles and played sports and was generally in constant motion. There was also more space indoors. Every house seemed to have a "den," rooms that were great for having parties where you could slow dance with boys without any parents being around.

But as the years went on and junior high turned into high school, what had at first seemed to be a wonderful dream came to feel more like an obstacle, a restraint that held my spirit back. I gravitated more and more to "the City," which for me was Manhattan or Brooklyn, anything but suburban Long Island. On weekends I met my friends from Camp Woodland, who lived mostly in "the City." Often I stayed overnight at my friend Ruth Wallach's apartment in Brooklyn. We went to see the great actor Eli Wallach, Ruth's uncle, perform in a Eugene Ionesco play off-Broadway, and got to hang out with him backstage. Both of Ruth's parents had been teachers active in the union. However, her father, who had been president of the union, lost his job during the McCarthy era due to his politics.

Traveling in packs, with guitars on our shoulders, we played and sang along with hundreds of others in Washington Square Park. The folk-singer/wordsmith Woody Guthrie was our hero and role model. We listened to the music of Ramblin' Jack Elliot, Dave Van Ronk, Peggy Seeger, and the New Lost City Ramblers, and eagerly awaited the hootenannies in Carnegie Hall where we heard the Weavers (Pete Seeger, Ronnie Gilbert, Lee Hayes, and Freddy Hellerman). At the Ethical Culture Society we folk danced. But often we just roamed around Greenwich Village for hours because just being together was a high. We would stop in at Israel "Izzy" Young's Folklore Center on MacDougal Street, a mecca for everything to do with folk music, where we would devour the latest issue of *Sing Out* magazine.

Some of my classmates in suburbia viewed me as a "beatnik" or a "bohemian." In truth, I was a bit young to be a full-fledged beatnik, but I was a wannabe. I wore peasant blouses, Mexican huarache sandals, never cut my hair, and had had my ears pierced at age 13. I bought dangly earrings at the Jewel Box store on 8th Street in Greenwich Village. Oh, and I religiously wore no makeup and, much to the chagrin of my mother, was totally uninterested in clothes shopping.

It was the end of the 1950s but I believe it was the foreshadowing of the political/cultural upheaval of the 1960s. Movements don't spring up full-blown without any antecedents. In the late 1950s there were signs and seeds of future events in the cultural garden of the time.

In October of 1958 I traveled to Washington, D.C., with a youth group from East Meadow, Long Island. We were heading for the Youth March for Integrated Schools, coordinated by Bayard Rustin and Herbert Wright. We joined ten thousand other young people who gathered at the Lincoln Memorial to "press for the laws which will guide and sanction our advancement to a fuller, more just, interracial democracy." My diary entry, at age 14, reports that:

> *Harry Belafonte, Jackie Robinson, Rev. Martin Luther King's wife spoke. A wonderful feeling to stand up for what I believe. Speeches were held at the Lincoln Memorial. Food for supper was lousy. New York weather was rainy but Washington was sunny. It was a six-hour ride each way. I saw many friends I haven't seen for a long time. Ike would not see the delegation. Maybe he was playing golf? Maybe he had nothing to say?*

In April of 1959 there would be a second Youth March in Washington and I became more active in the planning. We organized a busload of young people to travel to the April march in Washington.

There were reportedly 26,000 people at the march but my diary entry states only that the "Youth March was very exciting, of course, articles included." But the articles are missing and the rest of the entry deals with which boys I had crushes on at the moment, setting it all in my distorted teen perspective. I was becoming an activist, but I was still first and foremost an adolescent.

Despite my preoccupation with boys, I did continue to follow the action. I discovered that the Congress on Racial Equality (CORE) was holding picket lines outside local Long Island Woolworth stores because they discriminated in their hiring practices. So I began to attend those meetings as well and joined their picket lines.

Parallel to my involvement with what would become a full-blown civil rights movement, I was eager to act on the issue of disarmament as well. The Committee for a Sane Nuclear Policy (SANE) was a national organization that came into existence in the late 1950s. Its ultimate goal was for international and general disarmament with

At age 17, jamming in St. Croix, Virgin Islands: *"Since I Married Dorothy, She has me goin' crazy"*. Circa 1961.

intermediate aims such as moratoriums on atom bomb testing. It was the first to warn of the danger from radioactive fallout.

Many people supported both causes—civil rights and disarmament. The names of Harry Belafonte and Dr. Martin Luther King, Jr. were found on the stationery of both SANE and CORE.

In 1959, a friend and I attended a lecture of the Greater Roslyn Committee for a Sane Nuclear Policy. We decided then and there to join their movement, announcing a meeting at my house for all young people interested in a sane nuclear policy. The youth branch of the Greater Roslyn Committee of SANE was formed with me as the chairman. We sold tickets to a May 19th rally at Madison Square Garden. We distributed leaflets at a screening of the film *On the Beach* (about what happens in the world after a disastrous nuclear war). We ran an educational assembly at Wheatley, our high school. But the most exciting activity was refusing to participate in our high school Civil Defense Drill, the one where you crouch down in a hallway and protect your head from a nuclear holocaust. Instead, we handed out SANE literature and wore black armbands in protest.

The 1950s were characterized by repression and it went beyond the realm of politics. It infected all areas of life, including gender relationships and sexuality. However, the sexual freedom of the sixties was beckoning, presaged by the enormous popularity of rock 'n' roll, which confirmed that it was okay to have bodies. Our spirits were unleashed by the music of Bo Diddley, Chuck Berry, Fats Domino, the Everly Brothers, Little Richard, Buddy Holly and on and on. And of course there was Elvis, deeply influenced by gospel music, who gyrated his way to fame. Throughout high school I knew very little about contraception. Not a word about it was breathed in school. My mother, a free spirit in her own way, warned me that *"You don't have to marry the first man you sleep with."* That shocked my sensibilities. I told her it was a very premature statement and so we dropped the subject. However, I was very mindful that sex could lead to pregnancy and was determined not to go there.

In my senior year, I had my first serious relationship. Peter Nelson (a science geek!) and I became inseparable up until I went off to college.

He was a kind, intelligent guy who really appreciated me. But in retrospect I don't think I was quite ready for a serious relationship; I had too many places to go and people to see.

By the time I was ready for college, I had the consciousness to be part of an activist movement and had already taken some actual steps in that direction.

MADISON

I WOULD BE THE FIRST person in my family to graduate from college. My parents, although very excited about it, were not involved in the search for a school, and I made short shrift of it. When it came time to apply, my main criterion was the relative ease of the application. I completed the University of Wisconsin application in under half an hour with very little angst or, for that matter, thought. When I was accepted, that's where I went, sight unseen, in 1961.

Madison was a good fit for me. In the next years, college campuses started to jump off with radical political activity and Madison became a center of such activity. Of course phenomena like that don't emerge from thin air and Madison was no exception. There was a deep radical intellectual tradition at the campus. The national journal *Studies on the Left* was published out of Madison beginning in 1959. Every year when ROTC had their military ball, campus radicals and bohemians held an anti-military ball complete with satirical skits, costumes, and music. Although the rabid anti-communist Joséph McCarthy had been the Senator from Wisconsin, it was also true that the campaign to oust McCarthy had been led from the University of Wisconsin.

One of my best friends from high school, Diane Bland, went to the University of Wisconsin as well, and we were roommates off and on for four years. For us New Yorkers, Madison was culture shock. We had never seen so many blond-haired, blue-eyed, healthy looking Christian people, many of whom actually came from farming communities. I'm sure the culture shock went both ways as they were not so accustomed to loud-mouthed, opinionated Jewish New Yorkers. So it was an interesting mix.

It was also surprising to see a city so close to nature. This big city felt more like a small town. On an isthmus between two lakes, it was exquisitely picturesque. From the terrace of the Student Union, I could gaze at the crystal clear waters of Lake Mendota. Walking down the steep Bascom Hill where many classes were situated, my eyes reveled in the glorious autumn colors. In the winter I felt exhilarated by the clean fresh snowfall and the cold, cleansing air. On the other hand, getting up in the dark and racing to climb that hill to my 7:45 am class at below zero temperatures, I sometimes wondered why the hell I ever left New York.

My friends and I viewed the concept and even more importantly the practice of *in loco parentis* ("in the place of parents") as a holdover from Victorian times. What was most infuriating was the discriminatory way in which it was applied. The campus curfew for women was 10:30 pm, but men had no curfew. Except for the principle of the matter, it was okay with me since I had nowhere to go. But my good friend Nina wanted to be with her boyfriend John. The curfew was a problem for Nina but we worked around it. Nina was very interested in theater and I knew she could pull off an effective cameo performance. So whenever there was an unannounced bed check by the imperious housemother, I would report that Nina was in the bathroom, and then run to alert her by phone. Then ensued a mad dash for Nina, and for me as well as I ran to unlock the back door, and voila, she was there to show her smiling face.

My letters home the first year reflected the usual freshman angst: "I've grown up in many ways—I understand what it's like to be insignificant and can accept it." Although I enjoyed the readings, I found that "the classes were not more stimulating than high school; I have not found a truly intellectual atmosphere here." But I assured my mother that "I want to go to graduate school and don't intend to drop out like all other girls." Perhaps my disdain for my "sisters" can be forgiven since this was before the women's movement emerged, and I was determined not to "get married and settle down." Or at least I was in no hurry to do so, as I was later to prove.

Nancy in gown designed by biological paternal grandmother Ida Kahn, designer for stars of Jewish stage & screen, circa early 1960s.

I turned 18 that February of 1962, and in April, Malcolm X spoke on campus. He rocked the Madison campus while addressing a standing-room-only crowd in the Wisconsin Student Union.

I don't believe I have ever heard any speaker, before or since, of Malcolm's stature and charisma. The following year would find me in Washington, D.C. for Dr. King's famous address, but honestly, I recall little of his speech. Standing at under five feet, I was more preoccupied with the crowd surrounding me in D.C. than with the speakers. All that was in view was a sea of people.

With Malcolm it was different. He was just a few feet away from me with no distractions other than the high energy of anticipation in the room. At 6'3" he was an imposing figure, dressed in a dark single-breasted suit, a freshly starched white tab-collar shirt, and a skinny black necktie. It was clear from the way he carried himself and the timbre of his voice that he was comfortable and proud of who he was. With the final touch of his black-rimmed glasses, he could have been mistaken for an African Ambassador to the United Nations. Yet most importantly he said things that Black people had probably been saying to one another for years, but that the rest of us had never heard before. Expressing himself with stories and with wit, he was articulate in a way we could all understand.

I was impressed with Malcolm and also challenged. His ideas made sense but they were new to me. He was not talking the language of integration that I had been raised on since birth and reaching for since my high school years, yet I felt I understood what Malcolm was saying. I understood Malcolm's anger and believed we needed to rethink what we were trying to do. I also agreed that all white people shared in the responsibility of racism and had an obligation to do something about it.

That summer, the summer of 1962, I traveled to an Israeli kibbutz to visit my maternal uncle Miltie, his wife Honchie, and my cousins. I arrived at Kfar Blum in the Upper Galilee with great anticipation. My uncle was the head fisherman on this collective farm and I thought it sounded like a possibly superior way of living, a model for socialism.

I could rewrite history and tell you that I had disliked everything about Israel, since now for many years I have been profoundly disturbed by the settler behavior and mentality of many Israelis and, of course, the Israeli State. However, in 1962 my reactions were more mixed. I loved the physical challenges and worked hard at picking fruit in the orchards. I was proud to be evaluated as a great worker by the foreman of my work shift who tried to talk me into staying. She herself was a holocaust survivor and I felt I had passed an important test. I swam each day in the Jordan River that ran through the kibbutz. I loved the Israeli folk dancing and singing. I was also fascinated by the living arrangements on the kibbutz; the children all lived together, separate from their parents, and everyone ate together in a big dining hall.

I had been seeing a guy in Madison, Doug Baer, who was also in Israel at the time and would be staying on to attend Hebrew University in the fall. He tried to convince me to do the same, but at the end of the day, although I was still intrigued with Israel, I had some serious concerns.

Many of the workers on the kibbutz were Black Jews from North Africa, and Arabs who lived in the area. They were day laborers who went home to their villages at night and returned in the morning, receiving a small wage from the kibbutz. My first night there, an argument broke out between my uncle and my cousin. My cousin was born in Brooklyn as Steven but had become an Israeli at the age of 10 and was now known by his Hebrew name, Shimon. His father was my Uncle Miltie who had been part of the progressive movement in the U.S. and a target of the anticommunist campaign in the '50s. Shimon was complaining that the day laborers were all lazy and had a bad work ethic. That upset my uncle who said that's exactly what people used to say about workers in the U.S., and particularly about Black workers who had the lowest paid and most menial jobs. I listened intently and was surprised that my cousin Shimon, a member of my family and my generation, would have those views. I don't really believe in the concept of a "national character," but I did find Israelis, especially those on the kibbutz, to be less than warm and generous people. In a letter home I wrote that I was learning to be more independent and not to have to rely on others, a strange lesson to learn in a "collective" setting. I wonder now if that kind of thinking is part of a settler mentality.

By the time the summer was over, I left Israel with the words of Malcolm X still echoing in my head and the seeds of disillusionment with Israel in my heart. This was not an easy transition. I had always been so proud of being Jewish, so proud of my connection to a people who had struggled so hard against oppression. I had been sure that "we" were on the moral side of everything. But that summer was the beginning of a paradigm shift in the way that I viewed Israel.

On the other hand, back in the States for my second year at Madison, I continued to folk dance at the Hillel Center and elected to study Hebrew. That year Diane and I lived with two other friends in Dorothea House, a cooperative housing situation. There were 20 or so women who lived together in a big, old house. We had two rooms for the four of us, so we piled our bunk beds up and put our desks in the other room. In the basement was a big communal kitchen where everyone cooked and ate. The four of us took turns shopping and making dinners. The full-figured fairy godmother/housemother, Irma Hemer, was very cool, and a good time was had by all. Dorothea House was a big relief after the first year at Lowell Hall, a pretentious place where we had had formal dinners complete with uniformed waiters and mandatory meals with the very proper housemother.

When we returned to college for our sophomore year (1962), a pivotal moment in the civil rights movement was unfolding. James Meredith was risking his life as he attempted to be the first Black student to attend the University of Mississippi. That simple activity, his going to school, unleashed a white mob, 2000 strong, who attacked with guns, bricks, bottles, and Molotov cocktails. In letters home I wrote that Mississippi was on everyone's lips and "Kennedy's speech was very disappointing. I suppose I was naïve to expect more." In October there was a silent demonstration at the top of Bascom Hill in sympathy with James Meredith. I was responsible for contacting religious leaders to solicit their participation, although I didn't actually attend myself, because I had made a commitment to volunteer my time at the library in Mendota State Hospital, the state mental hospital on the other side of the lake, and felt I couldn't miss my shift. I did, however, have time to attend a fund-raising party for the Civil Rights Movement where I learned the "twist" and the "snake."

That first month back on campus, Diane and I joined Americans for Democratic Action. I was apprehensive because the ADA was known nationally for being somewhat anti-communist. I don't know if I considered myself an actual communist but I was definitely an anti-anti-communist! However, it seemed like the only well-organized action group on campus, and I respected the leadership. One of our first activities was to picket sororities and fraternities for their discriminatory practices. In a photo from the *Madison Capitol Times* newspaper, Diane and I appear wearing dresses and high heels as we walked the picket line as the clean-cut collegians that we were.

I was now spending a lot of time with someone I had met folk dancing—Marty Gold. He was one year younger than me and "a great boy to go out with, not at all oppressive or demanding." Did I love him? What a stupid question, I reflected in my diary. I wanted the companionship but was still nowhere near ready for love or sex or long-term commitment.

Life was exciting. I was biking, canoeing and ice-skating. And still playing the guitar and singing: at a college reception for 200 people including my teachers, on the University radio station, and at a coffee shop. Foreign films played regularly in the Student Union theater—*400 Blows, La Dolce Vita.* I was reading Marx in my Economics course and studying *The Beggars Opera* by Brecht in English class. I heard and saw the poet John Ciardi, the Modern Jazz Quartet, and Miriam Makeba, the South African singer and anti-apartheid activist. Films, music, books, life experiences, and sometimes classes fed one on another and, in that synergistic process, consciousness grew and a movement was growing.

I was having a great time until I contracted mononucleosis along with my roommate Susan, and ended up in the University Hospital with my mom at my side. I got better but struggled to stay in school that year. I dropped out of the Integrated Liberal Studies Department and developed a crush on my psychology professor, Dr. Mavis Hetherington, who became my advisor. With her as my role model, I decided to get a Ph.D.

in psychology, although I noted in a letter home that "becoming a psychologist and having children might be difficult."

The next summer, the summer of 1963, I spent in New York working at my father's office as a secretary. My boyfriend Marty worked there as well. However, he learned to actually process and print color film. I thought nothing of it at the time, but in later years wondered why he was given the opportunity to develop such a skill when it was never a consideration for me. I'm sure my father, if he reflected upon it at all, would have thought he was protecting me from those harsh chemicals and perhaps he was, but such were the subtle ways that sexism played out.

That was the summer of the great civil rights march where 250,000 people marched on DC and Dr. Martin Luther King gave his historic "I Have a Dream Speech" on the steps of the Lincoln Memorial. We were there—my mom, my sister Louise, and I. We took the train down to Washington, DC, and joined the march. What a thrill to be with my family among such a crowd of people all on the same exceptional mission.

In September of 1963, as we were returning to school, the KKK bombed a Black church in Birmingham, Alabama, killing three Black girls. I felt both depression and fury. On the 22nd of November, President John F. Kennedy was assassinated. Very honestly, I was not a big supporter of Kennedy. I felt he was not a strong force in support of civil rights. Nonetheless the assassination took my breath away and was further cause for distrust and apprehension about what forces dominated the American political scene.

During my junior year, I began working with a Neighborhood Center in the Black community, tutoring 10-year-old Larry, who had five other siblings and was being raised by a single mom. I also folk danced at Hillel House, went biking, played softball, and studied a bit of Kant, Hegel, and Marx in political science class. Diane got engaged and I had my wisdom teeth pulled, two approximately parallel processes in my mind: Diane got a ring and I got a lead apron to wear for dental x-rays. I continued to see Marty.

Summer of 1964, I worked as a camp counselor at Circle Pines in Michigan. Marty worked there as well but that summer we split up. I had no regrets about the time we had spent together but was quite relieved. I hooked up with Howie Emmer, who was still in high school in Cleveland, a good transition out of the relationship with Marty and possibly only a summer's liaison. Although Marty was upset, I knew he'd be fine and sure enough, before the summer's end he had a new girlfriend.

Circle Pines was a summer camp begun by the co-op movement in the early 1940s. It wasn't a hardcore 'commie' camp like Woodland, but it was a progressive place. I was a counselor in the Youth Camp, and two Black teenagers, one girl and one boy, were in my group. They were SNCC (Student Nonviolent Coordinating Committee) workers from Greenwood, Mississippi, sent by the organization for a vacation.

That was the summer that SNCC and an umbrella group, the Council of Federated Organizations (COFO), led a massive voter registration and desegregation campaign in Mississippi called Freedom Summer. Toward the end of June three campaign workers—Andrew Goodman, Michael Schwerner and James Cheney—were murdered by the Ku Klux Klan, sending a shock wave around the globe and certainly through me. I identified especially with Andy Goodman, who was from New York, had gone on the 1959 Youth March for Integration, and was also enrolled at Madison for the fall.

My last year in Madison I took a law course in Civil Liberties and read *"Freedom to the Free, a Report to the President by the United States Commission on Civil Rights."* It described all the legislation related to civil rights since 1863. The first week of school I decided to drop a course because, I wrote, "I intend to be active in civil rights." Soon after, I attended a Friends of SNCC meeting where I heard Stokely Carmichael speak. He came to campus dressed in the blue denim overalls that would become a SNCC uniform. His casual, down-home demeanor contrasted with the statesmanlike presence of Malcolm X. But with his infectious smile and the faint hint of West Indian roots in the lilt of his voice, he was just as compelling in a different way. His youthful passion for this righteous cause drew me in and by the time he left campus, I had joined Friends of SNCC.

When Barry Goldwater, the conservative Senator from Arizona and an opponent of civil rights legislation, was booked to speak on the

Capitol Steps, we organized a huge picket line. I was in charge of contacting academic departments to see if they wanted to participate and I also spoke at fraternities and sororities to solicit their assistance. By February of 1965 we were financially supporting 18 SNCC workers in the field.

1965 was a watershed year as the violence continued to intensify! On February 21, Malcolm X was assassinated. It was a shock to my system. Of course, Malcolm wasn't the first to be assassinated in the struggle for Black liberation. The murder of Emmett Till and of Goodman, Cheney and Schwerner were all still fresh in my memory. But I had never seen any of them speak and Malcolm had been such a powerful presence— a 6-foot tall charismatic figure who spoke with such a powerful, confident, poetic, and prideful brilliance. And I had been so close to him, I could have almost reached out and touched him. His assassination felt so personal, and I was flooded with an overwhelming sense that we had to do more. I had to do more. It was one rung in an increasingly repressive process that would drive me from protest to resistance and eventually toward revolution. On the heels of Malcolm's assassination came Alabama's Bloody Sunday, when 600 peaceful Civil Rights marchers were tear-gassed and billy-clubbed on a bridge in Selma.

Meanwhile as a senior in Madison I had one of my most memorable political experiences. It was my first encounter with direct action, other than picketing and demonstrating. The Madison chapter of the Congress on Racial Equality (CORE) decided to take on the Sears Department Store that refused to hire Blacks in sales positions.

Leaflets were printed describing the situation and calling on people not to shop there. A picket line was thrown up and the leaflets were handed out while about 30 of us, all dressed up and looking like serious shoppers, entered the store. My friend John Darnton (who later became a *New York Times* reporter) and I entered together, pretending to be a newlywed couple. We shopped all over that store, buying things I didn't know I knew how to buy. Then just before payment was required, I "discovered" the flyer in my pocketbook, inquired about their hiring policies and insisted we could not possibly shop in a store that discriminated.

Similar encounters were going on all over the store. Following these individual actions a group of us women converged on the dressing room, monopolizing them so no one else could try on clothes. The finale was a sit-in in the shoe department. By this time the store was topsy-turvy and the management called the police and those of us who were not willing to get arrested were warned to leave.

It was the first time I had ever seen anyone get arrested. I decided to leave but the decision was a difficult one and I was not fully comfortable with it. I had great respect for those who were going through with it. My first experience with creative direct action, with political theater, was a big success. Our goal had been to disrupt store activity and hurt business. We received a flurry of local media attention and shortly thereafter Sears changed their policy.

I was becoming increasingly radicalized and committed. When I arrived in Madison, the main game in town was the Socialist Club. It was dominated by male voices, and I could certainly never find mine in that milieu. There was an "inner circle" of radical intellectuals, largely scholars of history, and I would never be one of them. During the civil rights activities there was more participation of women, and I discovered at least a small voice of my own. I responded to my radical upbringing with a potential for participating in political activity, but it was civil rights and later on, the Vietnam war that broke through the insularity of groups like the Socialist Club and opened the door to wider participation for myself as well as many others.

My politics were shaping more and more of my life.

In the winter I joined the Green Lantern Eating Coop, a gathering place for people engaged in the political and cultural scene of the times. At each meal people would clink a spoon against their glasses to get people's attention and then stand up and make announcements about ongoing activities and meetings. I really loved the atmosphere as well as the idea of participating in a communal eating arrangement. The camaraderie of peeling potatoes and then eating together was great.

My decision to go to graduate school in Psychology at the University of California, Berkeley, was influenced in large part by my first woman professor. There were essentially no women professors in the early '60s. For that matter there were no women doctors or lawyers either; at least I never saw one. The entire four years in Madison I had only one professor or instructor who was a woman! I am sure I had never laid eyes on a professional woman until I encountered Professor Mavis Hetherington. Her area of concentration was Child Development and when she took the lecture stage to speak I was mesmerized. She was smart, confident, funny, and charming. With perfectly coifed red hair and freckles, she looked striking in her blue and green skirt suits, her high heels clicking as she paced and spoke. She spoke passionately with penetrating eyes that seemed to be directed right to me. Her lectures were fascinating and electric. I took every possible course with her, decided to major in psychology and then get a Ph.D.

Dr. Hetherington had previously studied at UC Berkeley. She initially went there to work with the renowned psychologist Erik Erikson—although, upon arrival, she found that he had left because the University insisted he sign a loyalty oath and he had refused. Still, she felt UC Berkeley would be a wonderful graduate school for me.

Beyond any academic considerations, I was also eager to attend Berkeley because of the level of radical political engagement there. From Madison I had followed closely the 1964 Berkeley Free Speech Movement.

Made uneasy by increasing anti-war and civil rights activism, the University of California (Berkeley) administration had been attempting to stifle it with stricter regulations, which the students ignored or defied, particularly in Sproul Plaza, the popular campus hotbed of radical organizing. So finally the administration called in the cops. Jack Weinberg was arrested for leafletting material deemed "unrelated to campus activities" and thrown into a police car. A crowd gathered. Someone shouted, "Sit down!" and hundreds did exactly that, surrounding and immobilizing the police car for 32 hours until a negotiated truce was reached.

Like students around the country, I had watched (on TV) when Mario Savio addressed the crowd from the roof of the surrounded police car:

> *"There's a time when the operation of the machine becomes so odious, makes you so sick at heart, that you can't take part. And you've got to put*

your bodies upon the gears and upon the wheels, upon the levers, upon all the apparatus, and you've got to make it stop."

In my heart, I was already part of that crowd.

A student strike followed, the entire university was closed down, and the students won a clear victory with the restoration of their right to organize. Inspired by the Free Speech Movement, in the spring of 1965 Berkeley radicals organized "Vietnam Day", a 36-hour, nonstop marathon anti-war "teach-in," which drew 40,000 participants. Many of them later tried to block troop trains heading to nearby Oakland, a shipping point to Vietnam for draftees.

I also knew about the Berkeley scene from the film "Operation Abolition." Shown to a packed audience in the Madison Student Union Auditorium, it was supposed to be a right-wing propaganda movie exposing communist "operations" against the House Un-American Activities Committee. The movie was a 45-minute documentary about protests in San Francisco in May of 1960. HUAC was holding hearings on subversive activity in California, and several hundred people came out to San Francisco City Hall to protest. The police arrested 70 people and blasted others down the steps of City Hall with fire hoses! But the protesters were undeterred and thousands returned, chanting the Nazi salute "SEIG HEIL!"

The movie had been produced by the supporters of HUAC and was intended to show what important work HUAC was doing. To us, however, it had the opposite effect: it signaled a new resistance to a previously unbridled red hunt. When it was shown to a full house in Madison, we were all cheering for the young people who were fighting to abolish HUAC in the face of police violence. I knew then that I wanted to go to California; "Operation Abolition" and the Free Speech Movement were more than I could resist.

It was 1965, my last year in Madison, when people I knew from the civil rights movement began organizing educational activities about the situation in Vietnam. About two years before this I had begun to hear about "U.S. advisors" being sent there, Buddhist protesters being killed, and monks immolating themselves. It all came to a head in 1964 with

Above: College roommates landing in NY airport from Madison, Xmas 1962:
Left to right: Jean Bardacke, Susan Stern, Diane Bland and Nancy.
Below: Me and my Martin New Yorker guitar, circa 1962.

the Gulf of Tonkin incident and a Congressional resolution, giving the U.S. military the green light in Vietnam. (It would later become clear that this "incident" had no more credence than the "Weapons of Mass Destruction" would have before the 2003 US invasion and subsequent war with Iraq.)

Diane and I would go down to the Student Union every morning for our usual nutritious breakfast of coffee, orange juice, and a glazed donut. In spring of 1965 I remember passing the newsstand and seeing the headlines in the *New York Times* about a U.S. bombing campaign called "Rolling Thunder." It was just the beginning of a campaign that went on for years.

Whereas a while ago I had never heard of Vietnam and had to consult a map to locate it geographically, now each day seemed to bring more disturbing news reports about the role that the U.S. was playing there. I was horrified that my country, my government, was responsible for such pain and suffering.

I paid attention and took it all in, and was drawn to the speak-outs on the steps of the Student Union. But I still maintained that the most important thing to deal with was the situation here at home, most particularly, Civil Rights. I feared that we would lose that focus.

However, it was Students for a Democratic Society (SDS) that helped me see the connections between what up until then I thought were simply separate issues. The war at home against Black people and the war abroad against Vietnamese people, foreign policy and domestic policy, were a product of the same economic and political system.

SDS took on organizing the first coordinated national protest against the war. This was a time when the official peace movement, groups such as the Committee for a SANE Nuclear Policy, as well as prominent individual pacifists and liberals, would not touch the subject of Vietnam because it was considered too controversial. Their response to the SDS call was negative. They criticized it for being one-sided, focusing on the evils of U.S. intervention, and not the evils of communism. They would have preferred "A Plague On Both Your Houses" to be the slogan as opposed to "U.S. Out of Vietnam." But SDS did not want to encourage an anti-communism stance that provided a rationale for aggression against Vietnam. SDS also accepted endorsements from anybody who agreed with them, even if they were communists. It was the beginning of a "non-exclusion " policy that became a hallmark of the New Left. This bothered certain prominent peace activists because they felt it tainted their efforts and left them open to attack by right-wing McCarthy-like forces. But I thought it was right on point.

On April 17, 1965, I traveled to Washington to participate in that first anti-war demonstration that turned out to be a huge success. Twenty thousand people participated, carrying signs that said "I Won't Fight in Vietnam." Paul Potter, the president of SDS, gave the main address. It was a wonderful speech that reached right out and grabbed hold of my heart and mind. He stated that:

> *"The incredible war in Vietnam has severed the last vestiges of illusion that morality and democracy are the guiding principles of American foreign policy …*
>
> *"There is no simple way to attack something that is deeply rooted in the society. The people of this country must create a massive social movement—and if that can be built around the issue of Vietnam then that is what we must do.*
>
> *"By a social movement I mean more than petitions or letters of protest, or tacit support of dissident Congressmen; I mean people who are willing to change their lives, who are willing to challenge the system, to take the problem of change seriously.*
>
> *"That means that we build a movement that … will not tolerate the escalation or prolongation of this war, but will, if necessary, respond to the administration war effort with massive civil disobedience all over the country, that will wrench the country into a confrontation with the issues of the war."*

I was excited by this speech. It articulated what I had been thinking and feeling, albeit in more embryonic form. We were not dealing with a momentary lapse of morality on the part of the government, but an entrenched system and we needed fundamental change. For that to be realized, we had to commit our lives to building a movement. It was not enough to attend a demonstration here and there; we had to make what became known as "the Movement" a priority.

It was at the Green Lantern Eating Co-op that I met "Guy" (as we will call him). He was a couple of years older than me. Blond and blue-eyed, he arrived from London just at the time of the so-called "British Invasion." I was already in love with the Beatles and the Stones, so it wasn't much of a leap. Guy was also sexually experienced, and I fell passionately in love.

I couldn't get enough of Guy and for the rest of that academic year we were inseparable. Then one day we went for a ride in the countryside in his powder blue MG convertible. At the end of the ride, he told me he had to share something with me.

"I feel very nervous telling you this. Please don't be angry at me. Remember I love you. I couldn't bring myself to tell you this earlier, but I am engaged to be married to a woman from Sri Lanka. She will be arriving over the summer to come and live with me. I didn't expect to fall in love with you. I feel great affection for her but I'm not in love with her. And I don't know what I will do."

I was beyond shocked. I had a really hard time believing it was true, let alone accepting it. It sent me into an emotional turmoil. I wanted answers.

"What does that mean? If you're not in love with her, are you going to break it off ? And don't you think you should let her know before she makes the trip?" The questions came tumbling out.

"I can't do that. I don't know what to do. I can't sleep or think," he said. "She is leaving her husband and her very young child to come and be with me. I have a big responsibility to her."

"Oh my God, she's married and is leaving her child! I can't wrap my mind around this!"

Not that he had promised me anything, but he had never mentioned a word of this. Yet instead of walking away, I continued to stay in the relationship. I was 21 years old.

That summer of 1965 I had decided to go to Cleveland to work with SDS on one of their ERAP projects. ERAP stood for Education, Research and Action Project. There were ERAP projects in cities such as Baltimore, Newark, Chicago, Cleveland, and in rural areas like Appalachia.

That same year Michael Harrington's *The Other America* was released with shocking revelations about the breadth and depth of poverty in America. SDS was talking about an interracial movement of the poor. I wanted to fight racism and poverty, to join a movement to change things somehow, somewhere, anywhere or everywhere.

ERAP was already on the west side of Cleveland in a poor, white working-class neighborhood where SDS had been for the past year. They were supporting an organization of welfare mothers that was challenging and attempting to reform Cleveland's welfare system. SDS was also trying to organize a Community Union around economic problems. This summer the work was to be extended to the east side, to the Black neighborhood of Glenville, as part of the vision to build "an interracial movement of the poor." I was assigned to live and work on the east side in Glenville.

In Glenville, all the SDS staff lived in one big house and we were expected to live at "subsistence" level. We paid about $200 to participate in the project for three months. Each of us raised the money before we came, and it went into the communal pot. We were then allowed a small amount each week for personal needs. We did all our cooking and eating together.

Some good work was done that summer. There were many problems in the community—lack of jobs, dilapidated buildings, overcrowded schools, inferior hospitals, and inadequate recreational facilities. We generally went door to door talking to people, letting them know about community union meetings that took place at different peoples' apartments. People were incredibly gracious to us, young white strangers knocking on their doors out of nowhere, and often invited us in to talk.

I also remember sitting in long, long internal SDS "house" meetings that seemed interminable, going around and around on different issues. We all agreed that participatory democracy was our goal, i.e., rule by the people through decentralized participation in the decisions that affect their daily lives. Participatory democracy became the watchword for everything we did. But even in our small project there were all sorts of questions about leadership and decision-making. What were our long-term goals? We wanted to make changes—get more stoplights, parks, more and better schools and hospitals—but ultimately what was really needed was to change who CONTROLS the institutions, not just fight for more or better institutions. These were theoretical discussions about what differentiated reform from real revolutionary practice. Although we tried to link theory to the everyday issues, I sometimes had to strain my brain to keep up with it.

I learned important lessons that summer through listening to others and by living in that community. The realization that in many ways conditions for Black people in the North were no better, and in some ways worse, than in the South was a bitter pill to swallow. I met many single mothers, as well as some men, who were struggling to survive and raise their children on a pitiful welfare check and in the face of abysmal hospitals, schools, streets, unresponsive local governments, and no political clout whatsoever.

It was a remarkable learning experience but I'm quite sure I myself contributed very little. In retrospect it seems that one summer is a very short time to really integrate into such a community project. From day to day I was tentative about what to do to be helpful. By the end of my stay in Cleveland, in August of 1965, Watts in Los Angeles had risen up in rebellion. The summer after my stint in Glenville, there was a major uprising in that very neighborhood, too.

The impossible conditions in the Northern ghettoes created tinderboxes and the sparks from one city seemed to set off the others. Black people were rising up in the face of the very conditions we had been trying to address. They were taking charge of their own destiny and the words of Malcolm X echoed in my brain.

Summer was over, and I was ready to go. Here I was, socialist by birth, but it was the Civil Rights movement that showed me the real possibility for action, change, bravery, courage, and integrity. It was in the Black movement and the first stirrings of the anti-war movement that I saw the authenticity that I longed for, and the creation of meaning and value that I'd read about in Sartre and Camus. I was ready for Berkeley!

BERKELEY

ACTUALLY BEING IN BERKELEY was another matter. I was lonely, for the first time away from home without any friends. I shared an apartment with three undergraduate women I hardly knew and had little in common with.

I was still very tied up in obsessing about my relationship with my London lover, who had remained in Madison with his betrothed Amayra. All summer he had written me at least one long letter a day, assuring me he wasn't in love with her and that they were no longer having an intimate relationship. But there were other problems. In one letter, he let me know he had slept with a friend of mine, insisting he hadn't enjoyed it. "It just fulfilled a physical need," he wrote. I felt hurt and confused both because of him and also my "friend." So I tried something I never had before. I slept with one of the other people in our SDS cohort when I wasn't really interested, and I definitely didn't enjoy it. When I told Guy (which may have been the reason I did it), he couldn't stand it and asked me to promise never to do that "to him" again. He started presenting the situation as if he had a condition that was beyond his control. The solution, he said, was to be together.

Shortly before I had left for California, Guy and I had a rendezvous in a Chicago hotel during which he asked me to go to graduate school in Madison instead of Berkeley. I considered chucking Berkeley altogether but fortunately did not. Yet I was in love with him and couldn't find it in my power to end the relationship. He promised he would come spend a month with me in the second semester when he wasn't teaching.

I studied pretty hard that first semester and got all As. In addition to classes, I worked as a research assistant to Dr. Mussen whose inquiries centered on the moral development of children. However, during the intercession of February 1966, I wrote home complaining about being swallowed up by academia and mused about dropping out. I'm sure my parents were not happy to receive that letter, but they exercised some serious restraint and remained quiet. To unwind I spent time at a free art class in the student union, throwing pots or at least throwing clay on the potters' wheel. I never made anything but I enjoyed the sensations.

Although I arrived expecting a five-year haul toward a PhD in Child Psychology, reality had something else in store for me. I immediately encountered the Vietnam Day Committee (VDC), a coalition of students, faculty and other community members opposed to U.S. intervention in Vietnam. Almost immediately I met Jerry Rubin. The leader of the VDC, he was referred to by some as "the P.T. Barnum of the Left," since the splashy activities of the VDC were generally considered to be his brain-child. His philosophy was: the more theatrical, the more confrontational, the better. The more people will hear about it.

Jerry had grown up in Cincinnati. His father, a supporter of Jimmy Hoffa, drove a truck delivering bread and became an organizer in the Bakery Drivers' Union. Although she had a college degree, Jerry's mother was a stay-at-home mom who played the piano. She died of cancer in her early fifties and her husband died a few months later of a heart attack. That left Jerry, in his early 20s, responsible for his 13-year-old brother Gil. He took Gil and set off for Israel where they spent the next year and a half. Jerry's experiences in Israel paralleled mine. Attracted by the lore that Jews from around the world were building socialism, he became disillusioned when he heard Israelis describe Arabs the way whites talked about Blacks in America. As he would later write, "My heart was Jewish but my head leaned toward internationalism."

Jerry had also traveled with *Fair Play for Cuba* on one of the first trips to the island in support of the 1959 Revolution, where he had the extraordinary opportunity of meeting with Che Guevara, the Argentinian who was a key figure in the Cuban revolution. Jerry was always very proud of this.

Jerry and I hit it off instantly, spending lots of time together—walking, talking, hanging out at the Mediterranean Café (affectionately called "The Med") eating and drinking coffee, and arguing about politics. I liked how Jerry looked back then. He was fairly clean-cut with short hair, starched white shirts, a sports jacket, and slacks. His handlebar mustache and swarthy appearance gave him the look of a classic Italian anarchist. I met lots of his friends and political buddies. Barbara Gullahorn and Marilyn Mulligan are two that I remember best. I understood that previously Barbara and Jerry had been in a relationship, and she was as involved as he was in the VDC, although she received less acknowledgement, consistent with the male supremacy of the day.

Jerry was a wonderful companion back then, loving and loyal to his friends. He enjoyed introducing me to others. I let him know right away that I was in a relationship with someone in Madison and that we were planning on being together soon. That didn't stop him from becoming my friend.

The VDC with its headquarters in a six-room house near the Berkeley campus was a beehive of activity. People came from all over to help out or just to hang out. On October 15, 1965, a month after I arrived in California, they organized a teach-in. The numbers were small compared with the past; perhaps 4,000 people attended. But toward the end the numbers grew and eventually 20,000 people streamed off the campus and into the street to march on the Oakland Army Terminal. I found it incredibly exhilarating.

We would shut it down!

However, I was still a member of SDS, having joined the Berkeley chapter. I felt it was a continuation of my work that previous summer on the Cleveland ERAP project. Embedded in the politics of SDS, I had mixed feelings about these huge Vietnam Day marches. The style and the process of SDS and the VDC were very different. On the one hand, I was committed to the SDS model of grassroots organizing, going door to

Nancy and Jerry Rubin, Berkeley, 1966.

door, speaking with people one on one and trying to build organization in a slow, deliberate process. On the other hand, I saw the power of the VDC educating huge numbers of people and agitating and providing outlets for action. Additionally, after the very successful anti-war march in DC earlier that year, the leadership of SDS had backed away from concentrating energy on trying to end the war. They felt that serious revolutionaries should not spend time trying to stop the present war since that was impossible. It was more important to expand ERAP and build a movement to fundamentally change American society. We would then be in a position to "stop the seventh war from now."

That didn't stop the foot soldiers of SDS, of which I was one, from voting with our feet. I was under the influence of SDS but clearly conflicted. I wanted to work for fundamental change and knew that could not be successful overnight, but I also wanted to end THIS war and be part of the momentum that was building. I never missed any of the big marches.

The VDC had its own internal political struggles. The day 20,000 of us marched on the Oakland Army Terminal, we started out with a commitment to get arrested, if necessary, in order to accomplish our goal of shutting it down. I had still never been arrested and wasn't sure what I would do if it came to that. My adrenalin was pumping and I became increasingly excited as we heard stories of anti-war activities taking place in 30 other cities. The anti-war movement was becoming a national phenomenon!

As we marched, we received information that we would be met at the city line by a phalanx of Oakland cops armed with gas and police dogs. Along the way there were fierce arguments among the leadership as to whether or not to turn back. In the midst of the turmoil, the steering committee of nine people actually met for a show of hands. The vote was split 5 to 4 and we turned back. Jerry felt quite bitter about the decision. I was disappointed as well.

As events progressed, the powerful impact of the VDC became clear. These activities were splashed all over the media, both local and national, and were forcing people to take sides. Intense debate was everywhere. People were changing before my very eyes. People who didn't know where Vietnam was were learning all about it. Those who were all for the war one day were against it the next. Public opinion was mobilized and politicians were being forced to take a stand.

In February of that year I wrote home:

> *"So today they bombed Hanoi again. It's really a nightmare. I spent the day marching to Oakland and sitting in at the Congressman's office. Not that I think it will change anything, of course, but it keeps dissent alive, it cracks that really rotten consensus, and I suppose most of all, it's an expression of the frustration I feel. Berkeley is an amazing place. Classes aren't in session yet but still a great number of people were reached, many who will go to jail if they have to. I'm not one of those in this case, but one of these days I may just be frustrated enough."*

The following day I moved into my own apartment on Spruce Street in a slightly more upscale neighborhood on the north side of campus and close to the Psychology Department. All that year Guy and I communicated constantly through letters and phone calls. By then Amayra knew all about me. Guy told me with certainty that their relationship was now purely platonic and that he would break it off with her.

Then one day he called to say, "I tried to break it off with her but then she stuck her head in the gas oven. I just had to back off. I really need to see you. I'll drive out right after my prelims." That spring he arrived for a month.

My style had always been general frumpiness as I had no interest in clothes. This lack of aesthetics bothered Guy and he now insisted on picking out my clothes. I can still remember the two tight-fitting dresses he bought, one black and white, the other purple. It's hard to believe now that I would allow a man to dictate what I wore, but it's the truth. What's more ironic is that after dressing me in slinkier clothes, he couldn't stand it if another man so much as looked at me and would become insanely jealous at even imaginary encounters.

Although Dr. Mussen wanted me to continue working on his research project through the summer, I didn't enjoy it and felt it was meaningless. Beyond all that, I wanted to spend the summer elsewhere with Guy. When school ended that year, he and I arranged to be at Cornell University for the summer. He would study economics and I would learn Russian. I already knew French well enough but needed to pass two language exams for my PhD. We rented a farmhouse in the Ithaca countryside and spent the summer swimming under the waterfalls and playing house. Again I wish I could say that I had some remorse about the fact that Guy had left a woman back in Madison who had given up a husband and child in Sri Lanka to come to the States to marry him. I wish I could take credit for some feminist consciousness, or just plain decency.

During that summer Jerry Rubin stayed in somewhat regular touch. By this time the VDC was only a shell of its former self. In April of 1966 the office had been anonymously bombed and destroyed. Differences had developed among the leadership about tactics and strategy. Perhaps the differences on the march to the Oakland Army Terminal about whether to go forward in the face of police opposition reflected larger issues of militancy in general. There were also differences about the role of electoral politics. Robert Scheer, one of our own, was running in the primary for U.S. Congress.

Jerry was one of Scheer's biggest supporters. An outspoken critic of the war and an editor of the left-wing *Ramparts* magazine, Scheer had written an 80-page pamphlet titled *How the United States Got Involved in Vietnam* that played an important role in convincing many people that this was an unjust war.

Although defeated in the election, Scheer presented a serious challenge—44 percent of the vote. Jerry had thrown himself into this campaign heart and soul. He never did anything halfway. I was quite conflicted about electoral politics and remained aloof. Most activists I knew were struggling with how to bring about real change and trying to learn from our experiences. That June of 1966 Jerry sent me an eight-page letter, along with clippings, describing the outcome of the Scheer Campaign. In his friendly way, he scolded me: "Nancy, do you realize that if you and a few others had worked on the campaign, it might be Congressman Scheer today? Do you realize that? Hang your head in total shame and picture while you are doing it napalm falling on innocent people in Vietnam." Although he was—in part—joking, it was also a critique of much of the Berkeley left. He felt they had missed a great opportunity to send an explicitly anti-war candidate to Congress and perhaps bring the end of the war one step closer.

The letter was, however, more than political. Jerry had more to say:

> *"My last three days in Berkeley were spent 'with you.' I talked with people we talked with, I sat in places we sat in (last booth in Kipps!), I talked incessantly and too much about you, I even slept in your bed. Every time I'm in any situation, what you would say flashes through my mind. I'm listening carefully and clinically to rock-and-roll songs. I wonder what you are doing now."*

The sad truth was, I had no idea what I was doing …

Despite a year's worth of letters professing his obsessive love for me, Guy would not arrange his life to really include me, while Jerry seemed willing to turn his life inside out to be with me. Plus, I was becoming more and more political. Guy had let me know that he might go to Thailand in the fall as part of his research in economics. I was beginning to question what exactly he was going to be doing in Thailand. I knew that his work had some connection to the United States AID program and wondered if it could have been some kind of CIA front. By this time even the Peace Corps was under suspicion since it served U.S. military and political interests. When fall came, Guy did indeed go to Thailand and chose to go without me or Amayra. "Perhaps I'll send for you later," he announced. That was it for me. I cut off all communication with him and moved on. (I saw him only one time again when we were both in our seventies. He was living with someone other than Amayra and when I inquired after her, he gave a very vague response. I could find no trace of the man I knew.)

That same summer Jerry received a subpoena to testify before the House Un-American Activities Committee as a result of his anti-war activities. The purpose of the hearings was to prepare a bill that would make opposition to the draft or the war a crime—treason, punishable by twenty years in jail.

Jerry sent me clippings from *The Berkeley Gazette* as well as his statement in response to the subpoena. He had already been involved in the creation of political theatre—troop train blockades, massive teach-ins, and confrontational marches. These had been theatrical productions as much as anything else. He found inspiration for dramatic protest in many places, and one of his favorites was the popular San Francisco Mime Troupe, a radical "guerrilla theater" outfit that performed on the streets, at demonstrations, wherever people gathered. So when Ronnie Davis of the Mime Troupe suggested that Jerry go to HUAC in costume, Jerry was all for it.

Returning to Berkeley that fall, I attended the rally where Jerry announced to the crowd that he would be going to the hearings in an American Revolutionary War uniform. "I will wear this uniform because my country was born in Revolution. All the arguments made against the Vietnam revolution could have been made against the American Revolution."

Three of the best lawyers in the land joined the fight, and our lives would continue to be intertwined with theirs in the years to come. When I met Beverly Axelrod I was bowled over. She was the first woman attorney I had ever met. It was exciting to have a sharp and feisty radical woman on our side. Arthur Kinoy, a 5'4" ball of energy, had been a stand-up movement lawyer for years. The third attorney was the charming, silver-tongued William Kunstler, with whom I would later spend a good deal of time in a manner I could not have imagined.

The hearings did, indeed, turn out to be a raucous affair. HUAC had clearly subpoenaed a new generation of protestors. Although the Communist Party and the National Committee to Abolish HUAC advised those subpoenaed to base their refusal to testify on the First Amendment and the right to dissent, Jerry and the others had a different idea. Also subpoenaed to HUAC were members of the Progressive Labor Party. Some told HUAC that they were communists and proud of it. Others took the oath with a middle finger uplifted or the Nazi salute when they took the stand. In the brouhaha that ensued, short, wiry, and bespectacled attorney Arthur Kinoy was dragged by the neck and ejected from HUAC by three burly federal marshals. It was front-page news throughout the land. Meanwhile Jerry, properly arrayed in tricornered hat and buckled shoes, was never called to testify. HUAC was not eager to interrogate a look-alike of a Revolutionary War soldier or to have that Tom Paine-like image go out over the wire service.

That fall Jerry and I began living together. We had spent much of the previous year in each other's company, and Jerry had been biding his time, waiting for my relationship with Guy to end. I left my north-side apartment and we rented a south of campus apartment on Regent Street. I was very excited to live closer to Telegraph Avenue, the strip filled with restaurants, bookstores, and cafes. From there it was just a short stroll up to Sproul Plaza, the epicenter of the movement, the free speech area where activists gathered daily, debating the hot issues of the day. For the next four years Jerry and I were inseparable and went through extraordinary times. Sometimes it felt like we were in control, changing the world according to our dreams. At other times, we were on a speeding train, way beyond our control. In the fall of 1966, however, I was still in graduate school and trying to hang in there on a thread.

It was a confusing year. The Vietnam Day Committee had run out of steam. The Scheer campaign had lost. However, our small SDS group remained standing, and we brainstormed about what to do next. Deciding that we could make an important contribution to the political scene by "organizing an educational and agitational meeting on the issue of Black Power," we began to plan an event to be held on the campus in late October.

We felt the mass media was distorting the message of Black Power and that we needed to create a platform for its advocates, be open and clear about our support, and indeed help to "create widespread community support for the new radicals in the Negro movement." We pledged in that one day to raise $5,000 in donations for organizers of the new Black Power movement. That was a lot of money in those days.

The university administration hit us with a barrage of restrictions and a web of requirements. We knew that in the wake of the Free Speech movement and the Vietnam Day Committee, that this was more than just one event. We did not want to concede to compromises that would have implications for future activism. Jerry's journalistic savvy made certain that the negotiations all played out in the mass media. The publicity generated by the controversy was our biggest asset.

And so, on a glorious October day, ten thousand people gathered in the Greek Theatre on campus. Seated in steep tiers open to the sky, the audience had a great view of itself and the excitement was palpable. Ten thousand people were exposed to the thinking of numerous Black Power advocates, culminating with Stokely Carmichael toward the end of the day. Most of the crowd had never heard anything like it before as Stokely explained that Black people were not the problem, that the problem was centered within white communities where racism and violence were the status quo. The advocacy of nonviolence for Black people was a way of maintaining the status quo and was never applied as a standard for whites. Stokely, like Malcolm X before him, challenged people in a way that people could understand.

Although the Black Power conference itself was a real success as an event, the impact on the small group that constituted our Berkeley SDS chapter was less clear. We had differences among us about what to do next. Stokely had said that white people should get out of Black communities and organize white people instead. But in what form and around what set of politics? There were differences both in national SDS where some leaders were still talking about building an "interracial movement of the poor" as well as within our local chapter. Jerry and I tried to digest what we had learned, and I attempted to continue my graduate studies.

Not long after Black Power Day, we were invited to a meeting over in the Haight-Ashbury, the center of San Francisco's burgeoning hippie counterculture. Some of the leaders in that community (yes, even hippies had leaders) wanted to explore closer relations with the Berkeley radical community. They were working on producing a "Be-in", a gathering of the "tribes." It took some mind-stretching for us "politicos" to understand what they were talking about or why it would have value. There had been sit-ins and now there would be a "be-in" where just coming as a person, a human *Being* was a statement. All such human beings would be welcome to celebrate BEing, and BEing together, to take joy in our common humanity. Everything would be free. It would take place in Golden Gate Park with free music provided by all the San Francisco rock bands. Jerry was invited to speak as a representative of "politicos."

I don't recall any other women being at that meeting, let alone speaking, at the Haight meeting. But I'm guessing they were there and they probably don't recall me either. I doubt that any women's voices were expressed or heard. However, today I never fail to notice the participation or non-participation of women.

But nonetheless I was taken with this new scene. Timothy Leary, the ex-Harvard psychology professor, LSD advocate and guru, had been traveling around the country telling everyone to "Tune in, turn on and drop out." Thousands of young people from all over the country, alienated by what society had to offer, followed Leary's instructions and were flocking toward the San Francisco Bay Area. Hard to believe now, but rents were cheap in the Haight and people lived communally. We were attracted to their way of life and their rejection of much of U.S. society. They emphasized cooperation and creativity over competition and profit-seeking, joy and love over hate and violence. Here was a community of mostly white people that we identified with. We thought we could influence them politically and they could influence us with their world view as well. We welcomed a blending of the two communities.

Twenty thousand people gathered in Golden Gate Park on January 24, 1967. Both Leary and the poet Allen Ginsberg were at that first be-in. Jerry spoke but was not very well-received. People wanted to dance and groove and not be "brought down" by negative political vibes. That experience, however, set the stage for our upcoming adventures.

Not long after this, Jerry and I dropped acid for the first time. Along with Michael Lerner (who later became Rabbi Michael Lerner) we tripped together and walked and talked and talked and walked. It was one of the very crispy clear Bay Area days. The sky was a deep, deep blue and the pastel houses of Berkeley sparkled. I felt like we had stepped into the Beatles song *"Penny Lane."* I remember Jerry kept obsessing about the written word. He was taken with the sensual nature of the material world (on LSD) and for some reason was thrown into a struggle about the written word which in his non-LSD world meant a great deal to him. But on this trip he was having some kind of epiphany about it.

As for me, a little nervous to begin with, I was pleased to find myself enjoying the heightened sparkling visual experiences and the friendly camaraderie of Michael and Jerry. Michael was a roly-poly, big-hearted intellectual guy. Although he was as self-centered as most of the other men in the Movement, I felt comfortable with him. Perhaps that was because he himself was seen as somewhat of a socially inept oddball, not a very "cool" person to keep company with. But Jerry liked and respected him, seeing beyond superficialities to his strengths. I liked that about Jerry. He befriended all kinds of people and wasn't overly concerned about what others thought of his friends.

Jerry and I took Stokely's message to heart about the importance of working within the white community. Nonetheless, it was difficult to figure out how to operationalize it in our daily lives. We were both looking for opportunities, and in Jerry's case, he was creating them. While I was trying to concentrate on my graduate studies, Jerry decided to run for Mayor of Berkeley. He knew he wouldn't win but it would provide a platform, a way for us to bring our beliefs and dreams to the community at large.

A group of us produced a 25-page brochure proclaiming Jerry's mayoral program. The campaign at a glance included withdrawing troops from Vietnam, fighting poverty, low-cost public housing, legalization of marijuana, and turning Telegraph Avenue into a mall, as well as planting trees and flowers. There would be free modern daycare centers for working mothers. The arts would be well-subsidized, including a significant Afro-American cultural center. The city would establish hitchhiking stalls and free bicycles to reduce the need for automobiles. It was a platform I could support even now.

Although the platform expressed what we all believed and desired, the campaign exacerbated tensions between Jerry and me, and also between Jerry and his other friends. He drove everyone around him crazy, working 24/7 and expecting the same from the rest of us. He didn't have a paying job and was living off the money his parents had left him. This was fine for him, but fulfilling his demands would have meant putting the rest of my life on hold. I was ostensibly still a student as well as a teaching assistant, and for me it was a struggle. In retrospect I think Jerry was continually trying to get me to drop out— which would validate his decision to do so and provide him with a constant companion. As much as we told ourselves that it was a collective endeavor, the whole structure of an electoral campaign places emphasis on the candidate himself. When all was said and done, the campaign belonged to Jerry as an individual. Our relationship came close to the breaking point during that time.

In the end he finished second with 7385 votes (22 percent) and won four precincts, all in the campus area. Although disappointed, I was not surprised. I always knew he wouldn't win. After the mayoral campaign, Jerry was at loose ends while I tried to turn back to my studies. We initiated a "peace torch campaign," a cross-country trek with an Olympic-style torch, organizing along the way. It never materialized. What I remember most clearly is attempting to present the idea on the steps of Sproul Plaza. I wasn't really sold on it myself, but Jerry thought I should speak since I was a student and he wasn't. Not only was my heart not in it but it was my first attempt at public speaking. I did a terrible job and Jerry screamed at me afterwards that I was an embarrassment to him. That should have been a signal to me about the quality of our relationship, but it wasn't.

The whole year that Jerry and I lived together in Berkeley, I don't remember ever leaving the Bay Area. We didn't have a car. I went everywhere in Berkeley on my bicycle. Here we were in one of the most exquisite areas of the globe, and we never once ventured out, not even up to Tilden Park. The furthest I remember is the Greek Theater, part of UC Berkeley, in the hills above the campus, and that was only because it was the venue for our Black Power Day event. It was politics 24/7, and if we left Berkeley, it was just for an occasional foray into San Francisco. The weather was beautiful much of the year, although in those days we were blessed with rainy winters. But I loved the rain. Especially after four years of Wisconsin winters. I felt I had died and gone to heaven.

It might sound like it was an insulated or suffocating existence. And yet, we felt we were in this incredibly vibrant community. Of course for me there was graduate school, although it was receding by the day. There

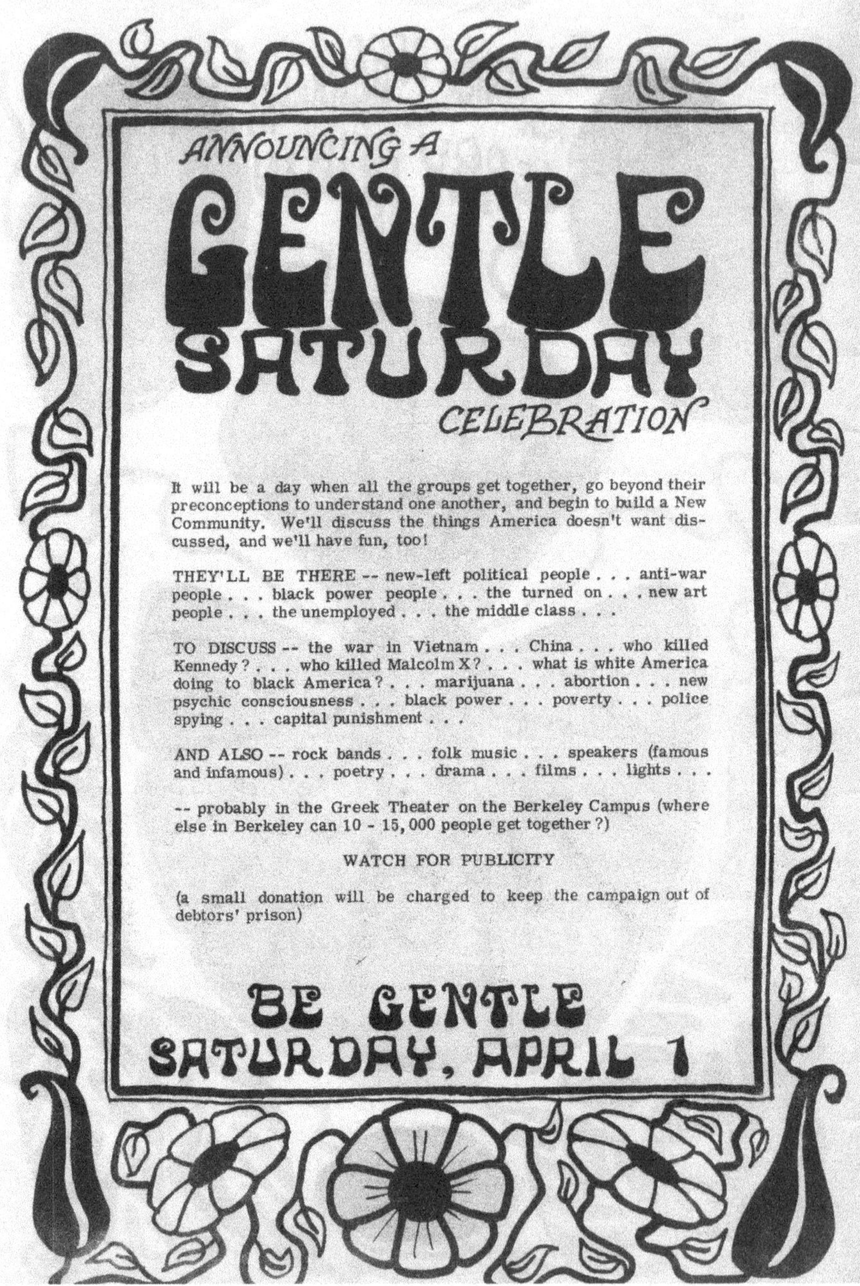

Jerry Rubin's run for Mayor of Berkeley, 1967.

Vote April 4th
Jerry Rubin
for Mayor of Berkeley

TABLE OF CONTENTS

Phones:

548-0436
841-0389
845-6215 (after 6 p.m.)

Campaign Offices:

2502 Telegraph, Apt. 2 (at Dwight)
2632 Regent St., Apt. B (at Derby)

If you like this program, please come by or call us and join the campaign.

Art work in this brochure by Tom Weller.

Jerry Rubin's run for Mayor of Berkeley, 1967.

Vote BERKELEY LABOR COMMITTEE Vote

Jerry Rubin for Mayor of Berkeley

Vote

AVAKIAN Council	CITY COUNCIL **RON DELLUMS**
HARAWITZ Council	SCHOOL BOARD **HAZAIAH WILLIAMS**
NEILANDS Council	**KALDENBACH** Auditor

30% UNEMPLOYMENT IN HOME BUILDING! CAUSED BY WAR IN VIET NAM!

THE DEPRESSION IN THE BUILDING INDUSTRY WILL NOT END UNTIL THE WAR IN VIET NAM IS OVER!! Housing is always last in line in a War Economy!!

70% of Federal Taxes go to the War Machine! This is the cause of the inflation prices! This is why Interest Rates are HIGH!

CARPENTERS, LABORERS, and other building tradesmen suffer UNEMPLOYMENT and many are losing Health Plan Benefits!

As Mayor of Berkeley Jerry Rubin and the Pro-labor Councilmen will ask all cities in the U.S. to join in DEMANDING AN END TO THE WAR IN VIET NAM. You know now that Republicans Johnson and Reagan support war!

BOYCOTT SOUTHERN FACTORY PRODUCTS!

Factories move to Southern states to profit from cheap wages, non-Union sweatshop conditions, and the poverty of segregation! The RunAway industry trend MUST BE STOPPED! Our JOBS are being STOLEN!! Republicans Reagan and Wallace Johnson have not acted!

- DYMO INDUSTRIES is moving from Berkeley to Georgia. 250 jobs GONE! They will want to ship their products back here.
- MARCHANT business machines (San Pablo & Ashby) ran off to Alabama!
- HEXCEL PRODUCTS (160 jobs) at 2332 - 4th St. is going to Texas!
- CABINET SHOPS like Paramount Fixtures and Millcraft Inc. have gone bankrupt (90 jobs) and Builders Cabinets on 6th St. has big layoffs BECAUSE THE University of California, Berkeley Schools, and BIG BUILDERS insist on using cheap cabinets from Segregated Southern Shops!!

JERRY RUBIN as MAYOR and the Pro-labor Councilmen will organize to BOYCOTT SOUTHERN MANUFACTURERS in Public and Private Purchasing!!!

JOBS FOR THE UNEMPLOYED • LOW COST PUBLIC HOUSING

Jerry Rubin's run for Mayor of Berkeley, 1967.

were so many interesting people to talk to and activities to participate in. We could spend hours at Sproul Plaza or on Telegraph Avenue, drinking coffee and spinning ideas at the Mediterranean Cafe, wandering through Moe's or Cody's bookstores to see what was new.

My intimate life with Jerry was another story. Jerry wrote about it long ago and so I'm not revealing anything when I say that we had no sex life. Jerry was too uncomfortable with sexuality and his performance. So we were not intimate with each other and most importantly, we couldn't communicate about it. Back then I didn't feel safe talking about it with anyone else either, and so I just repressed it all. Since we were involved in such a crush of activity, it was easy to do. Although I knew from experience it could be different, I accepted the situation and hoped it would change over time. It may sound corny or strange but I so wanted to be an activist, to change the world, and it was really exciting to be in a partnership with someone who felt, and more importantly, acted similarly.

That spring I was conflicted about whether or not to stay in grad school. Jerry was trying to convince me to leave and travel with him as representatives of *The Berkeley Barb. The Barb* was one of the most successful "underground" newspapers. As an alternative, often oppositional, voice to the mass media, counterculture papers were springing up all around the country, in college towns and in big cities. They were very popular and an integral part of our movement. Drawing on his experience as a professional journalist in Cincinnati, Jerry wrote for *The Barb* from time to time. Jerry and Max Scherr, the publisher, felt very affectionate toward each other and *The Barb* was always an available platform.

We were making summer plans to travel for *The Barb* when a call came from Dave Dellinger, the prominent peace activist from the East Coast. There was to be a large anti-war mobilization in Washington, DC, that October, and Dave wanted Jerry to be the Project Director of the mobilization. The sponsoring group was the National Mobilization to End the War in Vietnam. The offer was extended further—Jerry could bring along several friends to work as paid staff. That was it! This was an offer I was excited about. Discouraged with graduate school, informed by my professors that I needed to put more effort into my studies, and encouraged by Jerry, I decided to quit right then and there. Jerry left for New York while I tied up loose ends. New York was dear to my heart and I'd be close to my family again. I was enthusiastic about this new adventure that was about to begin.

THE SIEGE OF THE PENTAGON

In June of 1967 the Israeli military seized the West Bank and Gaza from the Palestinians in what came to be known as the Six Day War. Whatever lingering hope I had for Israeli socialism was now forever shattered. How could there be socialism at the expense of another people? Socialism was about sharing the wealth with all. It couldn't be built on land taken from the Palestinians.

That was once more a summer of serious urban rebellions in over a dozen major U.S. cities, among them Detroit, Newark, Atlanta, Cleveland, and New York. On August 9th, President Johnson approved sixteen additional Rolling Thunder targets and an expansion of "armed reconnaissance" in Vietnam. U.S. imperialism and its allies were moving on all fronts but there was resistance everywhere, from Black urban centers to Palestine and, of course, to Vietnam.

Jerry was already in New York assuming his new job as Project Coordinator for the October national demonstration against the war. While activists Stew Albert, Karen Wald and I got ready to leave Berkeley to join him, Jerry was already embroiled in internal debates about the nature of the October plans. The Mobe was made up of much more moderate elements than us West Coast radicals. Some of the main players were Women Strike for Peace, the New York Parade Committee, the Chicago Peace Council, Student Mobilization, and the Ohio Peace Action Committee.

Out west in California we all loved the idea of a huge national mobilization that included civil disobedience, and we felt it was important for the Pentagon to be the focus. Our argument went something like this: Demonstrations were always taking place at the Capitol, but it would be humdrum and we would never actually get past the door. We felt that the Pentagon, the symbol of U.S. militarism, was the real face of U.S. policy, and that demonstrating there would channel the anger that we all felt into a real political weapon. It wasn't only a clash of ideas. People were dying because of the war. We didn't want to target the civil government. We wanted to target the true center, the War Machine. We knew that our presence at the Pentagon would result in a confrontation, but we welcomed that confrontation in order to visibly demonstrate the true nature of the U.S.— to illustrate that it dominated not through its moral power, not through its Peace Corps, but by force and violence. We wanted to shut down the War Machine. More than that, we wanted to be the agents of history. We wanted to actually shut it down. "Shut It Down!" was the slogan we proposed.

Two processes had developed immediately upon Jerry's arrival in New York. One was Jerry's developing relationship with Abbie Hoffman. The other was the interaction between Jerry and the Mobe. He had to convince the Mobe that the targeting of the Pentagon was a good idea. Problem was, we Californians were in the dark about logistics. We didn't even know that the Pentagon wasn't actually in DC but was across the bridge in Virginia. Legitimate practical problems were raised and a team was sent to scope out the Pentagon itself. Bob Greenblatt, the coordinator of the Mobe and a Cornell Professor, Fred Halsted of the Socialist Workers Party and Jerry went off together to take a look. A discussion followed about the pros and cons. The Pentagon won out and our intention was to shut it down.

On August 28th, the Mobe held a press conference at the Overseas Press Club in New York to announce its intention to shut down the Pentagon in less than two months time. Participants ranged from Monsignor Rice of Pittsburgh to H. Rap Brown of SNCC. Father Hayes of the Episcopal Peace Fellowship announced:

> *". . . we will shut down the Pentagon. We will fill the hallways and block the entrances. Thousands of people will disrupt the center of the American war machine. In the name of humanity we will call the warmakers to task."*

Abbie Hoffman quipped that "We're going to raise the Pentagon three hundred feet in the air!" while Rap Brown noted that "I would be unwise to say I'm going there with a gun because you all took my gun last time. I may bring a bomb, sucker." Dellinger stated that there would be no government building left unattacked although it would all be done nonviolently. Jerry warned that "We're now in the business of wholesale disruption and widespread resistance and dislocation of the American society."

The Pentagon demonstration was off to a roaring start.

Meanwhile, Abbie introduced Jerry to a whole community of countercultural folks who would resonate to his theatricality and lead him to embrace thoroughly the "PT Barnum" designation. What began as a derogatory characterization coming from the "straight left" would now become a proud emblem for Jerry. His "P. T. Barnum" persona now served him well.

One evening Jerry called me back in California, ebulliently eager to share his excitement. His words just came pouring out and I couldn't get a word in:

"It was incredible. It's all over the media. A bunch of us got into the third-floor gallery at the Stock Exchange and threw handfuls of dollar bills down onto the floor! You should have seen those stockbrokers stop in their tracks and get down on their knees. They fought over the money while we shouted, "This is a paradise on earth. There's enough for all."

"Wow," I said. "Sounds like a great action! Who were all the people?"

"Abbie and a dozen of his friends", Jerry said in a clip. And barreled on to tell the rest of the story: "And then we set a handful of money on fire, to the outrage of all the Wall Streeters, and for all the media to photograph."

They hadn't forgotten to notify the press, and images of the event spread like wildfire. The burning of money at Wall Street was a precursor of yippie actions and would become an iconic moment in the history of the Yippies.

From that moment on, life changed. Back in Berkeley, we had been trying to figure out ways to meld radical politics with the hippie counterculture. But now here were these people actually doing it. What's more, Jerry and Abbie seemed to be soulmates. Both wanted to unite radical politics with the counterculture. Both understood the power of the media and wanted to figure out creative ways to reach people.

Jerry and I got an apartment just down the street from Anita and Abbie, a 4th floor walkup on St. Marks Place, right smack in the middle of it all. Our place was a colorful, zany space. It was basically one big room with a huge opening inside a half-wall between the two spaces. Today it would be marketed as an Open Floor Plan. But it was definitely not chic, not even shabby chic. Most everything was second-hand and it all worked fine for us.

One space was the kitchen/dining room and the other held a makeshift office, typewriter and TV, and beds that also served as couches. Both areas had red brick fireplaces, and I hung the walls and even the ceilings with posters: Che Guevara on the fireplace. COME ALIVE! JOIN THE UNDERGROUND GENERATION above a full-bearded Allen Ginsberg with welcoming arms uplifted toward his red, white and blue top hat. A psychedelic montage poster that read CAN YOU SEE ANOTHER WAY?, another of a psychedelic Dylan. There were photos of a crew cut Jerry shaking hands with Adlai Stevenson and longer-haired Jerry with Norman Mailer. Jerry dressed as Tom Paine for his first HUAC confrontation. And one of me and Jerry when we first met. There were paintings, peacock feathers, paper lampshades, yellow paper flowers, photos , etc., etc. It was all my doing, except the typewriter and TV which were Jerry's.

Talks were proceeding with a whole range of people in the countercultural scene about participating in the Pentagon action and there was great enthusiasm. Instead of behaving like the usual "Project Director" he was hired to be, Jerry was spending his time with his new friends who were planting the seeds of a Levitation of the Pentagon. Ed Sanders discovered that the five-sided polygon known as the "pentagon" was a baroque symbol of evil and oppression. So what better than an

Nancy and Jerry's St. Marks Place Apartment, NY; 1968.
Above: Nancy. **Below:** Sister Louise on bed, Mom in kitchen.

Nancy and Jerry's St. Marks Place Apartment, NY; 1968. Nancy on the phone, sister Louise on bed.

exorcism? A group of "Holy Men" ("Where were the Holy Women?" you might ask!) would encircle the Pentagon and conduct a ritual of drum-beating, chanting, incantations and incense that would raise the Pentagon a hundred feet in the air and exorcise the evil spirits. When we applied for a permit to exorcise the Pentagon, it was reported in the mainstream media that the government said okay, but no more than three feet off the ground. I was pretty sure that either Jerry or Abbie had planted that story.

Jerry, Stew, Karen, and I, the crazies from California published the first issue of *The Mobilizer,* a newsletter we would mail to peace groups across the country. The editorial stated:

> *"We live in a society which trains its sons to be killers and which channels its immense wealth into the business of suppressing courageous men from Vietnam to Detroit who struggle for the simple human right to control their own lives and destinies. We Americans have no right to call ourselves human beings unless, personally and collectively, we stand up and say NO to the death and destruction perpetrated in our name."*

We also included a piece by Keith Lampe. Lampe was a committed pacifist and anti-war activist who possessed a lively and creative imagination. Keith's article "On Making A Perfect Mess" suggested that, "a thousand children stage Loot-ins at department stores to strike at the property fetish that underlies genocidal war." When *The Mobilizer* came out there was a wave of indignation from the Mobe regulars and all hell broke loose. They confiscated the 5,000 copies of *The Mobilizer* and put out a new, respectable version featuring "Sid Peck Answers the Questions of Housewives About the October 21 Demonstration." (Sid Peck was the leader of the Ohio Peace Action Council.)

Dave Dellinger, who had invited us to come east, was out of the country when the conflict erupted. Dave was the most respected long-time peace activist, and editor of *Liberation* magazine. He was the people's ambassador for peace with a gentle, friendly demeanor, very much the consensus maker. He was the perfect coordinator but also as hard as nails in his own way. Dave very much wanted to see the anti-war movement advance "from protest to resistance." We counted on Dave to absorb and deflect the anger of the Mobe regulars but unfortunately he was not around for this skirmish. When he returned even Dave could not bridge that gulf.

We were upset. We knew that if we had a confrontational demonstration at the Pentagon, it would be young people who would be the troops. Yet here were these over-40 types who were censoring us and holding us back. They didn't like our writings. They didn't like our art. They didn't like our looks. They didn't like our levitation. They didn't like our militancy. They didn't like our resistance to U.S. society. They increasingly stressed the safe, the legal, and what I felt was the humdrum side of the demonstration and things were looking bad.

As for me personally, that fall I was having my own hard time with The Mobe. I was 23 years old and supposed to be the staff person in charge of the Midwest. I didn't have a clue about how to be "in charge of the Midwest." I tried to carry out by rote some tasks that I was given but it was too far outside my realm of experience and familiarity. I was used to talking to people, door to door, one on one. I was not experienced at being part of an administrative staff.

In addition, I was moving away from the "Straight Left." I feel a need to explain this further since I am often asked: "Were you really a Yippie? What would be the draw of sex, dope, and rock 'n' roll for a person like you? How could you make the mistake of elevating the hippie phenomenon beyond that?" But I looked at it this way. For the first time, the opportunity seemed to exist to really connect with masses of people in our society. There were thousands, maybe hundreds of thousands, of young people who were alienated from America. And it wasn't an opportunist connection; we really felt a part of them.

We had shared values, values that appeared to be very different from those of the dominant society, the older generation. A large number of young people had dropped out of society, rejecting the roles that had been assigned to them, just as we were. In some ways they were more communistic than we were. They lived communally, sharing food and material goods. They spoke of peace and love, not war. They believed in living for the moment and exploring with their senses and valued joy, laughter and the human imagination. Many were creative artists. They unapologetically preferred smoking marijuana above guzzling alcohol. They hated the police and the authorities as much as we did and were not afraid to commit illegal acts. We had a lot in common.

Hippies were developing counter-cultural institutions. In New York there was a Free Clinic and a Free Store. There were alternative newspapers like the *East Village Other* (EVO) and *The Rat.* Major rock bands identified with this counterculture. Country Joe and the Fish's "I-Feel-Like-I'm-Fixin'-To-Die Rag" was played everywhere and The Jefferson Airplane's "*Volunteers*" became an anthem. All these people identified with the counterculture. It was a much broader cross-section of America than those involved in "straight" politics. It was a force bigger than the Socialist Club, bigger than the Socialist Workers Party or the Communist Party. And it was way more fun. Hippies seemed to be in it with the whole of their hearts, minds and bodies. They were not going to school or work in the daytime and then having an occasional meeting or demonstration. They were talking about changing their entire lives. For me this resonated with what Paul Potter and SDS had been saying about turning our lives over to building a movement. It made sense in terms of what Stokely had encouraged us to do, to go into the white community and influence consciousness and behavior.

I always loved theater, music, all the arts really. They often reached me in a deeper, more powerful way than rational arguments alone or the written word. I felt the straight left was boring and formulaic, with only a few limited tools in their toolbox. So it was really about strategy for me. I thought we could use theater and art to reach other young people politically and influence them in a revolutionary direction.

Truthfully, I had to push myself to participate. The things it required did not come naturally to me. Neither did speaking in public, for that matter. But I wanted our movement to be effective in reaching people. If there could be a melding of the New Left and the hippies, I believed it could be social and political dynamite. I was not totally wrong.

I had dropped out of graduate school and now I dropped out of the Mobe. I spent time with Abbie, getting to know the "Free" community on the Lower East Side and talking up the Pentagon action wherever we went.

Jerry and I became good friends with Anita and Abbie in a couples sort of a way. By that I mean that Anita and I never spent much time together alone, just the two of us. However, the four of us spent a good deal of time together, often with others such as Krassner, Ochs and many more. Frequently we would just hang out in Anita and Abbie's small living room.

Being in the eye of the generation gap maelstrom had some personal implications for me. Returning to New York had accentuated the situation. It meant close proximity between Jerry and my parents. My mother and father had always been extremely supportive of me, no matter what I did. Anyone that I brought home, they would try to love, or at least accept. This had always been the case and there was no reason to expect it to be any different. But I hadn't considered Jerry and the baggage that he brought along.

I believed in the Generation Gap ("Don't trust anyone over 30!") but I didn't intend to apply that to my own parents. Jerry on the other hand, treated abusively by his father and orphaned at a relatively young age, had never really dealt with his childhood issues and could not accept my closeness with my parents. Perhaps the relationship was threatening to him in some way or another. I don't recall our having any adult, serious discussions about this. But I do remember that when I brought him to my parents' house on Long Island, he lit up a joint first thing. They let it be known very clearly that they had difficulty tolerating that. He and I were unwilling to gracefully compromise with them. We disregarded their feelings and responded by smoking in the bathroom. My parents were disappointed but they created no scene and life went on. In retrospect, it's hard to imagine that I would treat my parents so disrespectfully.

This was an instance of Jerry's bad influence on me. Most everything else we did together was consensual; I was in there, heart and soul, and would take responsibility for all my decisions. But I allowed Jerry to pressure me, to bully me into treating my parents shabbily and that I do regret.

While I went off to hang out with Abbie, Anita and others, Jerry kept working for the Mobe, although their mutual dissatisfaction was increasing. The Mobe had been meeting with Harry Van Cleve, a government lawyer from the General Services Administration, selected to do their negotiating. He said that if the Mobe planned to "close down the Pentagon," the government would not issue permits for any rally or march, not even a legal rally or march. In fact, our buses would not even be allowed to unload people in Washington at all. Well, that was the worst thing Van Cleve could have done for his team! When the negotiations hit the newspapers, suddenly people who had been lukewarm or opposed to the demonstration were calling in their endorsements. We heard from Martin Luther King, Benjamin Spock, and SDS among others.

As this support grew, the government was thrown into a quandary. Van Cleve telephoned, requesting another meeting, and in the next two weeks there were six meetings. They had a new strategy to defuse the impact in myriad different ways: can't use the preferred bridge, no sound at the Pentagon, can't arrive at the Pentagon until 4:30 (buses were returning to NYC at 5:00). Jerry was concerned that our whole vision was being compromised and wanted to break off the negotiations. I thought he was over-reacting although, uncertain of my own perceptions, I held my tongue. (It was also ironic, I felt, to be planning an illegal activity of civil disobedience while negotiating with those who would do the arresting.) On a deeper level, we both felt that the government really had to negotiate with the protest. If we stood firm, they would have to back down and grant us some of our vision. Ultimately, Dellinger signed what my friends and I believed was a less-than-perfect agreement. The unfolding of the day would render the agreement fairly irrelevant, but we had no way of knowing that in advance.

On Saturday, October 20, 1967, more than 100,000 (some say 200,000) people streamed into Washington for the legal rally at the Lincoln Memorial. The usual speeches went on for hours. I don't remember any of them. My friends and I were eager to get on with the Pentagon action.

Eventually a mass of people began the two-hour march across the Arlington Memorial Bridge with helicopters buzzing menacingly overhead.

I remember feeling that day that we were in some kind of a funnel, where the numbers of people kept narrowing. At the outset there were possibly one to two hundred thousand at the Lincoln Memorial with perhaps 50,000 continuing the march across the bridge. The majority of the demonstrators left Washington on the 5:00 o'clock buses after leaving us much of the food they had brought along, their final donation to our well-being. The crowd got younger as we headed out toward the bridge.

As we walked, we talked about what had happened the week before in California. *Stop the Draft Week* had erupted in Oakland with 3,000 demonstrators converging on the Oakland induction center. Some of the demonstrators were wearing helmets and carrying shields to ward off police attacks, but the cops had used Mace and attacked them with a vengeance, injuring about 20 and arresting 25. By Friday morning there were 10,000 demonstrators around the induction center, many of them using what came to be known as "mobile tactics." When the police began to attack, they blockaded intersections with whatever they could lay their hands on and then took off running. The stories of that confrontation rippled through the march and it was rumored that some veterans of that battle had driven across the country to join us. These were our people! I wondered which of our old friends from Berkeley had been involved and who was in the crowd with us.

We crossed the bridge with great anticipation. At some point, the police blocked us from marching toward our preferred route. In response we sat down on the bridge, tens of thousands of us as far as you could see, forcing the government to yield.

The government had brought in more than 6,000 Army troops. Twenty thousand were on alert around the country. Two thousand National Guard troops and two thousand Washington police were on hand. Eight hundred cops were stationed at the Capitol and Secret Service helicopters hovered over the White House. Their central command post was inside the Pentagon.

The Levitation of the Pentagon was one of the first successful aspects of the day, providing creative imagery of the fusing of politicos and acid heads into an activist community. Ed Sanders and Tuli Kupferberg of The Fugs, decked out in multi-colored capes, provided the music. Allen Ginsberg opened the ceremony with what would become his hallmark "Ommmmmmmmm..." Others led incantations of "Out, demons, out!" Truthfully while I loved the brilliant idea of the Levitation, I think the actual nuts and bolts of a levitation were not my area of expertise, since my mind is foggy on the facts. Or perhaps the levitation itself has just been overshadowed in my mind by all that followed—my first, though far from my last, arrest.

As we left the bridge area, there was a rush on the Pentagon by a militant contingent made up of SDS and a group calling themselves the Revolutionary Contingent. They broke down a fence and got right up to the doors. In fact, a few people actually made it inside for a brief moment until they were swiftly arrested. As more protestors came across the bridge (myself among them), this group that had rushed to the Pentagon began to swell into the largest contingent, putting ourselves in a direct confrontation with the troops who were lined up on the stairs at the main entrance to the War Machine.

SDS and the Revolutionary Contingent were joined by hundreds of other protestors who were willing to risk arrest, but at the same time a legal rally (people who were not planning to get arrested) was going on over at another nearby area. As evening came on, many of the people from that legal rally left and we were down to a couple of thousand people.

Though SDS was not a sponsor because of disagreements with the conception, they had joined the mobilization in the final hours and their contribution to the actual confrontation was significant. They were a group of people who were able to coordinate their activities and move as one. I remember feeling how we were just separate individuals: Jerry, Abbie, Anita, our friend Stew Albert, and I. You might think that we had some kind of tactical leadership role to play, or at least Jerry would have had. But that was not the case, as far as I can remember. As would happen many times in the future, we had helped to create the stage, had set up the situation as best we could, but had no clue as to how to influence the actual event. Inevitably there were others who would move in to fill that vacuum.

As the sun went down, it became cooler and cooler. The crowd was getting younger and younger. We were on our own. The protection of the older generation was disappearing. Even Uncle Dave was gone. We heard that Dellinger, Norman Mailer and several others had been arrested early on in a choreographed civil disobedience action, crossing over a forbidden line and being taken into custody. I had never been arrested before and I was apprehensive about what was going to happen. Ours was a volatile and unpredictable situation. We had no idea what would transpire. Would we be there for an hour or a day? Would they Mace us as in Oakland?

Maybe they would even shoot us? This was not a situation for anyone who needed to be in control, who needed to know for sure what was going to happen next. You had to go with the flow and some of the possibilities were really frightening.

As it played out, there were moments of exhilaration and community. And there were moments of outright fear. As we jockeyed for space there was physical, literally face-to-face, confrontation with the army. The scene became very tense very early on and finally, at the suggestion of SDS, we all sat down. When we started out that day we'd had no idea how many people would stay. Maybe it would just be a handful in the end. However, the actual numbers lifted our spirits; there were well over a thousand of us. But what's more, the group that remained seemed to beat with one heart and that gave everyone strength. We were on a mission and we knew we were right. We looked to the right and we looked to the left and we knew that all of us would remain up until the point of arrest. For hours there was an impromptu teach-in to the troops. People climbed up on a ledge and, using a bullhorn, spoke to the troops. There was an open mike (well actually a bullhorn) for anyone who wanted to speak. I did not have the confidence to speak but I was very proud of what people said.

It has been said that our movement was disrespectful of the troops but I don't think so at all. We were speaking the truth to them. Those truths had the potential to save their lives as well as the lives of millions of Vietnamese.

That evening at the Pentagon, my friend Stew Albert, a Berkeley non-student activist and future Yippie, addressed the troops:

> *"I went to PS 206 in Brooklyn, and when I was in school nobody liked the monitors. They were kids like us, but they worked for the strict teachers. We didn't like them when we were kids, so why should we like them now? We always considered the monitors to be finks. And now you guys are acting like monitors. Join us!"*

In unison, the crowd spontaneously chanted "Join us! Join us!"

We were right up against the troops. When Super Joel, one of the earlier levitators, stepped forward and placed a flower in the gun barrel of one of the soldiers, it became an iconic image. Other protestors followed suit. (Paul Krassner later pointed out that Super Joel's grandfather was the mafia boss Sam Giancana and that Super Joel had dropped out of the family business.) The confrontation between demonstrators and troops lasted thirty-three hours, all through the first night and until midnight of the second night. Especially during the night, the soldiers would every now and then make forays into the front of the crowd, clubbing a few people and dragging a few others away to be arrested. We sat, arms locked as tight as possible, to impede them as much as possible and to protect one another. In the end they dragged away everyone who remained. Well over a thousand people were arrested, with 780 of us held and several hundred released. Some people were beaten or gassed.

I was arrested alongside Anita Hoffman. It was the first time either of us had been under arrest. I would later learn that it was a very uncharacteristic arrest experience. They took hundreds of us, all women, to what seemed to be a huge dormitory. There were scores and scores of cots lined up next to each other, and away from the violence and uncertainty at the Pentagon, it was like being in a huge summer camp. Anita and I were able to stay together on cots alongside each other. The camaraderie was palpable and exciting. The nervousness about what would happen in court was somewhat alleviated by feeling there was safety in numbers. The next morning we were herded to court and (as counseled by our movement lawyers) we pleaded *nolo contendre,* meaning we don't say we're guilty, we don't say we're not guilty, we just don't contest it. This was worked out between the government and our lawyers. We did what we were advised, paid a small fine and went home.

Later, we learned that several paratroopers had left the line, saying they wouldn't be part of the military anymore, and they were now held in the stockade. Dave Dellinger reported that over the years he kept meeting veterans who said they were on duty that day and had been affected by the teach-in. Much later we learned that Secretary of Defense Robert McNamara had watched the entire battle from his fifth-floor office, accompanied by his young assistant Daniel Ellsberg, who later became the whistle blower of the famous Pentagon Papers.

Years later when asked about the hippie entry into the peace movement, Dave Dellinger offered this: "What I remember is just being thrilled and excited that this whole new element of humor and creativity and youthful zest was coming into things."

Were we right or wrong in our conflict with The Mobe? The final outcome of the Pentagon demonstration was awesome. It was one of the most successful activities I have ever been involved with. I believe its character was greatly affected by my friends and myself continuously agitating for a militant, theatrical, unpredictable scenario. We succeeded in adding mass civil obedience. This was our idea. It was those projections that attracted thousands of young people and forced the government to dig in its heels, threatening to deny our basic civil liberties. That denial then brought thousands of additional people into the protest. In the end, the victory was really a result of the energy and the numbers of the people that participated. Even the children of officials in the Johnson Administration were joining us. In a political sense the country was now really at war with itself. This realization seemed to hold within itself the possibility that we could end the war with Vietnam.

Elated and hopeful after the success of the Pentagon demo, Jerry and I returned to the Lower East Side with our New York friends. Radicalizing the counterculture was not only worthwhile, it was fun! We stayed busy organizing, networking, planning, but also lounging and laughing in Abbie and Anita's apartment.

The reader may remember that this was where the Yippies were born, on New Year's Eve 1967, and where Chicago 1968 was conceived: in the collective imagination of a bunch of stoned hippie activists. We spent the next eight months organizing for a Festival of Life at the 1968 Democratic Convention. What we got instead, as the reader now knows and indeed much of the world knows, was something very different: a Battle of Resistance and Repression. The Whole World Was Watching.

Much like the Pentagon siege, Chicago had been a success, exposing the brutal underside of American democracy. On American TV! Jerry and I had done our part, but we were glad it was over. We were exhausted and more than a little scared. It was time to go home, unwind, and take a break.

Who knew that Chicago '68 was far from over? This was just an intermission.

CONSPIRACY TRIAL

It had been a wild year; between the Pentagon, the birth of the Yippies, and the chaos of Chicago '68, Jerry and I returned to Berkeley for some much needed down time. Berkeley felt like our spiritual home, and we needed a safe haven. This was a lull in our lives. We didn't have clear "career paths" like other people seemed to, and had to re-invent ourselves anew each time we completed a major undertaking. Often we would look around in the quiet of ourselves and say, "Now what?" During the height of activity, we were certain. But during the valleys, the calm allowed self-doubt to creep in. This was one of those uncomfortable periods when we would have second thoughts about the path we had chosen. I experienced a feeling of temporary letdown but Jerry became intensely depressed. So we retreated to Berkeley, our spiritual home, searching for respite and perhaps direction.

Then, all of a sudden both Jerry and Abbie were subpoenaed to HUAC (the House Un-American Activities Committee) along with Dave Dellinger, Tom Hayden, and Rennie Davis from The Mobe. Their presence was required in Washington, DC, on October 1, 1968. So much for the quiet moments!

For Jerry this appearance was a repeat performance. The reader may remember that in 1966, when HUAC was "investigating" the Berkeley-based Vietnam Day Committee, Jerry showed up dressed as an American Revolutionary War soldier. This time, two years later, before the very same committee, Jerry dressed as an international revolutionary. His face was painted like a Native American warrior and he sported Viet Cong black pajama pants, a Pancho Villa bandoleer across his bare chest, and the black beret of the Panthers. With his wild hair and beard and carrying a toy M-16, he appeared as a nightmare to HUAC.

Not wanting to be upstaged entirely by the men, my friends and I got together in New York to plan our own response to HUAC. Roz Payne, Sharon Krebs, Robin Morgan, and I had all helped organize the protests at the Democratic Convention, yet not one of us had been subpoenaed! Here they were conducting a "witch hunt" and not a single honest-to-goodness "witch", not a single woman, was subpoenaed! We were being overlooked and decided to do something about it. We disrespected witches would put a hex on HUAC!

Our first public hex was conjured and delivered on the street in front of Gem Spa, the Lower East Side gathering spot for everyone who loved NYC egg creams. We were dressed in full black regalia, sporting witches' hats and the customary brooms. The hex we performed has been preserved for history, thanks to Roz Payne of the Newsreel alternative media collective:

In the Holy and Most Powerful Name of **WITCH**,

Women's International Terrorist Conspiracy from Hell.

We Sister Witches from the one true Underground

Announce our Presence and commence our spell.

In the Sacred Name of all our Sister Witches,

The original guerrillas and resistance fighters throughout the ages,

We cast our vengeful Magic on Hu-Wacky judges

Who dare conduct a witch-hunt without real witches.

They have created Subpoena Envy.

And then on to DC. As HUAC convened, Sharon Krebs and I, dressed in our pointed witch hats and armed with our brooms, walked up and down the aisles, burning stick incense and casting evil hexes on HUAC.

Nancy and Jerry at HUAC, Washington, DC, October 1968.

Historically, people had feared HUAC when they were called to testify. And for good reason: jobs had been lost and reputations ruined. And the specter of the Rosenbergs in the electric chair and Morton Sobell in prison still hung over HUAC.

Now HUAC was being turned inside out. All those called were defiant and we Yippies were making a mockery of the process. The emperor had no clothes! Once more Jerry unsuccessfully insisted on testifying. The government knew that his taking the stand in costume would bring even further disrepute to the process. We seemed to have won the battle with HUAC. Then in December of 1968, HUAC reconvened, calling the same people back to testify. This time Jerry came dressed appropriately for the season, as Santa Claus. Once again HUAC refused to allow him to testify, and once again we dominated the media. The Washington Post headline read "SANTA BARRED BY HUAC" over a big photo of Santa Claus Jerry Rubin on the front page. But all our magic and defiance were only able to hold back the forces of evil temporarily. In March, the feds struck back with a vengeance.

Relaxing after the HUAC circus, Jerry and I were finally settling into a rhythm in Berkeley when serious federal indictments jerked us back to Chicago. In March of 1969, with the Republicans less than two months in office, Jerry was charged, along with seven others, with conspiracy to cross state lines with the intent to incite riot. This "anti-riot" law was part of the 1968 Civil Rights Act and was often referred to as the "Rap Brown" Law, after the fiery leader of SNCC.

While proclaiming to the press that he was "honored" to be tapped for the Academy Award of the Movement, Jerry actually considered the conspiracy indictment somewhat of a relief. He alone had been indicted on similar Illinois state charges. If he went to trial on those charges by himself, it would have been a much smaller event and more difficult to fight. He also wanted to be at the center of the action, and he knew the Chicago 8 would be that center for the next year. I would have preferred to have stayed in California to pursue a less public life, but I knew I had to rise to the occasion. Given what ensued, I cannot say I am sorry that life played out the way it did.

The trial of the Chicago 8 has been referred to as one of the greatest trials in history, comparable to those of Socrates and Galileo. Well, maybe. But for sure it was a big deal. Graham Nash and Phil Ochs both wrote songs about it. Elliot Gould, Martin Sheen, and Peter Boyle starred in a docudrama with the dialogue lifted straight from the court transcripts. A 2008 release, *The Chicago 10,* utilized documentary footage and animation to portray the courtroom scenes. Myriad books, articles, and PhD theses have been written with the trial as the theme. Abbie Hoffman's first name is a frequent answer in the *New York Times* crossword puzzle. In 2021 Aaron Sorkin released his movie about the Chicago 8, which streams on Netflix. A recent Google search reveals 2,080,000,000 sites (unvetted) related to the trial. While the analogy to Socrates and Galileo may be a bit of a stretch, it was an incredible, fabulous, and fascinating affair. It certainly has become part of history, and I was fortunate enough to participate in that history.

The cast of characters was enormous. The stars were the eight defendants, two defense attorneys, and an extremely colorful judge. Six of the defendants were charged with crossing state lines with "intent to incite, promote, encourage, participate in, or carry on a riot." They were Rennie Davis, Dave Dellinger, Tom Hayden, Abbie Hoffman, Jerry Rubin, and Bobby Seale. The other two defendants, John Froines and Lee Weiner, were charged with teaching the "use, application and making of incendiary devices." All eight of the defendants were additionally charged with conspiracy, conspiring with themselves and others to commit the acts mentioned above.

There were four primary attorneys. Thomas Foran and Richard Schultz were the usual drab "suits" for the prosecution, in contrast with the defense attorneys who took center stage: a young, intense, intelligent, and disheveled Leonard Weinglass, and the older William Kunstler, a flamboyant lawyer with a deep Shakespearean voice who had been an active part of the civil rights struggle. Kunstler with his flair for the dramatic was the ideal lawyer for the Yippies: Broadway Bill meets the P.T. Barnum of the Left. But it was the judge, Julius Hoffman, who walked away with an Academy Award. Sitting high up in the federal courtroom in Chicago, his talking head looked strikingly similar to that of the cartoon character, Mr. Magoo.

From the beginning we embraced the concept of "conspiracy"; here I use the word "we" loosely, to include all of us around the defendants who considered ourselves part of the process. To conspire means "to breathe together," and we acknowledged that we did indeed breathe together. This was a widespread conspiracy. There were also 18 unindicted co-conspirators—named as conspirators but not charged at that time. Additionally, the indictment stated that there were "divers other persons, some known and others unknown to the Grand Jury." This was clearly an attempt to frighten the entire movement, to have a chilling effect on protest across the country. Rather than run away from the accusation that we were collaborators, we adopted the concept of conspiracy as our own and tried to project it as a positive phenomenon. We wanted to be part of a different kind of society, one that was based not so much on individualism as on cooperation. "Conspiracy" seemed to fit the bill. People all around the country came to feel part of it as well, and were breathing together with us.

The trial began on the 26th of September, 1969 and ended on February 20th in 1970. Hundreds of people would line up outside the Federal Building every morning to get a seat at the show. Every media outlet in the country was present in the courtroom every day, and although no cameras were allowed, there were court illustrators from each of the TV networks, creating a daily visual record. During the breaks the defendants held regular press conferences as well.

We had expected some semblance of legality in the courtroom, but that was not to be. Had Judge Julius Hoffman been willing to allow the defendants even a smattering of their constitutional rights, it might have been a more traditional trial. But it became clear from the jump that Julius was bent on suppressing, denying, and prohibiting the defense from doing anything. He ran the courtroom like a dictator. Jury selection was completed in a half day. He refused to question the panel on most of the defendants' requests. Almost everything the prosecution wanted was granted. Almost everything we wanted was denied. Hoffmann continually demeaned the defense attorneys. Yes, there was humor in the way he carried himself and how he spoke. Some observers were entertained, even charmed. Julius Hoffman was an entertaining character, but reactionary and mean-spirited to the core.

The Yippies wanted to bring to the courtroom as much of our Festival of Life as possible, the Festival of Life that we were thwarted from producing during the Democratic Convention. We figured the odds were against us if we accepted this courtroom's rules of the game. We would surely lose. Or we could confront the confrontation. We might still lose legally but at the end of the day at least we would have said something to the world. It seemed worth the gamble.

This approach was in conflict with others of the defendants, most specifically Tom Hayden. Tom's politics were as radical, perhaps more radical, than ours, but different. He felt that the courtroom was no place for revolutionary politics. He wanted to conduct a traditional defense, cut our losses, get out of the courtroom as fast as possible and back to the business of organizing real people, not in the media, but on the street. It might have been possible, even preferable, on a different planet, but it was out of touch with the forces at work in this trial—on both sides.

At first the differences between Tom and the Yippies had been subtle. Although we hoped to bring the Festival of Life to the courtroom, at that point we were also committed to organizing an honest to goodness legal defense. In an effort to do something helpful, I volunteered to work with Tom on tracking down different materials and people for our legal argument. I was going back and forth from New York to Chicago on a fairly regular basis, dealing with the publication of *DO IT!*, Jerry's forthcoming book. I was dealing with the publisher and working on the graphics with Quentin Fiore in Princeton, New Jersey, and traveling there as well from time to time. But when I was in Chicago, I tried to help Tom with some of the defense work. I offer that information as an illustration of the two-sidedness of all that we were involved with. Did we plan a real trial? Did we plan a circus? I think it's accurate to say that at least we Yippies were planning for a colorful trial but, as it turned out, we welcomed a militant circus.

When the trial first opened, Jerry was in Chicago's Cook County Jail. He had been serving a 30-day sentence in California for a Berkeley sit-in against the military. The day of my first visit with Jerry at Cook County Jail, *Chicago Sun-Times* columnist Tom Fitzpatrick interviewed me while giving me a ride there and wrote a piece about it—"Nancy With the Laughing Face."

I had agreed to the interview but wondered if we were going the most direct way. When the car stopped at a red light, I asked: "Are we going the right way? I want to make sure I get there on time, you know. I haven't seen him in a long while."

"We're less than ten minutes away," Fitz reassured me, and I felt my body relax.

Soon the concrete walls of the Jail appeared. "I'm nervous, " I admitted. "You never know what's happened to a person's life in jail. I'm always concerned about what I'm going to hear." I didn't admit that I was also nervous because only immediate family could visit, so I was going to present myself as Mrs. Jerry Rubin. This, of course, was untrue. We were not married but from then on, I became known as Jerry's wife.

Fitz dropped me off and I walked through the Criminal Courts Building, through the back yard and into the front door of the jail where relatives of the prisoners wait to be identified and searched. I was perhaps 24th or 25th in line.

When I reached the front of the line, the door opened and the jail guard said: "Your name and the prisoner you've come to see?" I showed him the white envelope addressed to Nancy Rubin that contained a notary's note saying that my married name was now Nancy Rubin. Feeling quite shaky I said in a quiet voice, "My name is Nancy Rubin and I'm here to see my husband, Jerry Rubin."

When I finally got to see Jerry, standing up and through a wire mesh, I breathed a sigh of relief but then was surprised and worried about how exhausted and nervous he seemed. He looked even more anemic because his hair had been trimmed way back, an army-style crew cut.

"Jerry, I'm so happy to finally see you. We couldn't get any information about where you were. And of course I missed you."

That unleashed a torrent of speed rapping that he had probably stored up:

"I was going out of my mind. They grabbed me out of my cell at Santa Rita in the middle of the night with no information. I didn't know where I was going or why I was thrown in the backseat and handcuffed to this other prisoner. That guy was hell bent on breaking away sometime during the trip which meant I'd be going along for the ride. I was probably paranoid, but I thought they put him there on purpose, to set me up or something. They wouldn't let me contact anyone."

"Oh my god! I'm so glad you made it here in one piece. Okay, not exactly here in Cook County Jail. But at least we can keep an eye on you here. I didn't mean to cut you off. Do you want to say anything else about it?"

"Only that luckily for me, there was no window of opportunity for him. Otherwise I might be dead meat. Those marshals do not fool around and they were fully loaded."

"And what's worse," he said, "Look at my head. I'm a shorn hippy. I tried to resist but they forced a haircut on me. And I will still be in jail at the opening of the trial. They'll bring me in from the lock-up. I feel so isolated from the other defendants and don't know what's going on."

I told him we knew he'd be shorn. But we had plans to deal with his hairlessness and keep his name on everyone's lips at the same time. I knew Jerry well enough to know that the little boy inside him would be feeling pretty awful after all he went through. Even the grown man would be feeling beat up. Anybody would be, but somehow I thought Jerry was exceptionally vulnerable.

"Time is up," said one of the guards. I blew Jerry a kiss and headed out. I'd have to save our plans for next visit.

On a later visit, Jerry told me that he didn't know what he would have done without Bobby Seale. Bobby was able to calm Jerry down, and help him get through those early days. Already in the Cook County Jail when Jerry arrived, Bobby was facing murder charges which looked like they might lead to the electric chair. He would later be acquitted of those charges, but at the time of the Chicago 8 conspiracy trial, they loomed over him. Yet despite his own dire situation, Bobby was able to

Sketch of Nancy by Spain Rodriguez, circa 1969.

compassionately reach out to Jerry and help him do the time. That is something I will never forget.

Together Jerry and Bobby came to the trial every day from the lock-up, escorted by U.S. marshals. And when the six other defendants left for the day, Bobby and Jerry were taken out of the courtroom by the U.S. marshals and sent back to Cook Country Jail for the night.

As Jerry had expected, his incarceration meant that he was unable to participate in the media frenzy that accompanied the opening of the trial. Quite honestly, this exclusion from the limelight of the media pained Jerry as much as the miserable conditions in the jail. He felt isolated and neglected by the others. To add insult to injury, there was the issue of his shorn locks. So as the trial opened, we put out a call through the underground press for a contest—Jerry Rubin versus Judge Julius Hoffman. We asked people to cut locks of their hair and send them to either Jerry or the bald Judge Julius Hoffman. Whoever received the most hair would win. Since Jerry was in custody, each day his mail was delivered to him while he sat at the defense table. And each day he would open the scores of envelopes and the hair would pour out, revealing the support of "longhairs" all around the country. It was quite a hairy scene. Needless to say, Jerry got way more hair than Judge Hoffman and won hands-down. These antics definitely lifted his spirits; though not so, Julius Hoffman's.

A few weeks into the trial Jerry's sentence was up and he came out, leaving Bobby as the only defendant in custody.

There was no chance of an orderly trial and it was Julius Hoffman who defined the terms of the situation. But it was Bobby Seale who took those terms and, from a position of apparent powerlessness, totally transformed the situation. Bobby was one of the founding leaders of the Black Panther Party. He was indicted along with the seven white guys. He had not actually been a major organizer of the demonstrations but had simply agreed to come and speak, to fill in for Eldridge Cleaver who was unable to make it. Bobby was in Chicago for less than 24 hours and hadn't met most of the defendants until they were arraigned in April of 1969. His circumstances dominated the trial for the first month.

Out in California, Charles Geary was THE attorney for the Black Panther Party. It wasn't easy for a Black revolutionary to trust any white lawyers, and most were white of course. But over time Charles Geary had proved to be more than trustworthy. The Panthers knew through experience that he was on their side. It seemed completely reasonable that we would get a postponement until Geary could recover from his surgery in order to be present as Bobby's lawyer.

But the motion to postpone had been quickly denied by Judge Hoffman. Therefore Bobby decided to defend himself. That should have been a reasonable backup position. Once again, Judge Julius Hoffman denied Bobby the right to defend himself. That set the stage for the drama of the next six weeks and really the entire trial.

At the outset of the trial, Bobby had been the most respectful of the judge, standing quietly as the judge entered the courtroom, as is traditional, while some defendants sat. But when he was denied his constitutional rights, Bobby refused to be quiet. He continually requested to have Charles Geary represent him and, if denied that, then to represent himself.

At first, Hoffman would just admonish him and threaten him with contempt charges. We held our breath. As Bobby continued to speak up, the judge escalated his repressive tactics. He would excuse the jury and tell the marshals to "Take that defendant into the room in there and deal with him as he should be dealt with." Then one day the marshals carried Bobby back into the courtroom with his hands and feet shackled to a chair. Even in that state he electrified the courtroom as he continued to demand his constitutional rights, his right to his attorney or to defend himself. The judge ordered the marshals to take him out again, and this time when they carried him back into the courtroom, it was not enough to shackle and chain his hands and feet to his chair. He was now literally gagged so that he could not speak. Even then he attempted to speak, although the sounds he made were not comprehensible. They carried him back out again and brought him back into court fully muzzled—with yet another rag tied around his head and under his chin.

Chicago reporter Bob Greene would describe it as "the most damaging thing I have ever heard of a judge doing. A Black man in an

American courtroom, tied to a chair with tape around his face and mouth, carried into the courtroom." Years later, even Prosecutor Schultz admitted that Seale "looked like a slave in the courtroom".

In the end Bobby Seale was severed from the case, to be tried at a later date, and then sentenced to four years for contempt of court. The trial continued as the Chicago 7 although we continued to call it the Chicago 8 in a salute to Bobby. It was Bobby's stance that defined the grandeur of the trial. A Black revolutionary, one lone individual, had gone up against a stacked, white, racist court system and had won the moral high ground.

Yet I remember feeling dreadful and paralyzed by the situation. I was not a journalist observing an atrocity; I was an activist trying to figure out how to respond. We were criticized by some people for not doing more to defend Bobby. We could have caused a melee in the courtroom when they bound and gagged Bobby. On the one hand, it was a complicated situation. Charles Garry and the Panthers from the beginning were somewhat leery of our Yippie antics and requested that we exercise self-control. They wanted Bobby to be able to define his own situation and not get tangled up with our agenda. We tried to respect their wishes in order not to detract from Bobby's situation. Jerry and Abbie restrained themselves accordingly, as did we spectators.

Nonetheless, when the repression reached the height of binding and gagging, others of us could have and should have acted. Spectators could have acted in the courtroom and movement people could have acted outside the courtroom and around the country. But it didn't happen. I wonder what held us back. Was it respect for the Panthers or fear of the consequences?

I had always admired Dave Dellinger but during the trial I came to respect him even more. He was indeed a resolute pacifist, imprisoned during World War II for his refusal to bear arms. I didn't agree with him at the time but I respected him enormously. I felt that if we were all Dave's kind of pacifist, we'd have a helluva movement. When the marshals came to get Bobby the final time, it was Dave who stepped between Bobby and the marshals, trying to prevent them from laying hands on

Bobby. He had to be pulled and pushed away. It was Dave who was punished with contempt charges for trying to defend Bobby. With his resolve he showed all who were watching that being a pacifist did not mean being passive.

I was being pushed closer and closer to real revolutionary commitment, radicalized by events both inside and outside the courtroom. While Bobby stood strong against the repression inside the courtroom, Panthers were under attack around the country. On October 3rd the Chicago police, with support from the Justice Department, raided the local Black Panther Party headquarters, riddling the place with bullets. These violent events kept on coming. I didn't have much time for processing this during the trial but these events deeply affected me. Symbolically my childhood nail-biting returned. And then it came even closer and bloodier.

While we slept, regaining strength to withstand another day of the prosecution's case in the Chicago 8 trial, in the early morning hours of December 4, 1969, over a dozen heavily armed men of the Chicago Police Department and the FBI assassinated Fred Hampton, the twenty-one-year-old charismatic leader of the Chicago Black Panther Party. An undercover police informant had drugged Fred earlier that evening. The cops waited until it was safe (for them), then in cold blood shot Fred, who was sleeping alongside his pregnant wife, and also killed his associate, Mark Clark.

Shock and terror, anger and grief washed over me and entered my heart. Our whole Conspiracy community was united in our mourning for these people we had all known, some casually, others well. In court that day, Kunstler requested an adjournment of the trial—out of respect for Fred Hampton and Mark Clark, and because of the emotional reaction of the defendants to what all of us on the defense side considered to be a wanton murder.

Of course the judge would have none of that and the trial proceeded as usual. Later we would all troop over to the West Side apartment where these two Black revolutionaries had been murdered. As I filed through the apartment along with hundreds of others who were also there to pay their respect, I was shocked and chagrined to see the bullet holes and blood-soaked mattresses. That experience intensified my anger at the government and also brought an icy chill, or should I say dread, to my heart.

Meanwhile, the mass anti-war movement was ballooning and I tried to stay connected to it. The defendants were allowed to travel although they had to file their travel plans with prosecutor Foran. One particular Friday I remember, during the prosecution's case, an undercover agent's testimony was dragging on and on. We were all itching to end early in order to catch planes to the National Moratorium demonstration planned for the next day in DC. Court ended in the nick of time and we made it to Washington for the 500,000 person outpouring of anti-war sentiment that unfolded around a stage right in front of the White House. At a subsequent Moratorium Day, the defendants wore black armbands to court and Dave read a list of the war dead on both sides.

Life during the trial was a surreal three-ring circus. For instance, while the intensely serious situation with Bobby was developing in Ring One, Ring Two was a photo shoot with the renowned photographer, Richard Avedon. He set up shop at the Palmer House, one of the fancier hotels in downtown Chicago, not far from the Hilton where just the year before we had all been gassed and clubbed. All the conspirators and their partners and family had their photos taken in various combinations. My sister Louise and Jerry's kid brother Gil (who was my sister's boyfriend at the time!) were wonderfully supportive and had traveled to Chicago to attend the trial. So our family Avedon photos consist of the four of us.

That was the same night that Abbie and Anita went skinny-dipping in the Palmer House hotel pool. They were the only ones in the pool that night. Although they weren't the only Yippies around, they were the only ones without inhibition. As such they were the stars in Ring Three.

However, most of our rest and recreation took place during the court's lunch breaks. Frequently Abbie, Anita, Jerry, Dave, Kunstler, and I, along with various witnesses and out-of-town friends, would head over to The Berghoff, a popular German restaurant adjacent to the Federal Building where a large, round table awaited us since we were regular celebrity guests. The surly, black-jacketed waiters joked around, and we would wine and dine, refreshed to do battle in the afternoon. Tom, Rennie, and Froines looked down on this behavior as "bourgeois" and would grab their lunch, along with Len Weinglass, at a more "proletarian" spot. What a conspiracy! We couldn't even agree on lunch.

Back in the courtroom the visual imagery brought into relief the differences between the defense and the prosecution. Their table was neat and clean. All their personnel were (and wore) "suits," very buttoned up and clipped. Our side was very sprawled out, as if sharing coffee at a messy kitchen table. Books, papers, food, tie-dyed shirts, and, as the trial wore on, longer and longer hair. There was, of course, lots of interaction with friends and supporters in the courtroom. Abbie would occasionally blow a kiss to the jury or suddenly do a handstand on the defense table at an off moment. On Bobby Seale's birthday the other defendants brought him a birthday cake since he was in custody. On what we thought was Ho Chi Minh's birthday we brought a birthday cake into the courtroom. (We were several months off.)

If Bobby defined the terms of the trial, the Yippies played a huge role in continuing to delegitimize the courtroom after Bobby was severed from the case. When it became the Chicago 7, the Yippies largely defined the tone of the courtroom and the nature of the defense. What an incredible drama it was.

When the trial first began we were worried that there might be some surprise prosecution witnesses, people we thought were friends, who out of fear or opportunism would choose to testify against the defendants. That did not turn out to be the case. Of all the thousands of demonstrators and movement activists, not a single person became a witness for the prosecution. This was not to be taken for granted and was very heartwarming for all of us.

Of all their many witnesses, only two or three were even civilians, and those civilians were unknown to us. The rest of the prosecution was a series of cops of one stripe or another—undercover and uniformed, from several different divisions of the Chicago Police Department, military intelligence, FBI agents, etc. One of the cops who testified as a key witness was Bob Pierson. He was the "biker" who had volunteered his "protective services" to Jerry during the 1968 demonstrations. We certainly hadn't thought of him as a friend, so it came as no surprise to us that he was a cop. He lied on the stand, putting words into Jerry's mouth that I'm sure were never said. They just weren't Jerry's style. And anyway, I would have heard them because I was with Jerry the whole time.

With Bobby Seale severed from the case and the droning of the cops completed, the defense took the stand from the first week in December up until the beginning of February. It was a frigid Chicago winter but inside the courtroom there was plenty of heat. Much of the "legal" defense played out in the form of high theater, but it was more than that. It reflected all the work and all the personal/political connections we had made leading up to the Democratic Convention. Everyone who testified for the defense had played some role in the actual organizing efforts. Many were well known figures in popular culture: Arlo Guthrie, Judy Collins, Country Joe (and the Fish), Allen Ginsberg, Norman Mailer, Timothy Leary, and Paul Krassner.

The musicians had intended to come to the Festival of Life before it became clear that it would be a mass confrontation. Now we brought some of them in as defense witnesses to attest to the fact that the Yippies had indeed invited them to perform, that our intent was to have a Festival of Life.

When Arlo Guthrie took the stand, he tried to sing "Alice's Restaurant," managing to get through the first two minutes of the 25-minute story-song before Judge Hoffman cut him off. Judy Collins sang the anti-war song "Where Have All the Flowers Gone" until the marshal was instructed to stop her. When Country Joe started singing, "One, two, three, what are we fighting for?" the judge instructed a marshal to deal with him. The marshal held him by his chin in an effort to prevent the singing.

Allen Ginsberg explained how he came to Lincoln Park, and in the midst of the tear gas and police clubbings, had sat on the ground and "ommed"

Nancy and the Chicago 8 (without Bobby Seale) Press Conference, 1969.

for peace. He struck a yogi pose right there in the courtroom and began "omming" in a deep, rich baritone until the judge demanded that he stop.

Yippie singer Phil Ochs took the stand to explain how and why we had nominated Pigasus the pig as our candidate for President. He was prevented from giving the whole story. Jerry had requested that Phil sing "I Ain't Marching Anymore," since it addressed the issue of Rubin's state of mind, his intent. Judge Julius forbade Phil from singing but allowed him to recite the words, as follows:

"It's always the old to lead us to the war,

It's always the young to fall.

Now look at all we've won with the saber and the gun.

Tell me, is it worth it all?

Call it peace or call it treason,

Call it love or call it reason,

But I ain't marchin' anymore.

No, I ain't marchin' anymore."

Abbie was one of the two defendants to testify. The other was Rennie. Jerry really wanted to be a witness but the group decided against that and once again he had to accept their decision, if begrudgingly.

Former Harvard professor and LSD guru Timothy Leary, of "Tune in, turn on, and drop out" fame, took the stand. He testified that before the Democratic Convention he and his wife, Rosemary, held a press conference at the Model Farm in Lincoln Park. His wife, Mrs. Leary, had held a lantern by a cow and they announced they were going to come to Chicago in August not with fire, but to bring light and peace.

All parties struck a respectful pose when Norman Mailer took the stand. The judge seemed pleased to have such a figure in the courtroom, as if his presence was an honor. Mailer's actual testimony itself was another story. He reported that Jerry, in recruiting Mailer's assistance, had explained his vision as follows:

"The presence of 100,000 young people in Chicago at a festival with rock bands would so intimidate and terrify the establishment, particularly the Johnson Vietnam war establishment, that Johnson would have to be nominated under armed guard.

And I said "Wow." I was overtaken with the audacity of the idea and I said, "It's a beautiful and frightening idea." And Rubin said, "I think that the beauty of it is that the establishment is going to do it all themselves. We won't do a thing. We're just going to be there and they won't be able to take it. They will smash the city themselves. They will provoke all the violence." (Tales of Hoffman, p. 204–7)

Journalist John Schultz and others believe that Mailer's testimony was most damaging as it gave a dark picture of Jerry's intent. Perhaps that was so. But, as Mailer said, the nuances are everything. Yippies were not romantically enamored of violence. At the beginning of our organizing efforts, we thought the confrontation would be symbolic. Later we realized it would probably be physical. However, we did not create the violence that we expected. It was there, just under the surface. It would be brought out for the world to see because it would be directed not just at Black and Vietnamese people but at primarily white middle class kids. The revelation of that violence would be our contribution to demonstrating the true nature of the system.

The defense subpoenaed LBJ, but the judge squashed the subpoena. Then the defense subpoenaed Chicago Mayor Richard J. Daley and the judge allowed it! Ours was not to reason why. The day he testified, many of our supporters were moved to the last row of the courtroom while the prosecution's people filled the front rows.

Daley, who during Convention week had slipped on national television and said, "The police are not here to create disorder; they're here to preserve disorder," took the stand. Kunstler tried but was not permitted to pursue most lines of questioning that would have revealed anything. The judge and marshals ran interference.

On the floor of the Convention, Connecticut Senator Abraham Ribicoff had accused Daley of utilizing "Gestapo tactics" on the streets and in the parks. In response to this dressing down, Daley was caught on an open TV microphone saying, "Fuck you, you Jew sonofabitch. Get your ass out of Chicago." In his questioning of Daley, Kunstler did manage to ask the Mayor, "Did you say to Senator Abraham Ribicoff, 'Fuck you, you Jew sonofabitch'?"

Of course Daley did not have to respond. As writer John Schultz noted in his book *No One Was Killed, The Democratic National Convention 1968*, "You could see and sense right there in the courtroom the vast complex of Daley's friends, cronies, and protégés, protecting him, using him, protecting themselves." (Schultz, p. 218)

During Daley's testimony it was difficult for our supporters and family to keep totally silent. Moans and groans slipped out and the marshals removed several people. I came close to being one of them. John Schultz describes one such encounter:

> *"Nancy Kurshan, sitting in the front bench behind the defense table on 'Daley Day,' cried out in disgust at one point, and 'Slim,' the tall black deputy marshal who had once been a Harlem Globetrotter, said, 'All right, Nancy, let's go,' gesturing with his thumb toward the door. She folded her arms, and would not look at him, and shook her head no. He repeated, 'Let's go.' She shook her head without looking at him again, showing that he would have to pull and carry her out. Probably because of the disposition indicated by the familiarity in his tone, he accepted her threat and relented."* (Schultz, p. 220)

When Daley left the courtroom, it was through the back door, generally used only by the judge and court personnel.

The defense planned on calling the former Attorney General Ramsey Clark as a witness. Clark had been opposed to sending federal troops to Chicago during the Convention, had refused FBI requests to wiretap the defendants' phones, and had also opposed the grand jury investigation that led to the indictments. On January 28th Ramsey Clark appeared, ready to testify. The prosecution objected and the judge ruled, as he had consistently, in favor of the prosecution. The former Attorney General of the United States was not allowed to testify.

On Friday, January 30th, the defense rested. But before everyone left the courtroom, Judge Hoffman reported that he had heard about a speech given in Milwaukee. He warned that if such a speech was brought to his attention again, he might very well terminate bail for that defendant. Dellinger acknowledged that he had made the speech and questioned Hoffman's motives. "Is it that I criticized your conduct of the trial? Why are you threatening me with revocation of bail for exercising my freedom of speech?"

On my 26th birthday, February 4th, the prosecution began their assault with rebuttal witnesses. Deputy Chief James Riordan was on the stand, telling lies about Dave Dellinger's actions in Grant Park, trying to impugn Dave's pacifism. Dave responded: "Oh, bullshit." A spectator yelled, "Right on!" and was arrested on Judge Hoffman's order.

That afternoon, outside of the hearing of the jury, Judge Hoffman revoked Dave's bail for the remainder of the trial with no argument permitted from the defense attorneys. He did this supposedly to maintain order in the courtroom. As a result, all hell broke loose. The official transcript reads "There was disorder in the courtroom." People were screaming from all points in the room and the marshals were evicting them. I cried out and suddenly a marshal grabbed me to drag me out. Rennie shouted, "This court is bullshit. Mr. Rubin's wife they're now taking..." At which point Jerry heard Rennie and screamed, "Keep your hands off her. You see they're taking away my wife! Everything in this court is bullshit. Why don't you put us all in jail?" Both the judge and The New York Times were unable to say the word "bullshit." It was referred to as "a barnyard epithet."

That night a debate ensued. Abbie and Jerry wanted to finally disrupt the trial enough so that the judge would revoke all their bail. They felt it would be a show of solidarity with Dave and would more clearly join the issue of his bail revocation. They argued that the pressure that would be brought to bear would more likely result in Dave's release than if it were just he alone. Others disagreed. Everyone went to sleep having arrived at no clear consensus.

So the next day, February 5th, Jerry and Abbie set out to do it themselves. As soon as they started to speak, the jury was whisked away. Then in the quiet of the courtroom they took turns speaking:

Jerry: Julius Hoffman is equal to Adolf Hitler today.

Abbie: You're trying to put us away on contempt because you can't do it in a jury trial. You know it's a hung jury.

Jerry: You're the laughing stock of the world. Every kid in the country hates you.... The judges in Nazi Germany ordered sterilization of defendants. Why don't you do that, Judge Hoffman?

Abbie: You'll have to cut out our tongues. We should have done it then, with Bobby Seale. It's the shame of this country that this building wasn't ripped down when that happened.

A marshal, without orders, said forcefully, "Shut up" to Abbie.

"I will not shut up," Abbie said. "I'm not an automaton such as you are." Then "*Shanda fur de goyim,*" Abbie shot at Judge Hoffman. (Shame before the *goyim*, front man for the Protestant elite.) He was hoping to hit Judge Hoffman's sensitivity about his Jewish background.

Judge Hoffman called a recess.

The following day, February 6th, I rented robes (I was often the "prop" person) from a costume shop and Jerry and Abbie marched into court wearing judicial robes. Standing back to back, like the Red and Black Queens in *Through the Looking Glass,* Jerry stated for the court, "These are judges' robes." This infuriated Julius Hoffman. He of course threatened them with future charges but did not revoke their bail. Shortly thereafter, the Court of Appeals upheld Dave's bail revocation, and he remained in jail.

The judge had stated continuously during the trial that the defendants would be "dealt with accordingly." On Valentine's Day, Saturday, February 14th, that time had come. The judge read his instructions to the jury and they then went off to deliberate. Immediately thereafter, Judge Hoffman began to sentence all the defendants for contempt:

Dellinger: 29 months and 13 days

Davis: 25 months and 14 days

Hayden: 14 months and 14 days

Hoffman: 8 months and 6 days

On Sunday Julius Hoffman completed the contempt sentencing:

Rubin: 25 months and 23 days

Weiner: 2 months and 18 days

Froines: 1 month

Then he turned to the attorneys:

Kunstler: 4 years and 13 days

Weinglass: 20 months and 9 days

The defendants were sentenced individually and, after an opportunity to speak, were denied bail and taken one by one to the lockup.

Over in the spectator section Tasha Dellinger applauded her father's speech and the marshals tried to drag her out. Jerry jumped up screaming "Heil Hitler" in a Nazi salute to the judge. When Abbie was taken away, he blew Anita a kiss and in a moment of levity reminded her to water the plants. When Jerry's turn came he told Julius Hoffman that he had "radicalized more people than we ever could!"

Jerry and I hugged and kissed and then he was taken away! One moment he was there and the next he was gone, sentenced at least for the two years two months on the contempt charges, but possibly much longer since we had no knowledge yet of how the actual trial verdict would come down. It could be many years before we would see each other outside prison walls. Although I had been trying to prepare myself for this moment, there was really no preparation that would protect me from the deep shock I experienced and the great unknown, no, the abyss, that appeared before me. I had little time to digest what was happening as the courtroom scene rolled on.

By the time the judge got around to sentencing the attorneys, they were the only ones left standing. The judge granted the attorneys bond until April since even Julius Hoffman understood it would appear over the edge to force them to file appeals for their clients from their own cells in the Cook County Jail.

On Tuesday the 17th, just four days later, the jury came back with a verdict. Before they announced their decision, Prosecutor Schultz proposed that the relatives be excluded since we couldn't be counted on to behave. I shouted out, "There will be demonstrations all over the country this week" as I was pushed out of the courtroom. On her way out, Anita

Hoffman screamed, "We'll dance on your grave, Julius." While some have interpreted that phrase as a threat, I believe that was Anita's "contempt sentence," an angry statement of fact that we were young and would still be here when he was gone. The judge was a representative of a violent, vindictive, and racist past. We had contempt for that past and we welcomed its death.

The verdict was a mixed bag. The jury was split. Most jurors wanted to convict on everything. Four wanted to acquit on everything. They finally made a deal and compromised. They threw out the conspiracy count for everyone and convicted five of the defendants on the inciting to riot charges. Froines and Weiner were acquitted of everything.

On February 28th the defendants were granted an appeal bond by the appellate court.

Although the trial was full of high (and low) theatre, the atmosphere of the courtroom was deadly serious. The intimidation of a federal courtroom, encircled by U.S. marshals, with the almighty power of the judge to hold people in contempt, should not be underestimated. What the defendants (and even the witnesses) did took a great deal of courage. The consequences were largely unknown. Five years in jail? Ten years in jail? And what about the contempt? That was completely unknown since it was at the discretion of the judge. Hoffman continually threatened the defendants that, "You will be dealt with accordingly." Yet people did what they felt was right to do without regard to the consequences! How often does that happen here in America?

An important part of our strategy was to capture the media's attention and use them to communicate our message. The dynamic with the press was a relatively complicated one, but largely favored us. Many reporters were at least politically liberal and some identified strongly with the growing youth culture. Additionally, many had been radicalized by the protests at the Democratic Convention and seemed to move closer and closer to us as the trial went on. We certainly gave them colorful news stories.

Two years later, a higher court primarily threw out the contempt charges. Only a small portion of the charges that related to Dave, Jerry,

Abbie, and Kunstler remained, and the judge imposed no sentence for those contempt charges. The appellate court reversed and remanded the trial convictions. The government could have retried the defendants but not on the conspiracy charge. They would have to be retried on the substantive charges, and retried individually, not as a group. The government chose not to retry them.

Jerry copped a plea and served another 66 days on the Illinois state charges.

Bobby Seale was never brought to trial on the Chicago charges. After the jury in his other case deadlocked 11 to 1 for Bobby's acquittal, the Connecticut charges were dropped by a Judge who stated, "I find it impossible to believe that an unbiased jury could be selected without superhuman efforts—efforts which this court, the state and these defendants should not be called upon either to make or to endure."

The real story about the Chicago '68 protest and trial is not about a few high profile individuals. Yes, several defendants were well-known media figures when the trial began and yes, they reached celebrity status as a result of the ensuing press coverage. But there would not have been any news if it weren't for the thousands of people, primarily young people, who were not afraid to speak truth to power even in the face of potentially serious consequences. The real story is that significant numbers of young people were decisively breaking with racism, war and a culture driven by greed.

It was the anti-war Movement itself that was on trial. A Movement that reached into big cities and small towns, into the army and into the schools, and even into the Democratic Party. It was manifested at dinner tables around the country and reflected in music, theater, art, literature, and sports. For every one of the ten thousand or so people that were at the Chicago protest, there were countless others back home who didn't make it to Chicago, but wished they had.

The Chicago 8 did not go to court alone. Scores of people adjusted their lives or put them on hold to come to Chicago to help. Hundreds and hundreds of people showed up to come to court to support the defendants. Thousands and thousands of others came to the rallies and joined the protests around the country.

That is what the trial was really about. That is what struck fear in the hearts of the rulers. They could no longer proceed with impunity. It was not just eight individuals that needed to be controlled. It was our Movement as a whole that needed to be contained. The police violence in the streets and the repression in the courtroom were attempts to silence a whole generation and for the moment, at least, they had failed.

In 2021 Aaron Sorkin's *The Trial of the Chicago 7* was released for streaming on Netflix. The movie is entertaining, sometimes moving and often funny. But it played fast and loose with the facts. As the reader knows, I was in the room where it happened. And I wasn't the only woman. The Conspiracy office was largely run by women and women were the most ubiquitous in the courtroom. Some were partners of the defendants; some were there as political activists and legal workers. Others were both personal friends as well as political and legal workers. Women were generally the grunts, doing all the day-to-day grind work in the office. That was true with regard to the Chicago 8 as well as other movement centers of activity. We were also a critical element in the courtroom dynamic. Prosecutor Schultz referred to us as "those girls who are always with the defendants." Author John Schultz (no relation) insists that we "girls":

> *"... had, in fact, intimidated many of the marshals. Their insistence on their rights, their vocal protest, their laughter, their way of acting forthrightly, and with a purpose when the spirit of declaration moved them, made many of the marshals think two or three times before "causing an uproar" by attempting to eject any one of them.* (Schultz, p. 284)

Perhaps the guards appreciated our power, but the defendants certainly did not. We were the supporting cast. Without us, the play could not go on. Despite that essential role, the defendants and those around them often treated us women like rock band groupies.

The most astounding aspect of the trial was the resistance of Bobby Seale, and the Court's physically gagging and binding him. Sorkin did a decent job in portraying that. The other incredible aspect, as I have described, was the Yippie defense, filled with imaginative, sometimes brilliant, testimonies from a dizzying array of people. There was not one word about that in Sorkin's version. Tom Hayden was the only one consulted on this movie, and I can imagine this was his view of what mattered in the trial. It is also probably more consistent with Sorkin's view of politics. But without the Yippie defense, the trial may never have become so widely known and there might not have even been a Sorkin movie.

Although the actors were great, Sorkin failed to reflect the essence of many of the characters. He showed Jerry as a violence-provoking buffoon, one who let a female FBI agent get close to him in the midst of what we had put our hearts and souls into for much of the year. The only woman who was next to him the whole time was me. And I knew Jerry's faults as well as anyone, which is finally why I left him. But I also knew his strengths. He had tremendous courage. Not Rambo courage. It was ridiculous to see him in the film talking about Molotov cocktails. He couldn't even make a smoothie! But he was brave. He stood up three times to the House Un-American Activities Committee (HUAC). He organized audacious protests and was brilliant at utilizing the mass media.

The one that Sorkin really got wrong was Dave. Dave was an incredibly firm pacifist and his behavior in the courtroom exemplified this. Remember, with a second to decide, it was Dave who stepped up and stood between Bobby and the guards when they went after Bobby. He was jailed for that, not for defending himself. And he would never have slugged a guard.

Sorkin also missed a most important aspect of Kunstler's courtroom behavior. What made him so different from many lawyers was that he had the greatest respect for his "clients," and most especially for Dave. And who didn't? We all loved and admired Dave, even if his stand as a World War II conscientious objector was difficult to come to terms with. I doubt Kunstler ever criticized Dave for his CO stance. And if he did, it would not have been in that offhand way.

Rennie Davis was not such a naive stick character. He might have looked like he was just an all-American guy, but he had traveled to North Vietnam, and Madame Binh considers him to this day as her adopted son. Although

I'm pretty sure it was actually Dave who read the names of the war dead in court, I was glad the film gave Rennie some respect by having him compile and read the names. But the unacceptable distortion by Sorkin was excising the names of the Vietnamese dead which had been read alongside the American names. Vietnamese lives mattered to us! That's what this was all about. How could Sorkin play it differently?

Sasha Baron Cohen did a reputable job, although Abbie was more charming, and both funnier and more serious. He was as good as most standup comedians but was serious in his devotion to social change. He had previously participated in the Civil Rights movement and in later life he became an environmental activist.

I believe Tom was, at that time, also a serious revolutionary. He made a mistake and misread the nature of the trial. He felt that the most important thing was to get the trial over with and go back to doing the real work that was needed to change the country. That's a reasonable argument. But it wasn't a reasonable trial, and it had been an opportunity to reach and mobilize people around the country and the world. Tom was slow to get that and perhaps didn't respect the Yippies enough to hear it sooner.

The Judge was meaner and more idiosyncratic than portrayed. He really was a nasty piece of work. The prosecutors were also creeps, and we did not have cordial conversations with them as depicted.

The missing element in the film was the rest of us, by which I mean the thousands of anti-war activists who came to the trial and waited out in the cold for hours to get into the trial. And all of us who joined the support effort and participated from the audience and were threatened or removed or arrested. Those folks were the engine that drove the anti-war movement, and among them were many WOMEN. In the absence of any of us being depicted in the movie, the fictitious burning of bras in Lincoln Park was demeaning. The only other women in this film were the phone-answering Bernardine (a ridiculous throwaway to Bernardine of SDS/Weatherman fame?) and the fictitious amorous undercover cop who "replaced" me. We might not have been out there in the limelight, but we were fighting just as hard, if not harder, than the men were to end the war and bring about a more just world. Sorkin could have had Anita, Tasha and me burning judges robes instead of bras. Our movement was shot through with male supremacy and with this, Sorkin inadvertently reminds us we have a long way to go.

Nonetheless the Sorkin film will now no doubt enhance the legacy of the Yippies. Even before the movie, many a high school and college student contacted me for their research projects, and Googling the Youth International Party produces 5,150,000 sites (unconfirmed) that one can roam through.

Nancy, circa 1970. Photo probably by Leni Sinclair.

GOODBYE TO ALL THAT

When the Conspiracy Trial had begun, I did not consider myself a feminist. By the following spring that had changed; I was slowly becoming a feminist, albeit a somewhat uneasy one.

I am sometimes asked why I was not indicted, and my response is always that the more important question is, why were no women indicted? I believe the answer lies in the pervasiveness of sexism, both in the movement and in society at large. Women were not recognized as leaders. The men who ran the movement and the men who ran the government were united in their contempt for women. Men dominated in our movement as they did everywhere, and women were not encouraged to become full leaders. The men were generally self-centered and all the media attention simply fed their egotism. Often we ourselves internalized that sexism, accepting male definitions of leadership and were not able to see ourselves as leaders.

Up to and including the Chicago 8, it was all men who were indicted for anti-war activities—the Spock/Coffin trial, the Oakland 7 trial, etc. Jerry welcomed the indictment, claiming it was the Academy Awards of the Movement. I am not saying that I wish I had been indicted (Best Supporting Actress?) or even that I deserved the "honor." I do believe, however, that if this were a non-sexist society, there would have been women defendants. As I said, women did the important work behind the scenes.

Across the street from the Federal Building was the elite Standard Club. One hundred years old and exclusive, it was where Judge Hoffman dined. Kunstler had received an invitation from an insider, and one day during the trial a group of us decided to accept the offer and dine there for lunch. A whole entourage trooped over—the cartoonist Jules Feiffer, the writer/publisher Jason Epstein, Tony Lukas of *The New York Times*, Norman Mailer, Saul Alinsky, Bill Kunstler and his wife Lotte, Dave, Jerry, and I. When we reached the Club, we discovered that it was a male-only establishment! All the men proceeded to enter in the blink of an eye, leaving Lotte and me on the outside feeling abandoned and humiliated. I was still a young upstart, 26 years of age, but Lotte was a mature, dignified woman with two daughters back home. We took little solace in the fact that Julius Hoffman, reportedly several tables away from the defendants, asked to have his table changed. Was it more important to get his goat or to show solidarity with us? The answer to that was clear.

So the trial, although exhilarating in many ways, was also, from my point of view, a negative experience in other ways. At times I felt psychologically battered. During the first weeks of the trial, when Jerry was in Cook County Jail, he was beside himself. He was reasonably enough freaked out by the conditions in the jail and was painfully unhappy about missing all the action on the outside. Despite the amazing help of Bobby, who knew how to "do" jail, the isolation and marginalization was driving him nuts. He had his own demons as well, and when he felt insecure he took it out on me by being verbally abusive.

Jerry would later write that his book *Do It!* was "Zapped by Nancy Kurshan," meaning that I shepherded his book to completion. This involved flying back and forth to New York to work with the designer on the layout, and dealing with the literary agent, the publisher at Simon & Schuster, as well as editor Jim Retherford. Jerry would provide me with long lists of things to do and I obediently tried to carry them all out. Often he would become frustrated and I would become the object of his discontent. Increasingly, I felt my identity being expropriated, as I was absorbed into the demands of his reality with no psychic space of my own. I didn't really understand it, but in those rare moments when I had

NEW YORK POST, WEDNESDAY, MARCH 18, 1970

Women's Lib Stages a Sit-In

Post Photo by Terrence McCarten

Members of Media Women occupy offices at the Ladies Home Journal, 641 Lexington Av, today, where they demanded that the magazine give women greater voice in operations Story on age 38

Nancy at *Ladies Home Journal* sit-in.

time to reflect, I was sometimes sad, unhappy and lonely. Only the occasional dinner and glass of wine with my old high school pal and college roommate Diane helped keep me grounded.

Meanwhile, the defendants were like rock stars! On weekends they would fly off to speaking engagements around the country where thousands would come to hear them and cheer them on. That exposure, combined with all the media publicity, was bringing their celebrity status to new heights. It was scary to see Jerry's individualism and self-centeredness reinforced as he was beginning to believe the hype. He also seemed to crave attention and excitement and wasn't able to enjoy quiet time with me.

Anita Hoffman and I spent a good deal of time together from 1966 through 1970. However, our friendship was a function of Abbie and Jerry's friendship. Traditional gender patterns ensured that our loyalties were with our respective partners. We each would "stand by our man," and since Abbie and Jerry had a tempestuous friendship, Anita and I were by turns in and out of each other's lives. We lived through intense and historic experiences in each other's presence, yet we never really shared our emotions or personal reflections. There was always a wall of caution between us that prevented a deep friendship from developing; a friendship that might have provided support and comfort in a time that was trying for both of us. Anita attended the Conspiracy Trial only sporadically, preferring to continue her life in New York. I think she was trying to hold on to an independent identity and not become completely subsumed in the frenzy of Abbie's existence.

This was still a time in which a bright young woman would defer to a man. Anita and I were younger and less experienced. To the extent we were conscious of the imbalance of power, it seemed to be "just the way things are."

However, while the Conspiracy Trial was coming to a close, the women's liberation movement asserted itself with a bang. A group of women seized control of The Rat, the most overtly political of the New York underground newspapers. They kicked out the men and produced the first all-women's issue. That feminist takeover of *The Rat* reverberated through the left. In that February 1970 issue, former Yippie Robin Morgan let loose a polemic against the "male-dominated left" in which she ran down the male supremacy of all quarters of the Movement and no group was spared. The piece was titled "Goodbye to All That," and in it Robin targeted the underground press, the peace movement, the old left, the new left, the Weathermen, the ecology movement, the hippies, and alas, the Yippies! She said goodbye to them all and she named names. She specifically called out Abbie and Krassner, and yes, Jerry.

> *"Theory and practice—and the light-years between them. 'Do it!' says Jerry Rubin in* Rat*'s last issue—but he doesn't or every Rat reader would have known the pictured face next to his article as well as they know his own much-photographed face: it was Nancy Kurshan, the power behind the clown." ("Goodbye to All That" in* Going Too Far, *Morgan, 1978)*

Robin completed the piece with a call to free about 20 women who were captives of the male-dominated political and cultural movements of the time: Free Kathleen Cleaver! Free Anita Hoffman! Free Nancy Kurshan! Free Bernardine Dohrn! Free Gumbo! (Just to name a few names from these pages.) With modesty and in recognition of the complexity, the final declaration was "Free Robin Morgan! Free our sisters! Free ourselves!"

Yikes, I was on that list! Much to my humiliation, my name was right out there. I could have taken the piece as a compliment but my dominant feelings at the time were shame and anger. I walked around with that piece reverberating in my head, challenging me for months and even years, perhaps even to this day. The women's liberation movement was impinging on all our lives and influencing our consciousness. For some of us the process was slower than for others but we were all affected in the end.

Robin Morgan, who had been one of our original Yippies, later went on to become the editor of *Ms. Magazine,* a prolific writer, and a feminist leader. I had attended a couple of meetings of a women's "consciousness-raising" group in Berkeley before the indictments came down. There I had felt pressured and had withdrawn. It was this same feeling that came over me when I first read Robin's "Goodbye to All That." I was very uncomfortable and vacillated between anger at Robin, anger at the men around me, and anger at myself. I was being challenged to change and was defensive about my relationship with Jerry. How could I call myself a feminist and remain in this relationship? I suppose change is often uncomfortable and confusing, and that's how I felt much of the time. Despite the discomfort, the overall impact was positive. I might have been angry at the Messenger but I got the Message, because it resonated with my own true life experiences. I imagine the same was true for many women in our scene although it was difficult for some of us to acknowledge our situation and talk about it openly at that time.

Robin broke new ground and helped change my life for the better. Certainly many of her ideas were not completely new. They had been hovering in the air, in part passed down by previous generations and informed by our own generation's experiences. However, Robin crystallized those ideas and wrote bravely, passionately and intelligently, explicitly bringing theory down to earth. There were many important concepts in her piece. She objected to the inaccurate blanket use of the phrase "male chauvinism," which she described as only an attitude. The more accurate term is "male supremacy" which, she said, is the "objective reality, the fact." She challenged the idea that freedom for women would come automatically with the advent of socialism, and she advocated an "ever stronger independent Women's Liberation Movement." All that began to make sense to me and pushed me to think harder.

However, in addition to the cognitive dissonance the piece caused because of my personal relationship with Jerry, I also had some real differences of opinion. Robin proclaimed an identification with all women: "Goodbye to all that shit that sets women apart from women…." and Robin bundled Pat Nixon right into that list. I was not ready, and am still not ready, to trade Jerry Rubin for a Pat Nixon or a Kristi Noem.

Robin also considered how to approach women such as myself who were "still in counter-left captivity" and cautioned that it was "not for us in Women's Liberation to hassle them and confront them the way their men do, nor to blame them—or ourselves—for what any of us are; an oppressed people…."

Yet that is how I felt, in part, when I read her piece—hassled, confronted and blamed. When she spoke of the Weathermen, she rightly critiqued their macho posturing but minimized the commitment of Weather women to revolution by berating them for rejecting "their own radical feminism for that last desperate grab at male approval that we all know so well." I don't deny that "male approval" was a factor, but I felt that to reduce it all to that alone is inaccurate and demeaning. I wasn't yet in the Weathermen, but I identified with the organization. Robin forced me to examine my own motives and practice. Yes, I had gone along with some pretty awful things. Most publicly, I had allowed misogynist imagery to appear in Jerry's book *Do It!* However, I had been an activist for at least ten years at that point, and to chalk it all up to the search for male approval was wrong.

Perhaps the most important difference for me was reflected in the fact that Robin no longer thought it was critical to protest events like the 1968 Democratic National Convention. While I felt protesting the Miss America Pageant was a good thing to do as well, I felt it was important to target the government, the state apparatus, particularly with regard to the war and racism but more generally, all aspects of life. I therefore made the choice to continue to organize for the Chicago protest.

A more mature movement, one quicker to change its practices with regard to women, would have embraced both protests, but the responsibility for that rested on all our shoulders. Ultimately I would have to say that as the years went on and I became more comfortable with myself, despite the differences that persisted I took inspiration from Robin, and my appreciation of her contribution grew. Decades later I learned that she was speaking at a NOW luncheon in suburban Chicago. I called to tell her I would be there and we arranged to spend some time together afterwards. I was eager to hear her speak but was wondering how things would be between us. She surprised me by asking me to stand, and described me as a long-distance runner to be emulated. Afterwards it was clear from the short time we spent together that we felt mutually affectionate after all those years of water under the bridge.

After the Chicago 8 defendants were sentenced on the contempt charges, they were sent to Cook County Jail without bond. In a certain way, the jailing of the defendants released the energy of the "support staff," many if not most of whom were women. In all honesty, I definitely felt myself making a leap forward.

Anita and I rented more judges' robes. We made a banner with the slogan "WE ARE ALL OUTLAWS IN THE EYES OF AMERIKA." Joined by Tasha Dellinger, we called a press conference and appeared in front of the banner in our judicial robes, and then took them off. Trying hard not to set my hair on fire, I sprayed the robes with lighter fluid while Anita struck the match. That image of the three of us, with fists in the air and the robes afire, was picked up around the world.

We had called for nationwide demonstrations the day after the verdict came down, referred to as TDA (The Day After). Sure enough, throughout the country people protested, many of them militantly. Anita and I, along with many others, organized a mass support demonstration in Chicago at the Federal Building and about 10,000 people showed up. It was the largest Chicago demonstration in support of the Conspiracy. I remember the worried anxiety I felt that Jerry, Abbie and the others were in jail, but also feeling a pride in our ability to organize and carry on without them.

March through May of 1970 were hectic, fast-paced months. During that time I didn't stop moving. Back home in New York I joined a women's liberation sit-in at the *Ladies Home Journal.* I pushed myself to accept whatever invitations came my way to speak about the Conspiracy Trial—Nassau Community College, Long Island; Cleveland, Ohio; Toronto, Canada.

I traveled with attorney Bill Kunstler to Isla Vista, the student area in Santa Barbara where the University of California is located. It was fun appearing with Bill. He was the star of course, with his Shakespearean voice and immense reputation. But he shared the spotlight, encouraged me, and gently led me out of my discomfort zone. We spoke in a huge outdoor arena that was packed with thousands of students and community people. Bill spoke to the controversy over fired anthropology professor Bill Allen and some scattered violence in Isla Vista,

Above: Chicago 8 Press Conference. Boys in jail. Anita Hoffman, Nancy, Susan Schultz Gregory, Ann Froines, Tasha Dellinger & Sharon Avery.
Below: Nancy speaking about the trial, 1970.

Nancy pouring lighter fluid with Anita Hoffman, Chicago 1970.

Nancy, Anita Hoffman, and Tasha Dellinger with fist raised, Chicago 1970.

including the attempted burning of a police car, that had preceded our arrival. "I have never thought that breaking of windows and sporadic, picayune violence is a good tactic," Bill told the crowd. "But on the other hand," he continued, "I cannot bring myself to condemn young people who engage in it." The crowd broke into loud applause. Bill understood, as did I, that it was the Movement that was inspiring us, and not the other way around. I set my shyness aside and followed with my first successful speech, ending with: "If there is no justice in the courtroom, the only justice is in the streets and I hope to see you there." That night, after the speeches and after the sun went down, there was a very militant protest driven by multiple issues including the firing of Bill Allen, and the Isla Vista Branch of the Bank of America was set on fire. Kunstler and I thought we stood a good chance of being indicted for inciting to riot, but that never occurred. It was the local people who took the brunt of the repression, and several were later indicted on charges.

In March the Long Island newspaper *Newsday* published a long four-page feature piece about me with several photographs, titled "THE MAKING OF A YIPPIE MRS." The article asked, "How did this L.I. girl go radical?" and reported that I had turned my back "on the middle-class values of the suburbs for a life of revolutionary participation." I had no problem with that. And when I read the interviews with my parents, teachers, and high school friends, I was touched to read that they were all supportive and protective of me.

My high school guidance counselor Robert Gorman remembered me as a "Stevenson Democrat" and my father was quoted as saying, "She's doing what she believes in and to a large extent we do, too." Even my college boyfriend Guy said, "I'm not surprised. It seems to me that in this day a Yippie is a natural thing to be. It's not Nancy who's changed. It's the country."

Of course, not everyone felt that same way as my friends and family. Shortly after the article came out, the following typewritten letter arrived at my parents' home:

1. *There is no limit to the deceit, degeneracy, and immorality of the kike.*
2. *The jew has been a cancer, contaminating every country in the world since time began.*
3. *Your daughter is a true dropping of the tribe—a commie whore.*

It went on and on, through to slur number 10. But you get the idea.

My parents always showed sterling character despite whatever disrespect was directed toward them as a result of my youthful pursuits. My high profile would result both in hate mail coming to their home and in the FBI attempting to interrogate them. They always remained strong, refusing to talk to the FBI and despising the hate mail, but never blaming me.

The defendants were soon out on bond but restricted from traveling. When an invitation was extended to attend and address the April Stockholm World Peace Conference, Judy Gumbo Clavir and I agreed to represent the Conspiracy. Although I still could not admit it to myself, Jerry and I were no longer completely joined at the hip and I was enjoying the opportunity to breathe on my own.

Although it was spring in New York, Stockholm was still in deep freeze. We stayed in the beautiful house of some Swedish peaceniks and were struck by the fact that they had a sauna in their home! We met up with several GIs who had gone AWOL from Vietnam and were living in Stockholm rather than returning to imprisonment in the U.S. They were active in the GI movement against the war and hungry for contact with the anti-war movement in America. It has always bothered me that the movement of the '60s was seen as contemptuous of the GIs. We actually had great relations with the many GIs who joined the movement.

Anxious about public speaking, especially at such a gathering, I very nervously addressed the conference. I was proud that I managed to do it (and glad that Jerry wasn't there to complain). In fact, something wonderful happened at the conference. Judy and I spent a good deal of time out in the hallways, talking with the Vietnamese delegation, an inspirational pleasure for us both. It was this encounter with the Vietnamese that was a life-changing experience. Here we were, face to face with

"The Enemy," and they appeared to be intelligent, friendly people. It was a joy to share our time with them.

Xuan Oanh was one of the key people in the Vietnamese delegation and he became our friend. While Judy and I each stood at almost 5 feet, Oanh was just a couple of inches taller. Perhaps 20 years our senior, he was slender and spry with a youthful demeanor. Oanh was a revolutionary who had lived through the French war, and also a poet and musician with a playful twinkle in his eye. He was interested in everything American, for political reasons of course, but also out of just plain curiosity. The feeling was mutual. Through conversation Oanh, Judy and I dreamed up a plan for a group of perhaps 50 Americans to meet with a delegation of Vietnamese. The Americans would be artists, singers, musicians, poets, cartoonists, actors, writers—all "cultural workers" who could then return to the U.S. and reach a wider audience. They would use the tools of their trades to help end the war. We would meet in a country open to the Vietnamese since they were not permitted to enter the United States. The Vietnamese loved the idea and invited us to come to Vietnam to further develop it!!

We were excited to get back home and start planning for that trip but first we had some unfinished business. After a quick visit to London, we made a final stop-over in Algeria to visit Black Panther leaders Eldridge and Kathleen Cleaver. Eldridge had written a book, Soul on Ice, which had catapulted him into the world of celebrity, and all us Berkeley Yippies had become friends with him through his lawyer, Beverly Axelrod (also one of Jerry's lawyers). Stew and Judy were especially good friends with Eldridge back in Berkeley. In fact it was Eldridge who had given Judy her nickname "Gumbo."

Now Eldridge and his wife Kathleen were in exile in Algeria. Tall and handsome, sporting a mustache and goatee, Eldridge was a big guy with a commanding presence. Kathleen, however, was the really striking one, her beautiful features framed by an extraordinary Afro. They were very gracious hosts although exile was clearly taking its toll. Kathleen was pregnant and they both felt isolated from the struggle and their people back home.

I remember roaming briefly around the winding, busy streets of the Casbah, but what remains most clearly in my mind is going to dinner at the North Korean embassy. The Koreans were very friendly with the "International Section" of the Black Panther Party, and they hosted a most gracious dinner that evening. However we were eager to get back home to organize our trip to Vietnam.

By the spring of 1970, Bobby Seale was still in prison, Fred Hampton had been assassinated, the Weatherman organization had become clandestine and renamed the Weather Underground, and the outcome of the Conspiracy trial still hung in the balance.

I entered the 1960s a young, wide-eyed activist, a democratic socialist. As a freshman in college I had campaigned for Robert Kastenmeier for Congress. The violence directed primarily at the Civil Rights Movement and later the Black Liberation Movement, had a decisive impact on my thinking. The assassinations of Che Guevara, Patrice Lumumba, Malcolm X, and Martin Luther King, assaults on the Black Panther Party, and the carpet bombing of Vietnam were all on my mind when I came to Chicago in 1968. Putting the pieces together, I believed it was the same system functioning abroad and at home. I saw the struggle of David and Goliath at every turn.

By the time the trial was over, I was almost ready to take my place as a soldier in the world revolutionary movement. The Democrats had been in power and both parties were complicit. I no longer thought the government was a force for good or that it could be reformed. However, I felt that it might be possible to end the war if we moved from protest to resistance.

By May I was also a nascent feminist, ready to begin an all-women's trip to Vietnam with one focus on exploring the role of women in Vietnamese society. The fact that it was a women's trip reflected the changes that were occurring in our movement. Judy was by now a full-fledged feminist, buoyed by her experiences in Berkeley. In an effort to have maximum impact upon our return, we invited Jane Fonda and Judy Collins to join us. They declined the offer, although it was not long after Fonda made the trip that won her the designation of "Hanoi

Jane." In the end our delegation was composed of myself, Judy and Genie Plamondon of the White Panther Party, a self-proclaimed revolutionary anti-racist hippie group that shared our belief that art and music were essential to revolutionary struggle. We needed financial help in order to make the trip and Judy Collins and Arlo Guthrie both agreed to contribute.

On May Day 1970 I attended a rally for Bobby Seale and Panther Ericka Huggins, who were on trial in New Haven, Connecticut. I came as part of a Yippie contingent that included Jerry, Abbie, Anita, and Allen Ginsberg. I wasn't feeling well because I had been shot up with all kinds of preventive vaccinations, because the next week Judy and I were to take off for Vietnam. And what a week that was! The U.S. was now widening the war and bombing Cambodia but the U.S. anti-war movement was widening as well. There had been immediate demonstrations all around the country opposed to the escalation.

On May 4 four students protesting the war at Kent State University were shot to death by the National Guard. Thousands more students across the country turned out protesting that atrocity as well as the war itself. Meanwhile Judy and I were on our way to Vietnam, to meet with the "enemy." I'm sure I was apprehensive but I mostly recall feelings of great excitement. These were tumultuous times for our movement, but for me it was also a time of personal growth as a woman and an activist.

MOSCOW

ALTHOUGH I WAS GOING THROUGH subtle changes about our relationship and would only be gone a month, my leave-taking from Jerry was hard. It felt like a trip into the unknown and all things were possible.

His parting words touched me and reminded me of the things I loved about him. "Stay away as long as you want and can. Experience it all. Don't let anything, not anything, back here worry or concern you. As far as I'm concerned you're gone for the now—no letters, phone calls, contact. I love you." I believe this was the best side of Jerry; at that moment he had my own personal growth in mind.

After a short stay in Prague, it was Tuesday, May 12th, when Judy and I arrived at the small Moscow airport. It was the women that struck me first. Teams of strong-looking Russian women wearing plain skirts and blouses, with scarves that tied back long, long braids. Teams of women constantly, continuously mopping, scrubbing, washing. On ladders cleaning pillars. On hands and knees scrubbing floors. Moscow's airport must have been the cleanest airport in the world.

Everything seemed great except for one huge problem. The plane to Hanoi was due to take off the next day but it was full! No reservations for you!! Next plane in two weeks!!!

Plus, we were told that since we had no visas to get into Moscow, we had to stay put at the airport hotel for now until this got sorted out somehow. So we dug in. The airport and its hotel all seemed very functional. No frills. They used an abacus instead of an adding machine. Curtains and bedspreads looked handmade, as if they'd been around for years, like Grandma's things. Everything had an old, well-laundered, clean look. There was a TV room with classical ballet on the screen and Russian magazines. At dinner I enjoyed eating globs of caviar for very little money.

We encountered two Swiss guys and asked them if one could get into Moscow without a visa. Their answer was, "Yes, for $35." We discussed it, but as guests of the Vietnamese, we decided it was best not to go around protocol and start bribing people.

We seemed to have our own personal Russian companion. Judy gave her the name of "House Frau." I offered her a women's liberation button and also our own button—deep purple background with neon pink Yippie letters that popped. She said, "Hippy, that's the one I want. More interesting." After a while, I began to wonder exactly who she worked for. The hotel? The KGB? But it was never revealed.

On Wednesday we were still in the airport, waiting for something to happen when the House Frau showed up with both Russian and Vietnamese visas. We then phoned the Vietnamese Embassy and learned that we had to spend a week in Moscow.

Our Russian adventure was about to begin. In those days nobody traveled to the Soviet Union without a planned itinerary. Yet here we were, footloose and fancy free! We were not on an organized tour. We were not to be escorted day and night by official government guides. We were set free in Moscow to do whatever we wanted and see what we could see. For Americans in 1970 that was an unheard of opportunity. In addition, we were guests of the Vietnamese and that afforded us a great deal of protection and leeway.

However, Russia was not a place that I admired. I felt that the Russian Revolution had been an earthshaking process with reverberations throughout the world. It offered the promise of a better world for all, but the Revolution had degenerated and the Russia of 1970 was not the Russia of 1917. I didn't believe the country was moving toward communism. Rather, the government had become a repressive bureaucracy. I felt there needed to be a cultural revolution and we were interested in understanding more about Russians who felt similarly.

On Thursday we were finally "liberated" from the airport and after two days there, we were more than ready to go. A reporter for the *Guardian* newspaper, Richard Ward, was in the same situation as we were. Representatives of the Vietnamese Embassy picked up all three of us at the airport and drove into town, about a half hour's ride. After a brief tour of Red Square, the changing of the guard, and the big department store known as the Gum (pronounced Goom), we were checked in at a huge, palatial hotel—the Hotel Ukraine—that was inside a gothic skyscraper built by Stalin in the 1950s.

Judy, Richard, and I had dinner in a large, open-spaced dining hall with Russian music in the background and long tables set with white linen. We shared champagne with a couple of East German guys who seemed to be largely apolitical. Somehow or another we started singing songs from the Spanish Civil War, songs that I had learned as a child at Camp Woodland, and all of a sudden, half the people in the dining hall were singing and the whole room was swaying back and forth with the internationally-known "*Freiheit*" (freedom). It was a fine evening after all.

Our relationship with the Western media in Moscow was interesting. On the one hand, I wanted them to help us get some publicity on our way back from Vietnam and I also wanted them to help us get in touch with various groupings of people in Moscow that the Vietnamese were likely not to associate with. On the other hand, I knew that many of them played a dual role of media person and intelligence gatherer. I didn't want to be part of that. Nonetheless, we proceeded.

We went out to breakfast the next day with "John," a Newsweek correspondent who had been out of the States for 14 years and had spent the last two in Moscow. Judy asked if he could help us meet freethinking Russians with whom we might have something in common, and he explained that there are three underground currents in Moscow: Marxist-Leninists who say there can be no socialism without democracy, social-democrat types, and Christian Marxists. And they would not be able to enter a place like the one where we were dining. I asked him what they thought of our anti-war movement, and he said, "They're so involved in their own dilemma, I'm not sure of their interest at all." I said that I did not want to meet with rabid anti-communists. He answered that he understood but that in this underground, people often made odd alliances because they were so in need of help. In the end, John said it would take a few days, but he would set things up so that we could meet with some people.

Meanwhile, the Vietnamese told Judy that she could travel with her Canadian passport and go through Beijing, but I most certainly could not. Relations between China and the U.S. were in the deep freeze. So those flights were out for me. I, of course, preferred that she stay but I also didn't want to serve as a brake on her. Judy decided to stay, and we'd travel together, along with Genie who had yet to arrive in Moscow.

We spent Friday afternoon in search of the University of Moscow via the subways and I was pleasantly surprised at the dazzling nature of the subway stations. Art museums in their own right, they had chandeliers, marble moldings and most notably, colorful, elaborate mosaics. Long, steep, swift escalators carried thousands of people, from level to level. The swift-moving sea of humanity awed even a hardened New Yorker such as me. We finally arrived at the University, only to be stopped at the main entrance by a woman who said, "No tickets? Have to get permission!" So that was that.

Instead of meeting students, we roamed around the neighborhood and ate all kinds of food and drink on the street. Ice cream, which was very popular with Russians. Some kind of watered down ginger ale that we thought was beer. It came out of an interesting machine with only one glass that was used over and over. When you set it back down, water sprayed up and rinsed it out. Again, nothing disposable about the goods here.

The subway ride back to the hotel was something else. It was rush hour and the pushing and shoving beat New York hands down. I have not before or since seen the likes of that. But no matter how fast things were moving in Moscow, the Russian people seemed always to have time to stare at us. Our purple and pink Yippie buttons were tremendously popular and we were referred to as the *dve devushkas* (two girls).

The Associated Press reporter, living across the hall from his office, invited us in for borscht. There were three Russians there—two women and a man. The man spoke English and one of the women spoke French. Judy was quite fluent in French and I squeaked by with my 7 years of school French. All three were poets. Alyona was the most interesting—with long black braids and peasant blouse, she looked like a San Francisco hippy. They asked us all kinds of questions about marijuana, LSD, hippies, Yippies, Williams Burroughs' poetry, etc. We seemed to be getting along famously until the conversation turned to Vietnam. The Russian man insisted that there was no right or wrong, and when I came out categorically on the side of the Vietnamese, he called me a Communist.

That night I felt very conflicted, like I wanted to take a long, long shower. I was angry with myself for hanging around with the American media people and their Russian acquaintances. If this was the Russian "underground," it seemed I had little in common with them. They didn't believe anything the Soviet media told them: if the Soviet press says the U.S. is wrong in Vietnam, then the U.S. must be right. Although I understood their position, there was no way I could unite with their way of thinking. For me, there was an international movement for liberation and socialism, and Vietnam was a dividing line. There was no doubt about that.

Judy and I stayed up until 5:00 in the morning trying to digest our experiences and also wrestling with whether or not we should demonstrate against the war at the American Embassy. Over and over again we were being told that the Russian government did not tolerate spontaneous demonstrations of any kind, even if it was on the same side of the issue that they were on. The spontaneity itself was threatening and might encourage their own youth to utilize the same tactics. And then there were the Vietnamese to consider, and this was our biggest concern. They would most likely frown on such a demonstration because their Russian hosts would be angry, and the Vietnamese would have to spend time and energy to get us out of hot water. We respected them too much to want to give them trouble.

On Saturday, we got up late and decided to check out a liberal arts college we had been told about. We were still looking for our political counterparts. Standing on a street corner, reading a map and looking helpless, we were approached by a young man from Mauritania who spoke French. He joined us as our translator, and we then somehow picked up two young Russians engineers and we all went off for coffee and ice cream. The ice cream parlor was filled with young people on their day off. We were seated at a table with two young women who were also engineers. It seemed that this was a country of engineers. In response to their questions, Judy explained to them that we didn't have traditional jobs. We were part of a revolutionary, anti-war movement and were supported financially by sympathetic people. They wanted to know where they could send us some money! They told us about their organization Komsomol (the Young Communist League) which met once a month, mostly around work issues. They said that when the United States invaded Cambodia, they had many meetings to condemn the invasion. I asked them what they thought about Czechoslovakia and told them that young Americans saw that invasion as similar to Cambodia. "Oh no, no," they responded, "We were invited into Czechoslovakia, to protect the working class." When I questioned them about Stalin, they said, "He was a great man, but he made many mistakes." They didn't seem to have any real anger toward the United States either. As the conversation became more politically confrontational, our Mauritanian translator turned to us and explained in English that he was a foreign student here and that this debate had been going on too long in public for his own comfort.

For all this argument, the Russians remained incredibly hospitable. One girl at the table suddenly pulled out a toy made of acorns and gave it to me. I gave her a women's liberation button that she very much liked, and the two guys invited us to visit their home. However, I was suffering with my period, so Judy and I went back to our hotel, along with the Mauritanian guy. He and Judy proceeded to have a long political discussion in French about the Soviet Union. Judy expounded on its non-revolutionary direction and he on its revolutionary economic achievements and how freedom is different under communism and capitalism.

I went to sleep reflecting on the cosmopolitan nature of Moscow. There were people from all over the world, but I had yet to meet one soulful revolutionary Russian brother or sister. In fact I had met an awful lot of apolitical Communists. Most of the Russians we encountered were extremely generous, warm, and friendly, but a revolutionary spirit was so far hard to find.

On Sunday our Russian poet friend, Alyona, invited us to her apartment. Her friends, all poets and artists, were there. They were offended by ALL politics; art was their only reality. Alyona and her family and friends were very warm and friendly—hugs, kisses, "I love you's," and then a grand exchange of presents. We gave them buttons, beads, a vest and pocketbook. They gave us very old Russian weaving implements and combs, straw slippers, a Ukrainian-type leather jacket with beautiful embroidery, and a peasant blouse. And food and drink and drink and food. They recited Russian poems and we talked about marijuana and LSD. These people were all at odds with Soviet Russia. Age 25 to 40, their art was "art for art's sake," not art executed for the ends of the state, not socialist realism, dictated from above. So in that sense these people were nonconformists, outside the mainstream of Soviet life, but they appeared to live a relatively carefree life. I wondered how they managed that.

A few days into our stay Genie appeared and so we were three young women with long, loose hair, sporting beads, buttons, fringe vests and, oh yes, pants! We needed no help in meeting Russians. Just the appearance of the three of us on the streets of Moscow was a magnet for young Muscovites. Before long a whole Russian posse had joined us.

Two of the young men came from families with more means than the others. Their parents had traveled to Western Europe and brought back records, and they were eager to discuss Creedence Clearwater, the Stones, and Jimi Hendrix. Intensely interested in Western rock 'n' roll and the American musical scene, they knew about the seamy side as well—the death at Altamont, the Hells Angels and Charlie Manson. They told us the Beatles had been to Moscow but had not played, and the Stones were not allowed in at all. Vladimir vainly combed his hair in public and was afraid to have his picture snapped. "Because of my job," he said. Strolling through Red Square, we spotted Soviet militiamen, and these two were the first to run.

The others appeared to be tougher, less fearful and somewhat less entranced with things Western. They took regular jabs at the first two for being from bourgeois families. As we went for a long walk around the Kremlin, they explained "there are hippies in all the other large cities of Russia and lots more who are sympathetic. Four years ago hippies used to sing and play music by the river, but now that is all wiped out because of scrapes with the police and the KGB." More political and militant than the two "bourgeois" guys, they described themselves as communists. When we pressed them about what sort of communism, they said "hippy." They wanted to fight for change and were split about whether it would need to be through peaceful or violent means. One spoke, no doubt with bravado, of assassinating Brezhnev. They also cautioned us that many hustlers tried to pass themselves off as hippies but actually were active players in the Black Market.

Our Russian hippy friends all had nicknames like "Zal of the Spoonful," "Jagger," "The Crocodile," "The Soldier," and "the one with the longest hair in Moscow." I was given the nickname of "Little Crow" because of my dark, dark eyes, they said. Before we parted ways, we agreed to all meet again at a later time. Someday.

On Tuesday, May 19th, the birthday of Ho Chi Minh (and Malcolm X), I took a taxi over to Newsweek and waited for a call I had arranged with Jerry in New York. Although I had to scream at the top of my lungs to be heard, the call was great. After the trial, Jerry and I both realized that we needed to be part of a real collective. Now he felt that it was coming together. I was excited to hear that Michael Smith, one of the Oakland 7, had moved into our apartment and Sharon Krebs was also around New York and interested in participating. Still, deep down I was uncertain of what I wanted for my future.

That evening at the Vietnamese Embassy we saw a film about the life of Ho Chi Minh in Vietnamese with Russian translation! However, the Ambassador, a wonderful man whom we had met in Stockholm, sat next to us and kindly translated from Vietnamese to French. The contrasting visual imagery was striking—the fragile appearing beauty of Vietnam and yet the fierce toughness of their resistance.

At the reception that followed, we struck up a discussion with several Russian women about the women's liberation movement. They asked us if we were members of Women's Strike for Peace, a more mainstream anti-war organization. I felt the conversation couldn't really go anywhere very interesting because they were there in an official capacity and seemed quite guarded in their remarks and willingness to engage.

When all the other guests had cleared out, we remained to take full advantage of the opportunity to converse with our favorite friends, the Vietnamese. We talked and talked about the horrific nature of this war that had brought us together. We agreed that Nixon was one of the world's greatest liars and they laughed when Genie told them that in America many young men are growing their hair long because they don't want to look like Richard Nixon and his cronies.

The next day we went to the Vietnamese Embassy again, this time for tea. Genie, Judy, Richard (our *Guardian* friend), and I were all invited guests. The table was exquisitely and delicately set with tea, mineral water and an orange liqueur from Vietnam. I learned something that day that would be reinforced during our stay in Vietnam: When a glass is empty, it quickly becomes full.

The Ambassador, Nguyen Tho Chan, was there as well as our old friend, Kim Lan, who had met us at the airport. Once again Judy's French fluency saved the day and my passing knowledge was put to the test. The Ambassador spoke of the torture and brutality of the war. He described how during his own imprisonment the Vietnamese puppets, those who did the bidding of the American government, had literally cut flesh from his side. Right then and there, he lifted his white shirt, pulled down his suit pants and revealed his tremendous scar. My heart fell through my stomach and a deep shame swept over me for being an American. This would be the first but far from the last time I would hear about and see evidence of such tortures.

The Vietnamese were prepared for our strong reactions, and they stressed over and over again the friendship between the American people and the Vietnamese people. This was a mantra we heard constantly in the following weeks, and I found myself wondering whether they really believed it or were just being diplomatic. If I were in this situation, I wondered would I be so generous? It was most definitely the official line of the government of Vietnam and many of the people seemed to genuinely believe in person-to-person friendship. The Ambassador insisted that our common enemy was *La Maison Blanc* (the White House). He gently encouraged us to consider a United Front against the war, suggesting that even people such as Cyrus Eaton and Nelson Rockefeller didn't approve of the war. He explained that he himself was not a Communist. In fact, he had been raised a Catholic and taught to hate the "Red Menace." However, now he and the Communists were united in fighting against the Americans.

Our time in Moscow was coming to an end. The next day we would head off to Vietnam. How fortunate I felt to have had real conversation with so many different Muscovites. Later, when Moscow went through profound changes, I would not be as surprised as many Americans. I certainly could not foresee the nature of the changes that would come to pass. Nor could I know how I as an American activist would feel about those changes. But we thought it probable that change would come to the Soviet Union. It was definitely blowing in the wind.

VIETNAM

THE AEROFLOT JOURNEY FROM MOSCOW to North Vietnam was far from an express trip. We stopped in Ulan Bator (Mongolia), Tashkent (Uzbekistan), Karachi (Pakistan), and Calcutta (India), letting passengers off, picking up new ones, and refueling. On every leg of the journey we were fed chicken, lots of chicken, repeatedly. In Ulan Bator, we saw nothing of the world outside. We sat in the airport restaurant that had the feel of centuries of civilization behind it, surrounded by ornate and colorful filigree, tapestry and tiling. We deplaned in Calcutta but never left the airport. Nonetheless, I could see through the floor-length windows the tiny shanties and the dire poverty that was literally right across from the airport. In the restroom there were women dressed in traditional saris, begging for small change.

And then, finally, we deplaned in Hanoi. Suddenly the black and white world was transformed into glorious Technicolor and I felt like Dorothy landing in Oz as Genie, Judy and I climbed down from the small Russian plane and were greeted as dignitaries, with scores of schoolchildren presenting each of us with multicolored gladiola bouquets and banners of welcome. We were taken to a lovely old French-style hotel, a legacy of the past colonial era, in the center of Hanoi. There were guests from around the world, most notably a large delegation from China and a number of individuals from the Soviet Union. I had my own room, a bed with mosquito netting, a ceiling fan, and my own bathroom. To this youthful Yippie, it felt like pure luxury.

Instructed to take our meals in the hotel restaurant, we protested, hoping to eat off the streets and share in the food that Vietnamese, not tourists, consumed. In the end, their instruction as well as our protest was irrelevant because we spent almost every minute of our waking time with the Vietnamese and meals became part of our adventures. On the few occasions when we did take meals there, the food in the hotel restaurant was wonderful, Vietnamese influenced by French cuisine. In the morning we were offered either a bowl of Pho, a soup with a hodgepodge of varying ingredients, or eggs French style. I loved it all.

As for clothes, we were immediately fitted for Vietnamese "black pajamas." These were not really pajamas, but loose-fitting outfits that had come to be identified as the uniform of the Viet Cong, the guerrilla forces of South Vietnam—baggy pants with an elasticized waist and a slightly tailored, long-sleeved button-down shirt. We were told that in the past when resources were less scarce there had been cloth of various colors, but during the war black was the only option. Thus the term "black pajamas." The material was black silk and had a delicate patterned weave. We were also fitted for sandals that were fashioned out of rubber tires that we wore our entire time in Vietnam and for years after in the U.S. The final item of clothing was a conical hat to keep us safe from the sun and rain.

Our host, the U.S.-Vietnamese Friendship Association, was accountable to the North Vietnamese government and in charge of relationships with American visitors. They attempted to tailor the trip to suit our interests. We traveled around in a large van that held the three of us plus our guides. These were four Vietnamese, three men and one woman, who were with us most of the time, including Oanh, our poet friend from the Stockholm conference.

Xuan Oanh had joined Ho Chi Minh and the Viet Minh Front in 1945 at the young age of 22. The Viet Minh was the national liberation movement that led the struggle for the independence of Vietnam from French colonialism, through the 1940s up until the 1954 Battle of Dien Bien Phu, where the Vietnamese finally defeated the French.

A poet, composer, musician, expert translator, and patriot, Xuan Oanh participated in some of the seminal diplomatic events surrounding the American War (the Vietnamese name for what we call the Vietnam War) including the Paris Peace Talks. In Vietnam he is best known for composing the revolutionary anthem, "August Nineteen." This warm and worldly poet and revolutionary was our host. Along with our "hero driver" (as we called him) and translators, he provided for our every need. We felt we were unnecessarily pampered but at the same time we were appreciative.

As an all-women's delegation we were particularly interested in the role of women in the revolution and in Vietnamese society. And in the American War! In this context we requested to go to the front, as far south as possible, to the DMZ (the demilitarized zone between North and South), as close to the fighting as possible.

When the Vietnamese defeated the French in 1954, the Geneva Conference divided the country in half with a demilitarized zone that came to be known simply as "the DMZ." The Viet Minh would control North Vietnam but South Vietnam would be under non-Communist control. In theory this would be a temporary arrangement and within two years there were to be elections and the country would be unified. However, it was soon clear to everyone that the Viet Minh would win the election by a landslide. Even President Eisenhower acknowledged that "possibly eighty per cent of the population" would have voted for Ho Chi Minh. So the U.S. began covert actions in South Vietnam to ensure that there would be no elections and no reunification of the country. Fifteen years later, in 1970, we were still mired in this now overt as well as covert bloody war, and it was a daily front-page conflict around the globe.

Although North Vietnam had experienced the war directly with severe bombing campaigns, it was South Vietnam that was taking the brunt. What Americans referred to as the Viet Cong was actually the National Liberation Front of South Vietnam (the NLF). The NLF led the struggle in South Vietnam. Like the Viet Minh, the most dynamic force within the NLF was the Communist Party, but many other patriotic elements participated as well.

Above: Jeanne, Nancy and Judy with civilian patriot and leader in the army of the PRG (Provisional Revolutionary Government) of South Vietnam; Hanoi, May 1970.
Below: Nancy joining hands with Thai Noir village elder in the mountains of Thanh Hoa Province; May 1970.

So we requested to go to the front. The U.S. was currently bombing the two most southern provinces of North Vietnam and we felt it was important to document it. We wanted to be able to describe the military destruction to people back home, to honestly say we saw it with our own eyes.

The U.S.-Vietnam Friendship Association welcomed us because we were anti-war activists; they hoped to strengthen our ability to fight the U.S. war machine and end the war. However, they did not want us to die in Vietnam. Their goal was to have us back in the U.S. better prepared to continue the fight against the war machine. So they said no to our visiting the DMZ. It was too dangerous. However, they would take us to the province of Thanh Hoa, a rural area about 150 kilometers from Hanoi, which had endured air attacks in the past but was quiet at the time. There we could see a very different way of life than in the city of Hanoi, more representative of Vietnam as a whole.

Before taking off for Thanh Hoa, we spent quite a few days getting acquainted with Hanoi and we immediately fell in love with the people and the city. In those days it appeared to be a bustling, thriving city but not in the ways of the West. There were few cars and buses on the streets; instead, we saw thousands and thousands of bicyclists going every which way.

People were all dressed simply, crisp and clean, similar to the outfits for which we had been fitted, although most of the women wore light-colored shirts, in contrast to the black "pajamas" of the Viet Cong. Genie at about five foot ten inches towered over most of the Vietnamese who were generally small in stature. I, on the other hand, at just under five-feet, felt like I had come home and was charmed by the idea that these small people were able to go up against the American Goliath. I don't think we saw an obese person the entire time we were in Vietnam. Neither did people appear hungry, underfed or malnourished. Generally speaking, the population appeared healthy, energetic, and yes, even happy, despite the fact that they were in the midst of this brutal war.

We walked around Hanoi, just taking in the scene. Everywhere we went people stopped to inquire as to who we were, and wide-eyed children followed along beside us.

The streets of Hanoi seemed safer than the streets of any big city I had ever been in and have ever been in since. One day Judy was saddened by the loss of her camera, but the next day it suddenly appeared, returned to her by our hosts. It was picked up by somebody and passed on until it found its way back to us. No one along the way had thought to keep it for him or herself despite the fact that it would have been quite a prize.

We visited a first grade class in an elementary school, quite spare by our standards. There were dolls and trucks and other toys in a cabinet but not the surfeit of materials that you might see in some American classrooms. There was a large chalkboard on the wall and at each desk sat two children. The girls wore short dresses and the boys wore the typical dark pants and light shirts. Most of the girls had short bob haircuts. The children performed songs and dances, boys and girls alike. Everywhere we went we were served tea. Flowers were the other constant, usually bouquets of gladiolas similar to the ones bestowed upon us when we landed at the airport.

We also met with a group of young medical students, among them a young woman from the Thanh Hoa minority who presented us with a bouquet of gladiolas. Wearing the colorful woven dress and headdress of her tribe and traditional jewelry, she explained that there were 60 different minority tribes in Vietnam, most speaking their own language. I told the medical students how sick I had gotten preparing for the trip, getting inoculations against Yellow Fever, Bubonic Plague, and Typhoid, all in one sitting since time had been short. The medical students had a good laugh and informed me that such diseases had been wiped out in North Vietnam.

We were hosted as well by the Women's Union. I knew that the leader of the Provisional Revolutionary Government (PRG) was a woman, Madame Binh. That alone impressed me because there were very few American women in public positions of power at that time. I was happily surprised to see so many Vietnamese women involved in political as well as military life. The Women's Union members spoke to us about the important role of women in the struggle for independence, both historically and in the present. We were told that Ho Chi Minh said, "Women make up half of society. If women are not liberated, then society is not free." In 1930 a woman named Minh Khai formed the Vietnam Women's Union at the same time as the creation of the Indochinese Communist Party. She has been called the founder of the long-haired army, the civilian movement composed largely of women who carried out much of the legal political work in the movement for national liberation. She was eventually tortured and executed by the French.

A woman from South Vietnam presented us with large silk scarves in the blue, red and yellow colors of the Vietnamese flag. I still have this scarf. It is framed on my wall, and it reminds me of my experiences in Vietnam. The four quadrants each contain a drawing of a Vietnamese woman, representing a different segment of the national liberation struggle. Two are armed with rifles, one in the uniform of the regular standing army and the other dressed in the black pajamas of the guerrilla fighters. The third wears the traditional garb of one of the minorities, carries a baby on her back, as well as a bow and arrows. The fourth is dressed in a blue and white Ao Dai, a traditional Vietnamese outfit made up of a long tunic and pants. She wears the familiar conical hat and carries the Vietnamese flag. She represents the patriotic civilians who participate in the political struggle. All four are honored equally. In Vietnamese, English and French is written "South Vietnam Women's Union for Liberation."

We were also introduced to a young woman who was part of the Army of the Provisional Revolutionary Government (PRG). She was wearing her army uniform with several medals pinned to her shirt. She described the torture she had undergone at the hands of the U.S.-backed South Vietnamese Army (ARVN) and how she relived her torture nightly. As with the Ambassador we had met in Moscow who had undergone a similar experience, we were reminded that beneath the goodwill and laughter there was a severely dark side to the experiences of these people.

We visited a military museum exhibiting the history of warfare in Vietnam dating centuries back to the invasion by the Chinese, the French colonial occupation and up to the present American war. The fight for independence was not new for the Vietnamese nor was it a fleeting preoccupation. An elaborate model of the Battle of Dien Bien Phu took up much of one room. The Vietnamese were especially proud of their defeat of the French, as it was the first time a non-European independence movement was able to defeat an occupying European power in a pitched battle. We also viewed remnants of U.S. planes that had been shot down in the current war and were shown useful household items that had been made out of the metal scraps.

Hanoi itself was peaceful while we were there but I knew it had experienced terror in the '68 U.S. bombing campaign, when school children had to be evacuated from the city to the countryside. We visited Bach Mai Hospital, the primary medical institution in Vietnam. (At Christmas 1972 it would be deliberately bombed and seriously damaged by the U.S. Air Force.) After visiting Bach Mai, we had the honor of sharing tea with Xuan Thuy, Chief Negotiator for the North Vietnamese at the Paris Peace Talks, a friendly, gracious grandfatherly man with a broad smile. An American diplomat described him as a "top drawer negotiator, a dreadful fellow to face across the table day after day." We wished him well.

After several days in Hanoi, we set out in our mini-bus for the countryside, the three of us and our four Vietnamese friends. En route to Thanh Hoa Province, we made a stop at the Gulf of Tonkin, the site of the infamous Gulf of Tonkin "incident" that had been invented or at least embellished by the U.S. in order to fool the American people into believing the North Vietnamese had initiated hostilities, the purpose of which being that the war could be seriously escalated.

There we sat with our Vietnamese friends, not another soul in sight, on the peaceful white sands of the Gulf of Tonkin and had long talks about Marxism-Leninism and our mutual work. They wanted to understand our ideology and our strategy and how we analyzed the forces at work in the U.S. They struggled with us to generally become more ideological as well as more systematic in our approach to our anti-war work. That afternoon Judy and I explained our idea for an American-Vietnamese conference and developed our collective plans. We would

Nancy with Xuan Oanh at the Gulf of Tonkin, Vietnam; May 1970.

organize a meeting between cultural workers in the United States—artists, musicians, cartoonists, writers, actors, poets, playwrights—and a Vietnamese delegation. They suggested we broaden it out to an Indochinese delegation that would include Cambodians and Laotians since the U.S. was expanding the war into the entire region. We agreed to hold such a conference at the end of the summer in Havana, Cuba. In a week we would leave Vietnam and return to New York to begin work.

After hours of such discussion, we continued inland on our journey toward Thanh Hoa province, about 93 miles from Hanoi. In Thanh Hoa we stayed overnight in a small guest house where I took a refreshing "shower" in a sheltered outdoor area, using a big ladle to scoop out water from a large bucket.

In Thanh Hoa it was clear that women of all ages and experience were playing an important role in the life of the village. The Mayor was a woman, about 35 to 40 years of age, and she served as our tour guide. She introduced us to a group of young women, anti-aircraft artillery fighters, who were all dressed in the black pajamas and military helmets that were commonplace. They showed us their artillery and proudly described how they had shot down two planes that had come to attack their community.

They told us that in the year 248 A.D., right there in Thanh Hoa Province, a 23-year-old woman named Trieu The Trinh and her brother led thousands of people to drive out the Chinese invaders. At first successful, they later were unable to hold back the invasion and Trieu The Trinh took her own life rather than live as a serf. Her iconic and inspirational words were, "My wish is to ride the tempest, tame the waves, kill the sharks. I want to drive the enemy away, to save our people. I will not resign myself to the usual lot of women who bow their heads and become concubines."

We left the village of Thanh Hoa and proceeded on a journey to visit one of the ethnic minority groups, the *Thai Noir* (or Black Thai). Traveling through some breathtaking landscapes, we crossed rivers and climbed up, up, up into the mountains. Leaving our mini-van behind, we were ferried over a river on a wooden platform, alongside a water buffalo that was pulling a cart loaded down with big barrels. One young man pulled out a Vietnamese musical instrument—seven thin bamboo tubes of different lengths—and played sweet, haunting flute-like sounds. There was music everywhere and I recorded it all—among the schoolchildren, of course from the musicians, and now out here, in the middle of a river, on a ferry. After disembarking, we hiked a ways and then took a VERY narrow ferry across the next river. It was basically poles of bamboo strung together, just a bit wider than I am. I sat on my haunches in true Vietnamese fashion and took the short trip to the other side.

We then entered the Thai Noir village. Hundreds of people came out to greet us—men, women and children. Escorted by the whole village over to a thatched roof house on stilts, I climbed the stairs and was greeted by the elders of the village, two women who were far more slender and petite than I. We sat on mats on the floor and exchanged greetings. They were wearing the traditional garb of their people, bands of colorful woven material worn around their waists. Their teeth were a brownish-red from chewing betel nuts, and they shared with us their rice wine that we sipped from a large common jug through multiple straw-like instruments. They also offered us *thoch lao*, which seemed to be a mild form of marijuana. We were told that it was mostly the elders who enjoyed thoch lao, an interesting reversal. They told us that the village was very excited by our presence and very rarely had visitors from other countries. In fact, most of the people who greeted us believed at first that we were Russians.

They then gave us a tour of the village where we saw the studios in which they wove the colorful cloth, and several youths entertained us with their drumming, on large drums suspended from a pole and struck with sticks. Here in this village, high in the mountains, I saw beautiful young women dressed in traditional garb with rifles slung over their shoulders. We were told that one of the tasks of the revolution was to integrate the 60 different minorities into Vietnamese society in a way that would preserve their culture and language, yet allow them to advance. It may have grown out of a Marxist ideal of equality for all, but it was also a military imperative. Discontent among some groups, known

Nancy and Judy Gumbo Albert in Moscow Airport, May 1970.

Above: Nancy and Judy with new friends who suggest this trip to country *dacha* to avoid eyes of the KGB, May 1970. **Below:** 3-person anti-war protest (Nancy, Jeanne, Judy) at US Consulate, Moscow, 1970.

as *Montagnards* (the French name for all highlanders or hill tribes), had been exploited by the French to sow opposition to the Communists. In this village, at this time at least, there seemed to be cooperation between the communist government and the Thai Noir. Actually, I would later learn that the large majority of Montagnards, as with ethnic Vietnamese in general, supported the revolution and the fight to defend their homeland.

On our return to Hanoi, I addressed the American GIs on Vietnamese radio. The station played American music interspersed with occasional commentary. I encouraged the GIs not to risk their life and limb in an illegal and immoral war. Even though I knew most of the GIs had been drafted, I believed that as human beings they were still responsible for their own actions. As a child of a Jewish family whose father fought in World War II, it was burned on my brain that many German people claimed they were "just following orders" and that silence was complicity. So I had an obligation to speak truth to the GIs. In between Sly Stone and the Beatles, I challenged them to ask themselves what they were doing in a foreign land attacking a people who had done no harm to the U.S. or to them as individuals.

The night before we left Vietnam, a banquet was held in our honor. All forms of unusual (to us) seafood dishes appeared on our plates and there was wine in abundance. Our hosts would have had us stay on and see more of their country, but as wonderful as the experience was, I was eager to get back home and get on with the work of fighting against the war. So were Judy and Genie. Therefore, after two amazing weeks in Vietnam, we headed home.

However, our route required us to return via Aeroflot to Moscow and then on to the U.S. from there. This time in Moscow I had a single-minded agenda. The three of us agreed to have that demonstration against the war that we had contemplated on the way through Moscow en route to Vietnam. We divided up the work and contacted all the media, particularly all the Western media, utilizing the contacts we had made earlier, and let them know about the protest. We tried to involve some of our Russian friends but they reiterated their fears of repercussions. I naively said, "Yeah but this is against the U.S., not Russia." "You don't understand," they reminded me again. "The Russian government does not tolerate spontaneous demonstrations of any sort, regardless of the content."

When we were alone, Jeanie asked, "So what do you think? Should we proceed?"

Judy immediately responded, "If there's to be a demonstration of three people, so be it. But how can we make it as dramatic as possible so we get some media coverage?"

Ever the prop gal, I suggested, "How about if we wear our black pajamas the Vietnamese gave us, along with our conical hats?"

Judy said, "Yes, yes, and carry big signs."

Jeanie concurred and together the three of us tried on various slogans and settled on "We are the Ameri-Cong! End the war in Vietnam!" and "Ho, Ho, Ho Chi Minh, the NLF is Gonna Win."

Today I think, my god we were spunky! And not surprisingly we got the attention of the Western media. They turned out and the Associated Press splashed our picture across the world in papers everywhere, well, everywhere but Moscow. Across the street our friends watched from semi-protected locations. And sure enough, the KGB of Russian intelligence was there as well. As we left the scene, we were followed for a while by a man in a green suit wearing one-way glasses. He probably left us when we entered our hotel and got ready to leave Moscow the next day.

Judy and I flew into Canada. Judy would stay to see her family and I would travel on to New York. The Canadians, despite being allegedly politically independent of the United States, immediately confiscated all the gifts the Vietnamese had given us. Later, thanks to some legal action, I would recover most of them, but I never did recoup my conical hat. Subversive, damning hats!

When I hit customs in New York, I was immediately detained and brought into a room by myself. I nervously waited for what seemed like hours—and then this great big, beefy FBI agent entered the room and started grilling me about where I'd been. "Moscow," I responded. "And where else?" he quickly retorted. I knew it was a felony to lie to the FBI, so I shrugged and said, "You can check my passport." It was of course clean since no one had stamped it with any evidence of Vietnam. I feared some future ramifications but there were none. It was the first time I traveled illegally but it would not be the last. It's a funny thing—I have never been to a country where I was not welcomed, and yet I have traveled a number of times to places my own "free" country has forbidden me to enter.

Although I was relieved to get away from the FBI, the intimidation fueled my defiance and would not stop me from my anti-war activities. I was fired up and ready to go. Inspired by the Vietnamese experience, I was more emboldened than ever to pursue an end to the war in particular, and to fight for equality and justice in all areas of life.

LIMBO IN CUBA

OUR TRIP TO VIETNAM HAD been a turning point for me. Vietnamese women appeared to be assuming more and more leadership roles in all spheres of public life: from Madame Nguyen Thi Binh, the foreign minister of the National Liberation Front, to the Mayor of Thanh Hoa as well as the young women anti-aircraft artillery fighters. Back at home the women's movement was mushrooming. The Vietnamese had talked to us for many long hours about the importance of organization, and I began to believe that with women's leadership we could build something more than a loose affiliation of Yippies around the country.

Upon our return to the U.S., Judy, Genie, and I jumped into organizing an alliance of Yippies around the country with the White Panther Party. We had meetings in Washington, D.C., Ypsilanti, Michigan (how about that, Ypsi Yippies!) and elsewhere, trying belatedly to pull people together in a new and more coherent way.

While in Vietnam, we had developed our plan to conduct a meeting between American "cultural workers" and a group of people from Indochina—Laos and Cambodia as well as Vietnam. After choosing a group of about 50 Americans, we would meet with the Indochinese that summer in Cuba for a gathering of about a week's duration. That would give us a way to both deepen the opposition to the war, and at the same time allow us an opportunity to try to build a more serious national organization.

Jerry was in jail once again, this time as the result of a plea bargain on his Illinois state charges, dating from the night he was picked up off the street in the Loop during the Convention. Meanwhile, his book *Do It!* had just hit the bestseller lists.

It was a schizophrenic time. Celebrity and repression seemed to be two aspects of the same coin. The celebrity side had been continuously intensifying all that year, through the trial and up into the spring. Jerry and Abbie were able to make a living giving speeches. They were superstars and could get a thousand dollars a pop through various speakers' bureaus. But the internal dynamics that all this celebrity encouraged were destructive, feeding the already confused egos of Jerry and Abbie. They saw themselves as larger than life and it distorted all their relationships.

But unlike Hollywood superstars, they also faced jail, both in the here-and-now and in the future. By this time Jerry was regularly taking Ritalin to make it through his daily commitments. He had already been in jail three times and when those prison gates clanged shut, he didn't feel sufficiently protected by his celebrity status. I was worried about Jerry but I was also becoming increasingly alienated from him.

The tensions in my relationship with Jerry became even more strained because I was increasingly feeling my oats. With Jerry in jail, I continued to grow independently as an activist. Judy and I got in touch with people all over the country to talk up the gathering in Cuba. Those who were interested included poets, artists, cartoonists, musicians, writers, guerrilla theater folks—as well as "just plain activists" like me. From California to Tennessee, from Michigan to Georgia and many parts in between, people wanted to join.

The trip to Cuba seemed to be shaping up well but I was soon dismayed by how many disputes and petty fights went on in Berkeley, Seattle, Madison, and other places, all revolving around who should go. Only about 60 people could go and people were battling.

Somewhere near the center of all the arguments over who should go on the trip was the issue of women's liberation, and it was present in other ways as well. It seemed to me that the men were sort of standing back a bit. Put less positively, they were using "women's liberation" as a rationalization for copping out, for sitting on the sidelines. I felt that if Abbie or Jerry were organizing this trip, the other men would throw themselves into ensuring its success.

With Abbie it was somewhat different. He wanted an active relationship with the project. However, once again there was some tension between Jerry and Abbie and Anita, and by extension, with me.

Abbie and I got together to talk about the Cuba trip. He was feeling marginalized and accused me of trying to cut him out of the decision-making for the Cuba trip. He wondered if I had brought him a ring back from my trip. (The Vietnamese had given us metal rings that were made from the remains of downed American fighter planes.) He chastised me for not giving his book to the Vietnamese. When I asked him if he had suggestions for the Cuba gathering, he reminded me that he had called a few weeks before, and although I had answered the phone, I hadn't asked him then to help with the trip or anything. I reminded him that, as usual, he hadn't asked to speak to me but had specifically asked only for Jerry, and that he got what his male chauvinism deserved. That took him aback, as he hadn't thought of it that way.

I thought it would be important to invite someone from Kent State to go on the trip to Cuba, so I got in touch with Ruth and Jack Emmer, who I had known during my summer experience at Circle Pines Center and then with the SDS ERAP project in Cleveland. They arranged a meeting with two people from Kent State. I flew into Cleveland and we met until 4:00 in the morning and then I collapsed in exhaustion. The Emmers (who would later play an important part in my life as the grandparents of my children who were not yet even a twinkle in my eye) fed me and pampered me, and I regained my strength.

Eventually the trip was all set, or so we thought. Judy and I were to go down to Havana in advance and work out last-minute details. When we arrived, however, it became obvious that things were more complicated than we had thought. It was uncertain whether or not the meeting would take place. We were housed in the luxurious Havana Libre. Built by the dictator Bautista, it was previously known as the Havana Hilton and was the tallest and largest hotel in Latin America. Ironically, in all my 26 years

I had never stayed in a place like that until coming to revolutionary Cuba. We were told to "sit tight," as were several Vietnamese comrades who had also arrived. The Cubans entertained us with trips to Hemingway's home and a beachside resort for Cuban workers. Had the situation been different, I would have been excited to be in Cuba, but under those circumstances I was preoccupied and anxious about the conference.

Eventually we were informed that the conference would not take place. The official reason attributed the cancellation to logistical difficulties on the part of the Cubans, but I was sure there were other issues that we would never know. I surmised that the possibility of a crew of potsmoking Americans was too risky or undesirable for the Cubans. Or could it have been a far different dynamic at work? We understood that there were tensions between the three Indochinese countries—Vietnam, Cambodia and Laos—and this was intended to be a unified effort. Perhaps such an effort had become untenable. Whatever the real reasons, I left Cuba very disappointed and returned home.

THE WAY THE WIND BLEW

I HAD PLENTY OF TIME to think while in Cuba and two things were churning around in my mind simultaneously—Weatherman and Jerry.

With echoes in my head of conversations with the Vietnamese comrades about the importance of organization, I was disappointed with the un-togetherness of the Yippie scene. We had had a great run, but I didn't think we could evolve into something more sustainable. I increasingly looked toward Weatherman. I had been having an ongoing dialogue with myself about Weatherman for some time. They seemed committed, serious and organized. They expressed the anger I was feeling. Yet at the same time, I had my doubts. They were small, several hundred, and I wasn't convinced of the efficacy of their efforts. A month after the Conspiracy trial began, they had staged the "Days of Rage" protest where one of their main slogans was "Bring the War Home!" Not many people responded to the call but those who did participate were dressed for confrontation—motorcycle or football helmets, heavy clothes that protected all areas of their skin, heavy boots, etc. The women as well as the men!

I was impressed by the militancy and revolutionary direction of Weatherman, but also concerned about the bravado tone of their militancy as well as their small numbers. So when Weatherman called for a "war council" in Flint, Michigan, on December 2, 1969, I decided to go to Flint and check it out for myself. I knew some of their history. They had started out as a faction of SDS, but had split with another major faction, the Progressive Labor Party (PL) over what I thought were critical issues. PL had denounced the Vietnamese for negotiating with the United States at the Paris Peace Talks. Similarly, while the Black movement was under severe FBI and police attacks, PL was denouncing the Panthers for Black Nationalism. A group like Weatherman seemed to be the answer to what Malcolm X and Stokely Carmichael had been advocating for white people, and what I had come to believe.

I was also attracted to Weatherman because of Bernardine Dohrn. I didn't really know her but had seen her a couple of times and knew her reputation as a strong leader. Still today in my mind's eye I can see the young Bernardine dressed in a black leather jacket and mini-skirt with high leather boots, all popular at the time. Her straight shoulder length brown hair parted down the middle frames her face. There is something about her face that radiates strength and determination. Perhaps it's the rectangular shape and angular square chin. Or perhaps it's just that she is strong and determined, speaks very distinctly, and with great intensity and confidence. As a woman leader at a time when men dominated the leadership of the movement, she was quite exotic.

But it was a big leap from Yippie slogans like "Abandon the Creeping Meatball," and even "Confront the Warmakers" and "Shut Down the War Machine" to the Weatherman's "Days of Rage" and "War Council." Ever since the Days of Rage I wondered how Weatherman could survive as a public organization. The Flint meeting made it official that the organization was making preparations to go underground. I was way out of my league. I had traveled there with a friend who was very interested in joining them and approached them to discuss the possibility. Right off the bat, they told her that she would have to abandon her baby daughter, that no children could be part of this process. I disliked the manner in which they had dismissed her. Knowing what I now know, they were probably right to do so. But to me it all seemed too way out there, too hard and cold. The atmosphere was generally frenzied and uncomfortable, with walls adorned with cardboard cutouts of machine guns and "PIECE NOW" written above.

Then, Bernardine's referencing Charlie Manson in what seemed like a positive light was the arsenic on the cake, although I think it has been overblown in an attempt to discredit the Weather Underground history altogether. If I haven't made it clear, violence has never been something I liked, even when I thought it was clearly necessary, as in the Vietnamese defense of their nation.

Three months later, in March of 1970, Weatherman was still preparing to go underground when a critical event took place that forced the process to accelerate. An explosion in a townhouse in Greenwich Village became a watershed event for Weatherman and for many others of us in the Movement. Three members of the organization were found dead inside. Two others, both women, had escaped with their lives and disappeared. The mass media proclaimed that the Townhouse was a bomb factory of Weatherman. And in fact, it was later revealed that they had indeed been building a bomb.

The presence of violence seemed unremitting. Three days after the Townhouse explosion two SNCC activists, Ralph Featherstone (30 years old) and William "Che" Payne (26 years old), were killed by a car bomb in Maryland. Police said they were carrying dynamite; friends believed that they were murdered.

The Townhouse explosion was on March 8th of 1970, and within hours most WUO members had disappeared. Some were fugitives trying to avoid prosecution and possible imprisonment. Others went underground to be part of the life of the organization and to help make revolution from what they thought to be a more strategically advantageous situation. By the time federal indictments came down for Days of Rage in April, the Weather people were nowhere to be found.

When I thought about Weatherman, the Panthers inevitably came to mind. The FBI along with local police departments had launched a fierce attack on the Panthers. This was later revealed to be part of the FBI's Counter Intelligence Program, otherwise known as COINTELPRO, especially targeting the Black Panther Party as "the greatest threat to the internal security of the United States."

Panther headquarters around the country were assaulted by local and federal police forces. False rumors and divisions were propagated that caused internal conflict in the Black movement. COINTELPRO left scores of Black revolutionaries dead, and many others imprisoned. In 1969 alone, 28 Panthers, including Fred Hampton and Mark Clark, were murdered by police forces and 749 others were arrested and/or imprisoned. As Sundiata Acoli has written:

> *"On April 2, 1969, I was arrested to stand trial in the Panther 21 case. Twenty-one of us were accused of conspiracy to carry out a ridiculous plot to blow up a number of New York department stores and the New York Botanical Gardens. Although the legal process took two years and the trial lasted eight months—the longest criminal prosecution in New York history—the jurors took only 56 minutes to acquit all the defendants of every charge."*

The Panther 21, indicted just weeks after the Chicago 8, became a central concern for our part of the radical movement, especially in the New York area. One of the defendants was Afeni Shakur who is now better known as the mother of the slain rapper, Tupac Shakur.

On May 21st Weatherman (now calling themselves the Weatherman Underground) issued their first communique. The eager underground press found tape recordings, slipped under their doors, not just written communiques. They were played on sympathetic radio stations, and I remember being held spellbound by the voice:

"Hello. This is Bernardine Dohrn. All over the world, people fighting American imperialism look to Amerika's youth to use our strategic position behind enemy lines to join forces in the destruction of empire.

"Our job is to lead white kids into armed revolution. Ever since SDS became revolutionary, we've been trying to show how it is possible to overcome the frustration and impotence that comes from trying to reform the system. Kids know the lines are drawn; revolution is touching all of our lives. Tens of thousands have learned that protest and marches don't do it. Revolutionary violence is the only way.

"Within the next 14 days we will attack a symbol or institution of American injustice. This is the way we celebrate the example of Eldridge Cleaver and H. Rap Brown and all black revolutionaries who first inspired us by their fight behind enemy lines for the liberation of their people.

"Never again will they fight alone."

I felt she was speaking directly to me. About three weeks later the Weatherman Underground bombed the New York City Police headquarters.

Though they had missed their first deadline, I was impressed. I believed only a movement that embraced armed struggle could be effective, and the WUO seemed to be the only real option for me. After the cumulative effects of the assassinations of Dr. King and Malcolm X, the Conspiracy trial conviction, the murder of Fred Hampton and Mark Clark, the attack on the Black Panthers in LA, the internment of the Panther 21, and now the murder of the students at Jackson and Kent State, I was ready to view revolutionary, clandestine violence as necessary. I wanted to be part of an organization that supported the Vietnamese and the Black liberation movements. And now Weatherman's political outlook seemed to be less crazy, less infused with the mania of the Flint conference and more open to the youth culture and the mass movement that seemed to be exploding.

Weatherman was far from the only group involved in armed actions in that era of political violence. By the 1969-70 school year there was roughly one such incident a day somewhere in the country. ROTC buildings, Selective Service offices, induction centers, federal buildings, and corporate offices were all targets.

I viewed Weatherman as reflective of a deep well of anger and resistance and it was in that context of mass resistance that I resonated to their words and actions. Their communiqué seemed like a personal invitation to join.

By 1970 it was clear that two completely intertwined processes were in motion. People were resisting, trying to transform the status quo both at home and around the world, and were having a real impact. Domestically that resistance was being led by the Black liberation movement. Globally the Vietnamese were blazing the way. The other process, however, was the response of the U.S. government—the unleashing of the power of their armaments against these forces for change. I thought that central to surviving repression and building resistance would be the nurturing of the underground.

But where were they? How could I join?

And then there was my life with Jerry. I needed to come to terms with what I wanted. Between us there was a built-in power dynamic that would have been challenging to overcome in any event. A man in a sexist society and six years my senior. I was 21 when we met; at that age, six years can be a lifetime.

For a long while, and with increasing intensity, I was feeling choked by the relationship. Everything I did seemed part of Jerry's agenda and it became harder and harder to find myself. His expectations and demands on me were exhausting. For a while I had been thinking about ending the relationship but unsure about letting go after all the intense experiences we had shared. It's difficult to leave someone you really care about and I thought it would be very hard for both of us. I was no longer in love, but fear of the unknown held me back. If I left, what would I do? Where would I go? I knew I wouldn't be able to stay in the same social/political milieu as Jerry. When the indictments came down, I put aside all doubt because I thought this was no time to jump ship. Then when Jerry was serving a California jail sentenced followed by the Chicago 8 trial, I had felt I couldn't abandon him.

Years later Jerry reflected in Growing (Up) at 37: "Since what I was doing was so 'politically important,' Ruthie [the name he gave me—to protect my privacy?] took the role of Mama, supporting me when I was down, feeding me, buying my clothes, washing my underwear, typing my manuscripts."

But buying his clothes was the least of what bothered me. In fact, I should have apologized to him since I had little fashion sense, even less about men's clothing. I was glad to read his "apology" but wished he had acknowledged that I, too, had done something of "political importance." Furthermore, I was the one actively oppressing myself, "taking the role," while he was simply the one passively being cared for, allowing himself to be cared for. I guess he forgot about the time he insisted I speak publicly about something I had little interest in and then let me know in no uncertain terms how terribly embarrassed I had made him feel because I was such a poor speaker; or the night he became depressed, and threw some kind of hissy fit until I agreed to go on a search for a steak somewhere and bring it home. Or the times he was in jail and wrote me many long lists of everything I had to do, chastised me when I couldn't complete it all ASAP, without any recognition of what it meant for my life. Jerry had little understanding of the way he enforced this inequality, of the impact of his demands on my life, or how little appreciation he expressed, or how destructive his denigration was for me. His regular use of Ritalin didn't help. Even now I want to say, "Yes, but ..." and tell you all the ways in which he was lovable and extraordinary. I don't know if that's generosity on my part or internalized sexism or both.

I had grown weary of all this and was ready to move on. I was pushed beyond my hesitancy when Jerry went to jail after the Chicago 8 sentencing. I had a chance to breathe on my own and work collaboratively with women. Anita and I burned judges' robes and organized demonstrations. Judy and I traveled to Vietnam and Cuba and organized a protest in front of the U.S. Consulate. And I began to secretly meet with a previous fling. Someone who would become the father of my children.

Although I couldn't find the Weatherman organization, I did find a member. On my return from Cuba and the disappointment of our failed conference with the Indochinese, I made another trip to Cleveland, Ohio to speak at Case Western Reserve University.

Ironically I have the FBI to thank for helping me write this memoir. When I later obtained thousands of pages of my FBI files through the FOIA, they were severely redacted, full of inaccuracies (they confused me with my mother!), and replete with unflattering descriptions. But they did refresh my memory, for which I am grateful.

Their informant described me as "from the bottom of the barrel, as she is brazen, uncouth and repulsive." I prefer to think they were wrong. But at least I got the last laugh because thankfully the FOIA files remind me that "the audience seemed to like certain expressions she used as they would laugh and applaud ... [She] used the word 'bullshit' many times in referring to the actions of the courts and the U.S. government

… At the end of her talk, subject indicated that there was no justice in the United States courts, so they have to take justice to the streets. Subject's talk was accepted by the audience with a standing ovation."

As it happened, I reconnected on that trip to Cleveland with Howie Emmer, with whom I'd had a summer relationship several years back as a camp counselor at Circle Pines Center in Michigan. Part of the Weatherman faction of SDS, Howie had been a very effective campus organizer at Kent State the year before the four students were killed. So effective that James Michener describes him in his book *Kent State*:

> *"…a young man who in certain light looked as if he might have been a Manchurian or an Eskimo. His mouth was enormous and his eyes piercing. He wore his hair long but was without beard or mustache, and the dominant characteristic by which people remembered him was the acuity of his intellect. He was not well versed in a wide subject matter, for in many areas he was deficient, but in revolutionary tactics he was a master. He had one attribute which made him invaluable to the movement … He was fantastic at face-to-face persuasion. He listens to what you are trying to say, then picks up where you left off and shows you the consequences of your reasoning. Even people who disliked what he was trying to peddle liked the way he presented it." (Kent State, page 84.)*

In the spring of 1969 charges were filed against more than 100 students at Kent State for anti-war activities, including Howie. These charges stemmed from anti-war activities and protests such as demands to abolish campus ROTC. Therefore, although Howie was part of the Weatherman, he was in jail on a six-month sentence when the Townhouse explosion occurred and when the four Kent students were killed. Upon his release, the rest of the Weatherman organization was underground. Terry Robbins and Diana Oughton, two of those killed in the Townhouse, had been his close friends and when I met up with him he was profoundly grieving for them.

Howie and I reconnected immediately. He was a kind breath of fresh air, a real mensch, and accepted me as an equal right away. I felt my own identity returning. It was a bonus that I already knew and loved his family!

Howie and I discussed the blanket of fear that had descended upon

Kent in the aftermath of the May 4th killings. Many people were frightened and argued that there should be no activities planned for the anniversary of the murders because of possible repression. We both disagreed. Kent had become a symbol and we felt it would be especially important for the struggle to continue. We also discussed the joining of Yippie sensibilities with the politics of Weatherman, especially in light of the sizable youth counter-cultural community in Kent.

Enjoying the new romance, disgruntled with both Jerry and the political scene in New York, I decided to move to Kent with Howie and help organize. Once I made up my mind, there was no stopping me. I returned to New York, explained to Jerry that I was leaving, packed up a couple of things, and headed out the door. Jerry was shocked. He screamed and yelled and tried to block my way, but I was far stronger. I know it might seem like the decent thing would have been to have had more of a conversation with Jerry. Before you decide I'm an ice queen, let me say that I was scared to do so. I feared he would unravel and take it out on me.

Jerry later wrote this about his response to my leaving: "I furiously destroyed my apartment, running through it naked, crying, screaming, at the top of my lungs. I alternated between rage and getting down on my hands and knees to beg Ruthie [aka Nancy] to stay. I was mad, insane; I could not bear to be alone and insisted that friends sleep over, to keep me company."

I knew that was coming and didn't want to be there for that because I was afraid I couldn't get away if I stayed. Jerry's abuse and pleading would all be directed at me. So I self-protectively fled.

I left Jerry and New York, didn't look back, and burned my bridges with most of the Yippie/hippie/ Lower East Side crowd forever. That was October of 1970.

NEW MORNING

In December of 1970 the Weatherman Underground for the first time issued a communique unrelated to an action. Titled *New Morning, Changing Weather*, it reflected the organization's attempt to come to terms with what had happened in the Townhouse explosion, stating that "the townhouse forever destroyed our belief that armed struggle is the only real revolutionary struggle ... This tendency to consider only bombings or picking up the gun as revolutionary, with the glorification of the heavier the better, we've called the military error." *New Morning* was also an explicit acknowledgement of the importance of the counterculture as it connected with events happening around the country in the mass movement: "The demonstrations and strikes following the rape of Indochina and the murders at Jackson and Kent last May showed real power and made a strong difference."

Significantly, the name of the organization changed once more. "Weatherman" had previously changed to the "Weatherman Underground" and now had morphed again. It changed from an "Underground" to an "Underground Organization" representing a shift toward placing political (as opposed to primarily military) considerations in command, and had dropped the exclusively masculine nomenclature. From then on it would be known as the Weather Underground Organization (WUO). The women's movement had penetrated its shield, although to what extent has always been a live debate among those in the know. I was far from their center, living in the heartland, and knew nothing of their internal struggles. I simply welcomed the change.

New Morning was met with mixed reviews. I applauded it. It seemed to parallel the changes that I was going through, trying to merge revolutionary politics with the mass movement and the counter-cultural scene. Although I thought armed struggle and clandestine organization were important, I continued to believe in the necessity of militant and public mass struggle. Situated in Kent State I could feel the organizational void that was created when the Weather Underground disappeared from public view. It was just at the moment of the disappearing act that youth communities around the country had exploded with energy and force. I felt there was no national organization that could provide coherent leadership and help ensure that this upheaval would result in sustained struggle. This would become a theme of the next few years.

By January Howie and I were living in a funky old house in Kent and found some like-minded folks to live and work with. I can't remember how we supported ourselves although I do remember that we got food stamps and then sold some of them for money. We also did some amount of petty shoplifting during that time and lived very much on the margin. According to my FBI file, we "operated" a Yippie commune at 718 Stowe Street in Kent and the Cleveland bureau was to advise the central FBI of our whereabouts every 45 days. I was designated a "Non-Weatherman Support Individual" and it was reported that "extensive physical and electronic surveillance ... did not disclose any contact with the Weatherman Underground."

We called ourselves Weather/Yippies and our little group published an underground newspaper called *Kent Dragonfire* that included local as well as national and international news thanks to the remarkable Liberation News Service (LNS), an alternative radical wire service. Howie was banned from the Kent State campus because of his previous arrest, and so, despite the fact that I was not a student, I became a campus organizer, now joining the ranks of the "outside agitators."

It seemed like everyone was looking for the Weather Underground: I was and so was Howie; the FBI certainly was, placing Bernardine Dohrn on the Ten Most Wanted List; and then a new element was introduced. One day I was sitting at home in Kent when the phone rang. I picked it up and on the other end of the line was June. June and her boyfriend, Sam, had been arrested for several bombings directed at the military and war-related corporations. Sam was now in New York's Attica Prison, but rather than appear for trial, June had become a fugitive. Although we were not close friends, I had known her in New York. Now she was asking for help and hoping to find the Weather Underground. I was somewhat nervous about it since she was so indiscreet in her method of contacting me.

My concern for her safety and wellbeing trumped my fears and I agreed to help her out. We asked friends in Cleveland if they would be willing to put her up, only for a few days but without too many questions asked. They agreed. Their willingness was not that unusual in those days. The Weather Underground could not have existed for so long and so well without the existence of hundreds of such supporters.

A few days turned into weeks and then into months. We were concerned because we were high profile, public activists, and as time went on June seemed to have less and less concern for security, almost as if she wanted to get caught. Eventually we had to ask her to leave since the whole setup seemed wrong and dangerous to all concerned. June said she was looking for the Weather Underground Organization since she was all out there on her own. I felt concerned for her but, in truth, I too had no idea how to reach them at that point in my life.

In February the U.S. launched an all-out invasion of Laos and revealed that they had been militarily engaged in that country for a while. We organized a substantial demonstration on campus. There were enough protestors to afford me cover (or so I thought) to spray-paint "U.S. Out of Laos" on the campus walls. That would have consequences for me later on.

In retaliation for the expansion of the war, on March 1st the Weather Underground bombed the U.S. Capitol, declaring:

> *"We have attacked the Capitol because it is, along with the White House and the Pentagon, the worldwide symbol of the government which is now attacking Indochina."*

We were thrilled by the audacity of the act and the fact that they were able to penetrate the capitol of the most aggressive and powerful country on earth. It was David versus Goliath, and even though they were only able to deliver a bee sting, that was okay because it represented a possibility of more militant activity.

Later that year our tiny group at Kent put together a collection of the WUO communiqués and statements in a low-tech, mimeographed form. On the cover it said HAPPY BIRTHDAY WEATHER UNDERGROUND and displayed a rifle crossed with a hash pipe.

I wanted to be part of the rising feminist tide that was reflected in the name change of the Weather Underground Organization. Along with several other women, I formed a group called New Nation Sisters, and two of us hitchhiked to a women's conference in Bowling Green, Ohio. Those were hitchhiking days, but I don't recommend it. I was sitting in the front passenger seat when the driver, with his left arm on the steering wheel, inched his right hand onto my lap. Taken aback, I gently pushed it away. But he came back at me. This time I strongly and unmistakably shoved him away. That seemed to put him off, but I was really frightened and felt captive. When he stopped for gas and went inside to pay, my friend and I made a mad dash and hid until he took off. We made it to the conference but I can't remember how as the emotionality of that man intruding upon my person is what remains with me to this day.

Fanning the flames of my feminism was the fact that soon after moving to Ohio I became pregnant. I had given up taking birth control pills because of the mixed scientific reports regarding their side effects. I was instead using a diaphragm. I had no intention of getting pregnant which is why I used a diaphragm. But it failed me. For all those who think all birth control is foolproof, let me just say, yup, I got pregnant while using a diaphragm.

I was by now a feminist and believed 100 per cent that women should have control of our own bodies and healthcare. I was in a relationship with a very caring man, and so Howie and I discussed it together and agreed I would have an abortion if I could figure out a safe way to do that. I always wanted to have children, four if possible, preferably all girls as in Little Women. (So you can see I had no clue at that point about what it would take to care for children.) However, both of us loved kids and wanted to be parents someday. But this wasn't the day. We were at the beginning of our relationship, still young we felt, and had very little money, no stable jobs or home, and we were determined to continue movement work. I had no qualms, no angst about it. I was just really scared by the specter of the process and the fact that it was still illegal in most places. I had heard so many stories about women getting really sick and women dying in back-alley abortions. I worried about finding a safe abortion provider. But I was determined.

It would be another two years until *Roe v. Wade*, but I did some research and learned that abortion was now legal and available in New York City. (I love the Big Apple!) I made an appointment and traveled to the Women's Medical Group on the upper east side, where I had a vacuum aspiration, effective with pregnancies ten weeks or less. The folks at the medical group were kind and thoughtful, and the procedure was pretty painless. I then wrote an article for *Dragonfire* about my experience, since I believed that talking about it was very important. I explained how worried I had felt and what a relief it was to have a safe and legal abortion. I encouraged women to think seriously about their circumstances when making their decision and acknowledged, "Having a baby can be beautiful whether or not you're married, if you are really into it. It's your decision, your life." I also cautioned that abortion is no substitute for birth control and exhorted my sister witches to "take our broomsticks to the streets and demand better information and access to birth control." I signed the article "Wanda the Wippie Witch." I'm not sure why I didn't use my real name since it was a legal abortion. Perhaps it was a matter of the stigmatization that existed then and still substantially exists today. (How many women do you know today who feel comfortable enough to talk openly about an abortion?)

Then came a call for a Women's March on the Pentagon on April 10th. Three of us jumped into my tiny second-hand green convertible Karmann Ghia and headed for Washington, D.C. Somewhere in Pennsylvania I took a wrong turn and ended up on a windy and wet country road where the car skidded out of control and overturned.

Miraculously, we were able to crawl out of the car with only scratches! Looking up we saw a man and a woman, dressed all in black with large crosses around their necks. It flashed through my mind that I had gone to heaven. Or was it hell? However, they were merely two mortals from a nearby seminary, who were kind enough to help us get cleaned up and deal with the police. The car was totaled but we were determined not to miss the march. We hopped a bus and continued our journey to D.C.! There we joined thousands of young women who had converged from around the country. My FOIA file states that a "source" reported that both myself and one of the other woman [whose name is blackened out] "thought it was the best march we'd ever attended."

Toward the end of April I was informed that the *Akron (Ohio) Beacon-Journal* and the University News Service were about to issue a press release calling me an "outside agitator." I acted preemptively and asked the student paper, *The Daily Kent Stater*, to interview me. The interview ran on Thursday, April 22:

> *"If people consider me a threat because of my connections with Jerry [Rubin], I just want them to know that I consider myself a threat to the American way of life in my own right because I know what I want and I'm willing to fight for it."*

The next evening, I recall panhandling in downtown Kent and my FOIA file kindly reminds me that I was trying to scrounge up enough money to see the movie *Little Big Man*. Suddenly two beefy cops appeared from nowhere, grabbed me and placed me under arrest, not for panhandling as I had assumed, but for "malicious destruction of property"! Somebody had seen me spray-painting U.S. OUT OF LAOS on a campus building, and apparently turned me in to the cops.

I was stunned and spent 14 hours in the Portage County Jail reading one issue of *Ladies Home Journal* from cover to cover, and then again. (I think that alone was enough of a price to pay!) But in truth, I was now really worried. Sometimes Kent felt like a small Southern town. And the specter of the four murdered students was always on my mind.

I had been arrested before but never for a felony. The malicious destruction of property charge was a felony because it cost over a hundred bucks to sandblast the slogan off the building. So I now faced up to five years in prison. I reminded myself that felonies often get broken down to misdemeanors in the plea-bargaining process. That thought calmed my nerves and I was hopeful that this would happen in my case.

Friends collected money for me on the street and I posted a $300 bond, pled "not guilty," and went home. In an article titled "Nancy Nabbed" that I wrote for *Dragonfire*, I reported that the following evening I was able to see Little Big Man and learned that "Cheyenne" means "human being." I insisted that the malicious destruction we should be concerned about was not the property damage from the spray painting but the destruction of people: Indians in this country, the Indochinese people, and Allison, Bill, Jeff and Sandy—the four students who had been shot by the National Guard the previous year. I ended my article by saying: "But then, they're only human beings. What's in a human being?"

Meanwhile other Movement women were making big news. The FBI was out to get somebody for the bombing of the Capitol. On April 28th they arrested 19-year-old Leslie Bacon, a public organizer of the upcoming May Day protest in D.C. She was picked up in D.C., flown to Seattle and held incommunicado for weeks in a hotel where she was interrogated and denied access to everybody but lawyers. On May 1st the Weather Underground issued a communiqué addressing Leslie's mother:

> *"Your confidence in Leslie is justified because she is completely innocent of any involvement in the bombing of the U.S. Capitol. We know this for a fact because, as the FBI and Justice Department well know, our organization did the bombing."*

Toward the end of May, my old Yippie pals Judy Gumbo and Stew Albert were subpoenaed by a federal grand jury investigating the Capitol bombing. Judy along with Stew audaciously held a press conference in front of the Capitol building. Judy stated that, "The Weather Underground bombed the Capitol to bring a smile and a wink to all the kids in America who hate their government. We didn't do it but we dug it." From my perch in Ohio, it strengthened my resolve and made me smile.

For the first anniversary of the Kent State shootings, May 4, 1971, the University planned to have a memorial program. Our May Day Coalition had something different in mind. We announced at a campus rally on April 28th that we would hold our own remembrance. We felt that the conditions that inspired last year's protests were still the same. In fact, the war had escalated in Indochina and that in order to do justice to the memory of those who had died, we needed to continue to protest. We planned to have a nonviolent civil disobedience action as an explicit alternative to the University program. By this time the school administration had become concerned about the participation of non-students such as myself, insisting that we were barred from attending and warning that they would be checking student identification at all of their events. We were elated when the student body president, Craig Morgan, announced that he would not participate in the official events.

As reported in my FOIA files, the University did their thing and we did ours: "During this memorial service a group of individuals moved against the KSU ROTC Building and staged a sit-in which closed the building down." The action continued throughout the night with several hundred people staging a sit-in and effectively blockading the doors. By early morning, some people had come and gone and some demonstrators were still blocking the doors. The May Day Coalition had chained shut the doors to the building and declared victory but a few stalwarts insisted on remaining. I was not one. I felt it would be difficult to sustain the sit-in and we had shown that despite the killings of the previous year, the students and non-students at Kent were not afraid to protest. Besides, the truth is, I was exhausted.

On May 20th several hundred protesters gathered on campus to protest a ROTC ceremony, chanting and shouting and throwing marshmallows at the ROTC members. That night and the next there was a rebellion in downtown Kent. The police read the riot act, blocked off the streets, and made mass arrests. FOIA files indicate that there "reportedly was quite a bit of 'trashing' going on with damage being inflicted on buildings, cars, etc." That was Kent in 1971 and Kent was not exceptional in this regard. The early 1970s saw a broadening of mass militant activities in youth communities around the country.

Despite the spontaneous nature of these militant activities, the authorities saw Howie and me as instigators. By now I had decided to plea-bargain my way out of the malicious destruction of property charge. They broke it down to a misdemeanor on the condition that I would plead guilty, pay a fine and for the sandblasting, and most importantly, get out of Dodge. I had to agree to leave Kent. By that time I was ready and so was Howie. We had received telephoned bomb threats when we were in our home and I felt like we were under attack. In retrospect, I suspect the FBI had something, if not everything, to do with the bomb threats. Taking our leave seemed to make sense because we were, after all, non-students with limited access to the University. Our "outside agitator" days were over and we needed to move on. Additionally, we had not yet found the Weather Underground.

Unsure about what to do next and completely broke, Howie and I moved in with his parents in Cleveland, Ruth and Jack Emmer, and went to work. The Emmers deserve a special place of honor in this memoir. They were as tolerant, progressive and supportive as my own parents. In fact, Howie was a Red Diaper Baby like me; his parents had long been pillars of the Cleveland peace and justice scene. Jack was a social worker and Ruth was a preschool teacher.

One evening Ruth told me a story. In 1962 she had been subpoenaed to HUAC and had refused to testify. The story was front page in the *Cleveland Plain Dealer*, and a neighbor had rushed over, eager to help out. "Ruth, there's another Ruth Emmer who's a Communist, and you need to tell them it's not you!"

"Come on in and have a cup of coffee," said Ruth. "We need to talk." That was Ruth, with cream and sugar.

In the 1970s, Ruth became known as the Weather Mom. She welcomed all exhausted activists when they needed a home-cooked meal or a good night's sleep. Anyone who was fighting for justice was welcome in her home. Jack was the same. Just not as good a cook! Howie and I were to learn they were also wonderful grandparents.

For most of that year in Cleveland, I was a waitress, first in one Jewish deli and then another. Howie was employed by an auto parts place and between the two of us we were able to pay off our fines.

The murders of the Jackson brothers, about a year apart, stood like bloody bookends on our time in Ohio. 17-year-old Jonathan had died in 1970 attempting to free his brother from prison in what is referred to as the August 7th Rebellion. Then on August 21, 1971, George Jackson was gunned down on the yard at San Quentin. By then his resistance had become legendary and his books, *Blood in My Eye* and *Soledad Brother,* were passed around in Movement circles, inside and outside prisons, until they became dog-eared.

Stephen Jay Gould, the evolutionary biologist, critiqued Social Darwinism and sociobiologists like Cesare Lombroso who argued that "criminals are primitive savages who are evolutionarily backward compared to normal citizens." Gould would refer to George Jackson in his book *The Mismeasure of Man*:

> *"George Jackson ... died under Lombroso's legacy, trying to escape after 11 years (8 1/2 in solitary) of an indeterminate one-year-to-life sentence for stealing $70 from a gas station."*

I realize there are those who see George Jackson in a different light, but I agreed with Stephen Jay Gould back then and still do today. Apparently many others do as well because for years afterwards, August 21st would be a day of commemorating George Jackson throughout the country, both inside and outside prisons. On August 28th the Weather Underground blew up the offices of the California Department of Corrections in San Francisco to protest the assassination of George Jackson. Were they in San Francisco?

Three weeks after George Jackson's death, on September 9th, a major rebellion broke out at Attica Prison in upstate New York. Although driven by the racist and sub-human conditions within the prison itself, it was sparked by the murder of George Jackson. The uprising lasted for four days until Governor Rockefeller sent in the National Guard to mow down the rebellion. When the smoke cleared, it was obvious that the siege had left 39 dead bodies and over 100 seriously wounded. Among the dead was Sam, who had been the partner and codefendant of June, the fugitive who had stayed with our Cleveland friends.

Howie and I were angry and felt helplessly frustrated. Could we ever hope to stop the madness! We participated in a march thrown together by various peace groups in Cleveland, but we felt we had to do something more. The best we could do was to go out under cover of darkness and spray paint "Long Live Attica" all over Cleveland Heights.

On September 17th the Weather Underground bombed the New York Department of Corrections to protest the murders at Attica. Once again it felt as if they had read my heart and mind. They had issued a statement of support to those most disenfranchised inmates who had dared to rebel against their wretched conditions.

That fall Howie and I went off to Washington, D.C., to join Rennie Davis and the People's Coalition for Peace and Justice in their continuing effort to end the war and fight racism, poverty and repression. I was arrested while participating in civil disobedience, but the demonstration paled considerably when compared with the previous May Day activity in D.C. Howie and I found ourselves at a crossroads and were pretty much out of funds so our options were limited. There was an offer to do anti-war work in New Hampshire during the period leading up to their primary. We volunteered and up to New Hampshire we went, without any serious winter clothes or any funds. The Concord Quaker congregation gave us the use of a car and a small stipend, and we lived rent-free at a Portsmouth hippie commune of sorts. We organized a couple of peace demonstrations, handed out lots of leaflets and went on a trip to Quebec City where we picked up an anti-war film from Vietnamese diplomats to use in our anti-war work.

Returning to Cleveland in March 1972, totally broke, we found jobs in an effort to save some money. That May, Nixon massively bombed North and South Vietnam, mined the harbors and bombed the dikes. On May 19th the Weather Underground bombed the Pentagon.

We drove to Miami in the summer of 1972 to participate in the protests at the Republican Convention. I remember very little, other than that it was dark and chaotic and full of tear gas. We slept outside in a big parking lot with many other people. I was uninspired by the whole turn of events. A respectable number of folks had turned out and there was plenty of media coverage. Who knows what impact it had? That is, most of the time, hard to measure. I don't know how to explain my feelings other than to say it felt fragmented. I didn't feel part of a coherent whole. From my old-age perch, I wonder if it was because for the first time I was participating in a national action that I had not helped organize. In a sense I was on the outside looking in. Perhaps that was a part of it. But the anti-war movement was becoming more fragmented even as more and more of the country was coming to agree with us.

Howie and I were also at an impasse politically. After my felony bust, we couldn't return to Kent in any meaningful way. We were still in Cleveland working full time to pay off court fines; me slinging hash and Howie stocking shelves in an auto parts store. We were seeking direction for what to do next. And we were exhausted. In those days movement folks had no conscious philosophy about self-care as exists today. We just knew we had to find another way to live and engage in political work. But we also needed some R & R, and yearned to be in nature. With our meager savings, we bought a van and took to the road.

OFF THE GRID

I LOVED THE BAND AND "*The Weight*" was my favorite song. We named our newly purchased, used Dodge van "Fanny" in reference to the refrain "Take a load off Fanny." We built a bed in the back and headed out of Ohio. Little did we realize what my FBI file later revealed—that the agency had us under surveillance at the actual moment we pulled onto the turnpike.

It was September of 1972 and our sights were set on the West. If we couldn't find the WUO, we would head for the countryside of the Northwest. We'd heard it was beautiful and we were ready for a change.

It was a very carefree couple of months. We made a short stop in Chicago to visit my high school pal Diane who was now living with her second husband. He suffered from agoraphobia and seemed quite uncomfortable with our presence. He went off to bed, however, and Diane stayed up with us late into the night. At her request we sang all the old labor union favorites, a throwback to other times. It was fun and I was so glad we had stopped by.

In the morning we took off to the countryside around Madison where we deposited our cat, L'il Screecher, and her new litter of kittens in the good hands of some folks who lived on a farm. They were friends of Howie's older sister Toby. Toby would run for sheriff of Madison in the fall 1972 election, on the left-wing Wisconsin Alliance ticket. It was a protest campaign; she expected to lose and she did. For years I held onto her campaign poster—a picture of Toby grinning from ear to ear, with her long blond hair, casually dressed in jeans and sandals, sitting in a rocking chair on a front porch with legs crossed and a shotgun in her hands.

Leaving Wisconsin, we camped overnight in Iowa and Nebraska and then headed for the Badlands and the Black Hills. We spent one night in a pine forest on a placid lake, playing guitars with people we met along the way. Then a few days in Custer State Park where we were the only human beings around. Grazing in a nearby field was a herd of 300 bison, unconcerned with our presence. In the morning four mountain goats joined us and Howie fed them bread right out of his hand. It was a magical place.

We spent time with friends, or friends of friends, all along the way. We imagined what it would be like to live in a small mountain town when we visited Ward, Colorado. Potbelly stoves, no running water but plenty of fresh spring water. We felt very peaceful in this rustic space as we split wood, played guitars, and took long mountain hikes despite the unaccustomed and challenging altitude.

Then on westward to the Anza Borrego State Park and Joshua Tree National Monument.

This apparently was a confusing time for the FBI. Despite the fact that we didn't know we were under surveillance and did nothing to purposely throw them off the track, they had difficulty getting a handle on our whereabouts during this traveling period. My FOIA file states:

> *"From September, 1972, until June, 1973, Subject's location and residence were unknown. During that period of time she was in a travel status most of the time and apparently just went from one place to the next. After arriving in a particular place she would stay a short period of time and then move on."*

Your FBI at work: vague perhaps but, at least in this case, undeniably accurate!

After the intensity of Chicago '68 and its aftermath, followed by my experiences at Kent State, this journey was a soothing balm. We were actually off their grid! It was comforting to learn we had friends and

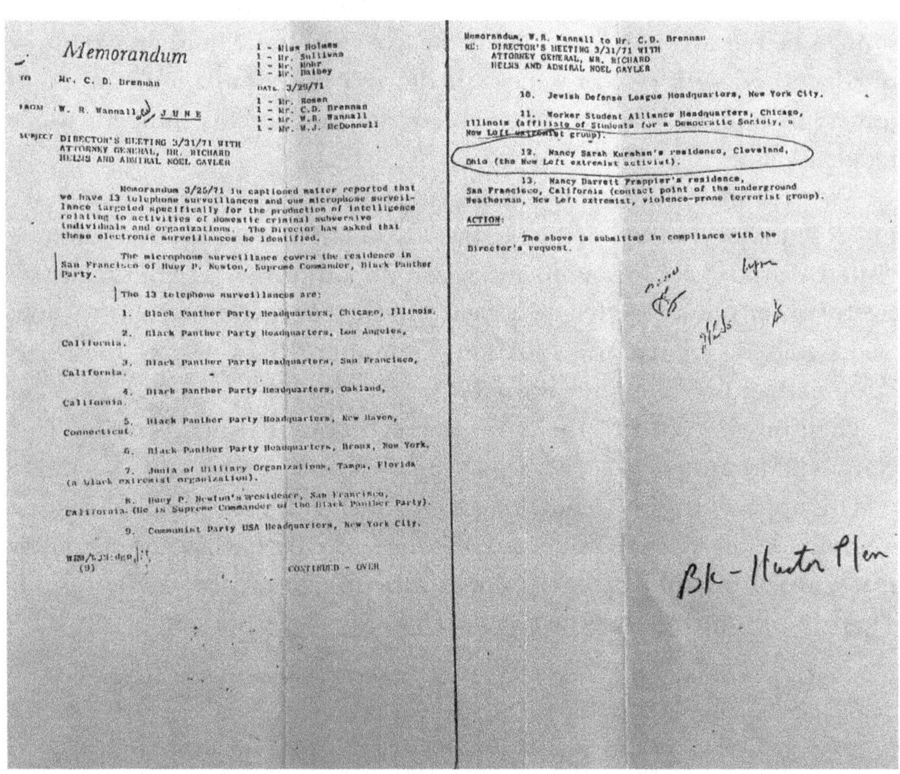

Memorandum

1 - Miss Holmes
1 - Mr. Sullivan
1 - Mr. Mohr
1 - Mr. Baisey

TO: Mr. C. D. Brennan

DATE: 3/29/71

1 - Mr. Rosen
1 - Mr. C.D. Brennan
1 - Mr. W.R. Wannall
1 - Mr. W.J. McDonnell

FROM: W. R. Wannall, J U N E

SUBJECT: DIRECTOR'S MEETING 3/31/71 WITH ATTORNEY GENERAL, MR. RICHARD HELMS AND ADMIRAL NOEL GAYLER

Memorandum 3/25/71 in captioned matter reported that we have 13 telephone surveillances and one microphone surveillance targeted specifically for the production of intelligence relating to activities of domestic criminal subversive individuals and organizations. The Director has asked that these electronic surveillances be identified.

The microphone surveillance covers the residence in San Francisco of Huey P. Newton, Supreme Commander, Black Panther Party.

The 13 telephone surveillances are:

1. Black Panther Party Headquarters, Chicago, Illinois.

2. Black Panther Party Headquarters, Los Angeles, California.

3. Black Panther Party Headquarters, San Francisco, California.

4. Black Panther Party Headquarters, Oakland, California.

5. Black Panther Party Headquarters, New Haven, Connecticut.

6. Black Panther Party Headquarters, Bronx, New York.

7. Junta of Military Organizations, Tampa, Florida (a black extremist organization).

8. Huey P. Newton's residence, San Francisco, California. (He is Supreme Commander of the Black Panther Party).

9. Communist Party USA Headquarters, New York City.

WRW/LJM:dgo
(9)

CONTINUED - OVER

Memorandum, W.R. Wannall to Mr. C.D. Brennan
RE: DIRECTOR'S MEETING 3/31/71 WITH ATTORNEY GENERAL, MR. RICHARD HELMS AND ADMIRAL NOEL GAYLER

10. Jewish Defense League Headquarters, New York City.

11. Worker Student Alliance Headquarters, Chicago, Illinois (affiliate of Students for a Democratic Society, a New Left extremist group).

12. Nancy Sarah Kurshan's residence, Cleveland, Ohio (the New Left extremist activist).

13. Nancy Barrett Frappier's residence, San Francisco, California (contact point of the underground Weatherman, New Left extremist, violence-prone terrorist group).

ACTION:

The above is submitted in compliance with the Director's request.

Bk - Hunter Plan

An FBI list of surveillance targets acquired by Attorney Weinglass 10 years later and forwarded to Nancy. List includes Huey Newton & many Black Panther chapters but also the residence of Nancy, "the New Left extremist activist".

allies in many places, on farms and in mountain towns, on college campuses and communities and in national parks. Where we had no two-legged friends, we had met our four-legged friends—the bison and the mountain goats. We felt connected. We were young and the future seemed to hold great promise.

We intended to make it to the Northwest, but by the time we hit the San Francisco Bay Area, we were completely broke. That was clearly the end of the road. As events evolved, our trip turned out to be a pastoral interlude, a bridge between intense periods of political activity.

If the FBI was there to watch us as we left Cleveland, they were also ready for us in the Bay Area. We moved in temporarily with Howie's childhood friend, Mickey Tenenbaum. Thanks to a live human being—the postal worker who delivered the mail—I was warned that there was a "mail cover" on the house; that is, all mail addressed to me was being monitored. Were they tracking everyone who wrote? Was there an illegal phone or house tap? Whatever their methods, it was clear the FBI was back on the job.

GUESS WHO I SAW TODAY?

We settled down into life in the Bay Area. I worked any number of odd jobs, most memorably running Crazy Dave's Juice Stand at the corner of Bancroft and Telegraph in Berkeley. After two years in a UC Berkeley PhD program (followed by six years in the Movement), there I was in a juice stand at the gate of that very same campus. That was definitely not the progress my parents had had in mind for me.

Never one to give up, I went back to school at Oakland's Merritt Community College to get an Early Childhood credential. It was a great program, and I became a firm believer in universal early childhood education, from infancy on up, and the importance of play. For some time, Howie and I ran a daycare program for toddlers, quite a challenge that involved lots of diaper changing. The parents of the kids were all political activists, two of whom were ex-members of Weatherman. Others worked for Non-Intervention in Chile (NICH), a group in defense of the democratic process in Chile.

Howie and I had closely followed the news about Chile since 1970 when a socialist, Salvador Allende, won the presidential election. But now, in California, we followed it even more closely. Many people that we knew had traveled to Chile and were involved in various informational and support efforts.

In America today, there is only one September 11th. However, for people throughout much of Latin America, September 11th has another significance. On that date in 1973 the democratically elected government of Chile was violently overthrown in a military coup backed by the United States. President Salvador Allende, a medical doctor and a Marxist, was murdered in the coup. Allende's victory had been a watershed for progressive people throughout Latin America and indeed the world, and the coup was a horrendous reminder of the nature of U.S. imperial power.

I was not surprised by the coup. Anyone who followed the developments could not be totally shocked. But my heart ached as I cried along with much of the world. I felt hatred toward my own government for enabling the crushing of this experiment, and I will never forget *The New York Times* picture of the bespectacled, professorial Allende wearing a helmet and carrying a Kalashnikov, a present from Fidel Castro inscribed "To My Friend and Comrade in Arms, Salvador." This would be the last image of Allende as he went down with his ship, the Popular Unity Government.

Just 17 days after the coup, the WUO bombed the ITT Corporation "in support of the people of Chile." ITT was a U.S. corporation that had been complicit in the coup against Allende. This was the first time the WUO had targeted a corporation, accusing ITT of subverting the Allende regime. I was thrilled and happy that some people could do something about Chile besides cry.

On September 11, 1974, one year after the coup, the Weather Underground bombed the Anaconda Corporation in Oakland, California. That same year Phil Ochs organized a benefit concert in the memory of murdered Chilean folk singer Victor Jara, calling it "An Evening With Salvador Allende." Bob Dylan, Pete Seeger, and Arlo Guthrie all performed that night.

On September 4, 1975, to mark the second anniversary of the Coup, the Weather Underground attacked the national headquarters of Kneecap Corporation in Salt Lake City, Utah. The communiqué stated that the action was in solidarity with the heroic revolutionary struggle of the Chilean people.

Ready to hop into political activity after our pastoral interlude, Howie and I joined the Ruchell Magee Defense Committee shortly after we reached the Bay Area. Ruchell Magee was the lone survivor of the August 7th Rebellion when Jonathan Jackson was killed. Ruchell was indicted for the incident, along with Angela Davis, and charged with murder, kidnapping and conspiracy. [In 2023, after 67 years of imprisonment, Ruchell was granted compassionate release and lived only 81 days in freedom!]

In 1973 I took a job working for the National Lawyers Guild in San Francisco on their Grand Jury project. Federal grand juries were the descendants of HUAC, often employed as a way to destroy radical movements. I was hired as a non-legal person to help put out a newsletter and organize activities in opposition to grand juries.

Ironically, as I later learned from my FBI files, I was working for the Grand Jury Project around the time the FBI was considering subpoenaing Howie and me to one of their grand juries.

Howie and I lived in several different situations but the most extraordinary was the Bachenheimer houses on Parker Street in Berkeley. The Bachenheimer complex was a cluster of houses that went on rent strike for several years. Bachenheimer was the name of the landlord/slumlord in charge of overcharging and under-repairing everything.

Being on rent strike meant that none of us paid rent to the landlord. We treated the houses as if they were our own, tearing down walls and rehabbing as desired. The backyards of the buildings ran together so there was a large outdoor common area.

The rent strike meant much more than simply not paying rent. We, like so many others, had rejected the traditional materialistic values of U.S. society and were looking for more meaningful, cooperative and creative ways of living. The rent strike was a collective decision and action taken by all the Bachenheimer houses. We weren't out to con the landlord. On the contrary, we believed that people had a right to decent and affordable living conditions, and we put our rent checks into the escrow account every month—payable when and if Bachenheimer brought the houses up to code.

The nature of that community was not lost on the FBI. My FOIA file indicates that: "This department had not had any success in developing any sources or informants ... in the 2200 block East Parker, Berkeley, California ... Because the residents of this block are "hippie type individuals," their attitude toward any type of authority or law enforcement official is somewhat negative, therefore, communication with them is also somewhat limited."

I wonder if any left organization was better guarded against snooping FBI agents or undercover informants than the Bachenheimer houses. Although the rent strike may have been exceptional, there were communities of similar character all around the country.

Bachenheimer eventually took us to court and, ironically, I was called to the jury pool for that trial. I, of course, had to disqualify myself. What a small world is Berkeley!

Decades later, I went to see my friend Paul Samberg who was still living in what was once a Bachenheimer house. He said he had bumped into Bachenheimer years after the strike and felt sorry for him; our old nemesis seemed like a sad, pathetic man.

In January of 1973, Vietnam and the U.S. signed the Peace Accords. That night thousands of people poured out into the streets of Berkeley in a spontaneous mass celebration. Shortly thereafter, the WUO issued a communiqué called "*Common Victories.*" Howie and I reproduced it by the thousands and distributed it around the Bay Area.

One Saturday afternoon I was sitting at home reading when Howie burst into the house with news he couldn't wait to deliver. "Guess who I saw today? At the Alameda Flea Market!" "Haven't a clue," I said, thinking he must be referring to the Nancy Wilson song. "Bernardine! Bernardine Dohrn! I didn't recognize her at first. She looked so different. I didn't notice her, but she walked right up to me and said, 'Howie?' and as soon as I heard her voice, I realized who it was. We arranged to meet, you too, next week." Howie hadn't seen her for several years, since before he went to jail for his actions at Kent State in 1969.

We had finally found the Weather Underground! Who would have thought to find them at the Alameda Flea Market? They were excited about our serendipitous encounter as well. Howie had been a key Weatherman organizer at Kent State before his incarceration. Bernardine and Bill also appreciated my past history as a central Yippie organizer and visitor to Vietnam.

Perhaps most importantly, they had seen our publication of *Common Victories*, and heard that we had produced it. At that time, many of their supporters were afraid to reproduce WUO materials for fear of being too publicly identified with the WUO. One of the benefits of having no real ties with the WUO was that we felt no compunctions about publicly supporting them. Perhaps because we had nothing to hide, we were unafraid. That was all about to change.

Bernardine and Howie had arranged for a secure way of communicating and eventually the two of us met with both Bill and Bernardine, beginning a series of meetings that quickly led to our joining the organization. From that point on we were part of the Weather Underground Organization, and that step would define the next 15 years of my life.

I liked both Bill and Bernardine but was especially drawn to Bernardine. Connecting again in 1973, I remember being struck by how different Bernardine was from the image of the younger Bernardine in my head. Purposely altering her appearance so as not to be detected, her red-hennaed hair was cut very very short. Gone were the miniskirts and black leather. The high boots were replaced with Chinese slippers. She dressed very casually and simply, yet with taste. She wore the same scent all the time—Kiehl's musk oil—and cooked us a delicious vegetarian soup. Her chosen name was Rose. Bernardine seemed very comfortable in this persona.

But it was more than a matter of changed appearance. The Townhouse explosion and three years of living underground, and the Bernardine of the Flint War Council had given way to someone quite different. The macho bravado was gone. Bernardine was softer around the edges and, despite the mythology, quite essentially sober in her approach to life. She was, of course, as politically determined as ever.

Bernardine was a leader but I also felt like we were becoming friends. She was a good listener and questioner, not so common a trait among movement "heavies," and nothing like what you'd expect from someone on the FBI's Ten Most Wanted List. Despite all that must have been on her mind, she was thoughtful as well. On my birthday she gave me a bar of sandalwood soap and a pair of chopsticks that I have to this day.

Bernardine and Bill kept their physical distance from public political activity but they stayed informed about what was going on both around the U.S. and internationally. Because of them, my political horizon expanded exponentially. They would bring us books and magazines, things I'd never heard of, and we would have great discussions—international works by and about revolutionaries: *Racism and the Class Struggle* by James and Grace Lee Boggs; *The Weapon of Theory* by Amilcar Cabral, the revolutionary leader of Guinea Bissau who was assassinated by agents of Portuguese colonialists in 1973; *The Wretched of the Earth* by Frantz Fanon; *African World,* a newspaper about the African continent; *The Disinherited: Journal of a Palestinian Exile* by Fawaz Turki; *Claridad,* the newspaper of the Puerto Rican Socialist Party. We also began studying Marxism-Leninism, beginning with Lenin's *Imperialism, the Highest Stage of Capitalism.*

The organization had studied the manual of the Tupamaros, the revolutionary guerrillas in Uruguay, and adopted some of their procedures for clandestine survival. Usually we spent a couple of careful hours getting to a meeting and then a couple more getting home without retracing our steps. It was difficult, but necessary. One day there was a knock on the door of our Oakland apartment.

"Who is it?" I asked. I never opened the door without asking.

"Your neighbors from across the street," a woman's voice replied. "Can we come in? We have some information you'll want to know."

I opened the door and in walked two young women.

"I'm Rhoda and this is Susan. We live directly across the street," she said, pointing to her house. "We thought you ought to know. The FBI has been living in the apartment upstairs from us and they have had an arsenal trained on your house. They just moved out yesterday. We're ashamed we didn't tell you sooner but we were afraid. Now they're gone and we thought you ought to at least know."

So. we had real enemies but friends as well, at least in Oakland. Years later when I received my FBI files through the Freedom of Information Act, there was a picture of me with my newborn baby in my arms, stepping out on the porch of that apartment to look around. Others were looking back.

Occasionally we spent an entire weekend "underground," staying at Bill and Bernardine's apartment, where we'd eat homemade soup—Bernardine always made soup—and mostly we'd just talk, talk, talk.

Being with them was like a parallel universe. We were no longer Nancy and Howie; we had transformed into Nina and Sandy, names that we chose. I chose Nina for the wonderful Nina Simone. Bill and Bernardine were wiped from memory; I thought of them only as Joe and Rose. There was a whole lingo constructed so that if a conversation were to be overheard by the wrong people, no red flags would go up. I liked the language. The WUO was referred to as the "Eggplant" while the clandestine part of the organization was the "Forest." The knowledge of the WUO was referred to as the "Joke." So you might ask whether so-and-so knew the "Joke." Different groups within the organization were known as Tribes while the FBI was the "Shoes."

Soon we met other people in the WUO and became part of a collective that met regularly with organizational leaders; Kathy Boudin, one of the survivors of the Townhouse, met with us once or twice. Later our collective of five got together on our own to study and discuss the program and strategy of the organization. We were all public activists but secret members of the WUO.

The organization was moving in a new direction. There were probably several hundred members nationwide and many more supporters. But feelings of isolation—isolation from any mass political activity—were growing. The WUO had gone completely underground at the time of the most widespread disaffection with the war. The move to clandestinity meant increased capacity to carry out actions undetected. It also avoided likely imprisonment for some members who were fugitives. On the other hand, the organization had lost touch with large numbers of people who were then in motion.

With the war coming to an end, it was definitely time to rethink what we were all doing. I was glad to be part of this organization, to join the work of this group of committed people.

Subsequent events increased our sense of political isolation. The Symbionese Liberation Army (SLA) was a predominantly white group located in the Bay Area. Their leader was a Black exprisoner who had taken the name Cinque, the West African man who led a mutiny aboard the Amistad slave ship. We had first heard of the SLA in November of 1973 when they assassinated Marcus Foster, a Black man who was Superintendent of the Oakland Public Schools. He had set up a controversial ID system in the schools, but I couldn't understand why that would justify his assassination. The act seemed so essentially negative. Much of the Movement was condemning the SLA, some accusing them of being agents of the government sent to sully the name of the Left. It was tempting to join the choir. However, this was the same choir that often tried to isolate the WUO, accusing us of being "radical extremists" or even "agent provocateurs." We had seen the government use these kinds of divisions against the movement itself and didn't want to foster such processes.

Then in February of 1974 the SLA kidnapped the newspaper heiress Patty Hearst and held her hostage, demanding that food be distributed to the poor of Oakland. Indeed, a food distribution ensued with thousands of people lining up to receive paper bags full of food. This Robin Hood scenario was more understandable.

While most of the Left was trying to distance themselves from the SLA, the WUO issued a nuanced communiqué emphasizing the injustice of so many hungry people alongside huge accumulations of wealth, and warned the Left not to "do the enemy's work" by positioning their organizations as the "moderate" alternative, the "legitimate" Left in juxtaposition to the SLA.

In May the police trapped the SLA in a safehouse in Los Angeles. The police set fire to the house with incendiary bombs when they refused to immediately surrender. The horrifying inferno was shown on the evening television newscasts. The six SLA members inside (much of the membership) were all either burned alive or shot as they fled the building.

In June the FBI came by our house to question us about the SLA. Neither Howie nor I had ever met any of the people involved. We didn't know the SLA but we did know the FBI. Therefore, we would never talk to FBI agents about anything because they were clearly the enemy and had no positive agenda, only one that would cause pain and suffering to friends or allies. We also understood that once you said anything to them, they would stick to you like flypaper in the hope that you would become an informant, give them information about other people and perhaps testify against others in court. So we said nothing: standard movement procedure.

The few remaining SLA members were soon captured, and while Joe Remiro and Russ Little were being held in the Oakland jail awaiting trial, I visited Russ several times. Although critical of what they had done, I believed that they were revolutionaries and deserved to have sympathetic visitors.

The public position of the WUO denounced the government attack on the SLA, and I agreed with that. However, I also privately felt that the SLA had gone off the deep end. The murder of a Black man, an educator, even if he were misguided, was indefensible and incomprehensible to everybody. I don't think I encountered one person who supported that action. Who were they hoping to organize? More than ever, I felt it was important to devise a plan to connect with a larger mass movement and to unite in practice with a broader group of allies.

PRAIRIE FIRE

The Monty Python movie *The Life of Brian* satirizes the tendency of Left groups to spend more time splitting and bickering than in fighting their common enemy. In the movie, the People's Front of Judea, the Judean People's Front, the Popular Front of Judea, the People's Liberation Front of Judea, and the Campaign for a Free Galilee all wasted time and energy fighting with each other rather than actually opposing the Romans. Funny, for sure, but too close to reality to be comfortable.

The Communist Party U.S.A., founded in 1919, was the mothership of the left-wing political scene for much of the mid-20th century. There were other organizations but even they were defined, in large part, by their relationship (even if it was oppositional) to the CP. Then with the anti-communist witch hunts of Joséph McCarthy and the Stalin revelations, all those groups became less relevant or disappeared altogether. Influenced by the civil rights movement, the 1960s left was dominated by "New Left" organizations such as Students for a Democratic Society. The CP still existed but it became a shadow of its former self while other left-wing organizations also had minimal impact. Then in the 1970s there was once more a proliferation of Marxist and Marxist-Leninist groups of various stripes such as the Revolutionary Union, the October League, the Progressive Labor Party, Workers World Party, Socialist Workers Party, etc., as well as many more local collectives around the country. Some were supporters of China or Albania or Russia. Others considered themselves "Trotskyite," meaning they were followers of the revolutionary Russian leader Leon Trotsky.

We in the WUO hoped for something better than the Monty Python scenario. We were moving toward Marxism-Leninism but felt we had to have a collaborative approach, reaching out to other groups and individuals. We needed to have a solid political idea of what we ourselves believed, but also a willingness to engage in real discussion with others.

Vietnam had served as a central orientation and organizing focus for our movement. Now with the peace treaty in Vietnam, conditions were very different. The WUO wanted to rethink the situation. It was decided that after considerable internal struggle, a political document would be written that explained the politics of the WUO. The discussion and writing of the document would be important for the consolidation of the organization. It would then be produced as a book and used to stimulate discussion with other individual activists and groups. Printed and distributed secretly at first, it would later be reprinted and distributed as widely as possible.

The debate about the content of the book had been going on before Howie and I met up with Bernardine and the book was in fact now close to publication. After several months of meetings and study with the WUO, Bernardine explained, "The first printing of the book will be a clandestine operation. It has been written, discussed, and revised and is nearing completion. We're beginning the process of typesetting, illustrating, laying out, printing, binding and then distributing. This will all be done clandestinely. But we need your help for the next phase. We're proposing that the two of you work on a public reprinting of the book. It will be a different edition, with supposedly no connection to the Underground, with different design, graphics and all, to give it a different look."

Our first step was a visit to the Red Dragon Print Collective, where the clandestine version was being printed. The trip was a cloak-and-dagger affair. We flew into a distant airport and were met by two WUO members who blindfolded us in preparation for our journey by car to the destination. Information in the organization was generally on a "Need to Know" basis, a basic principle of clandestine practice. Most members knew very limited information about others in the organization. We didn't know people's real identities, who participated in what activities, or where people in clandestinity lived and worked.

Howie and I didn't actually need to see the Print Collective, but the Weather Bureau (as the leadership group was known) thought it would be an inspiration. And it most certainly was. How remarkable to be able to put together such an operation while being sought by the government and functioning with refashioned identities. Not only was the organization able to survive and carry out militant actions, I reflected, it was able to advance in other sophisticated and important ways. I was impressed. I returned to California more excited than ever about the work ahead.

One night in July of 1974, *Prairie Fire, the Politics of Revolutionary Anti-imperialism, Political Statement of the Weather Underground,* was released. The name of the book, "*Prairie Fire*" was a reference to a quote by Mao Tse Tung: "A single spark can cause a *Prairie Fire.*" The 158-page book was distributed around the country, secretly under the cover of darkness, to bookstores, Movement printing presses, community groups, newspapers, etc. Anonymous phone calls the next day advised bookstores that they could either sell the books or give them away free.

The appearance of the book caused quite a stir. The UPI wire service reported that the books were "snapped up within hours by radicals wanting to know the current thinking of the group." *The Citizen Journal* of Columbus, Ohio stated that the books "mysteriously were left outside store doors across the nation ... Within hours the books were gobbled up by radicals eager for the current thinking of the group." News stories and book reviews also appeared in such diverse places as: *The New York Times, The Minneapolis Tribune, The San Francisco Chronicle, The Berkeley Barb, The Guardian,* the Madison, Wisconsin *Daily Cardinal,* and *Crawdaddy.*

Not surprisingly, it was Black, Puerto Rican, and Native American activists who felt the most unity with our politics. Ramon Arbona of the Puerto Rican Socialist Party (PSP) reviewed the book in their publication *Claridad,* applauding the WUO's emphasis on "anti-imperialism as the central force that defines its struggle and gives it direction." He went on to say that the WUO's position on the Puerto Rican struggle is "the best of all the positions advanced by the different left organizations in the U.S."

Others were excited by the self-criticisms as well as the general line of thinking presented by the book. *The Michigan Free Press* praised the book and welcomed the WUO's self-criticism of "its macho romantic sexism." They also committed themselves to raising money to reprint 3,500 additional copies of *Prairie Fire.*

A number of the reviews expressed political differences, but a general openness to engaging in dialogue. *The Columbus Free Press* reported that:

> *"Underground newspapers received one copy, a bookstore got 50 copies, a prison library project was sent 100 copies. Nobody knew where they came from.... There is probably not a single FP staffer who agrees with all of the Weather people's politics. But we all recognize the importance of the existence of an underground strong enough to carry on 5 years' worth of study and armed struggle, and collectively write, publish and distribute a whole book of revolutionary theory."*

An anonymous criticism appeared, titled "WHY ARE GAY PEOPLE SO ANGRY? A criticism of *Prairie Fire* from a Gay Man." All he could find in the book, he said, was "something vague, detached, patronizing, and reflecting all of the oppression that the New Left inflicts on gay people, especially gay men." His criticism presaged important developments that would deepen in the next decade: an activist gay movement spurred on by the AIDS epidemic with a profound critique of U.S. society, from gender relationships to the healthcare system. However, at the time of his criticism, I have to honestly admit that my own heterosexist lens kept me from seeing the power of this man's argument.

Some old friends weighed in as well. I hadn't seen most of them since I'd left the Yippies in 1970, and I doubt they knew I was involved in the *Prairie Fire* project. Nonetheless the ideas of the WUO, despite whatever disagreements existed, were important enough to demand engagement and comment. One such person was Pun Plamondon, my old White Panther Party pal, whose wife Genie had been one of my traveling companions on the Vietnam trip. In the early '70s, Pun was indicted for the 1968 bombing of the Ann Arbor CIA office, placed on the Ten Most Wanted list, spent some time as a fugitive and then close to three years in prison. Writing in *The Ann Arbor Sun,* he now took issue with what he saw as *Prairie Fire* positing all forms of struggle as equal. He asserted that at this time "mass struggle takes precedence over clandestine struggle, peaceful over violent ... To promote armed struggle at this initial stage is a needless waste of beautiful revolutionaries, as the SLA debacle clearly proves."

An old Berkeley friend, Michael Lerner (later reinvented as Rabbi Michael Lerner) wrote a piece in the liberal/ moderate socialist *New American Movement* (NAM) newspaper. He decried the WUO's "lack of vision that still keeps the Weather Underground from seeing how an American working class could be a creative and central part in the revolutionary struggle."

My old Yippie friend Stew Albert, writing in the pages of *Crawdaddy,* welcomed the book. He asked, however, "What event will change the worker's head, and what can we do to consciously speed up the process? A few sentences about 'going to the people' just won't suffice."

The reliably radical William Kunstler admired the "plea for unity and the fact that the book does not condemn any Left organization," adding that "an active underground is the healthiest thing in a country like this."

The only woman to write her own review was Maisie M writing for *Plexus,* the Bay Area Women's newspaper. She stated that "*Prairie Fire* is Marxism at its most constructive ... To integrate a consciousness of racism and sexism with a Marxist class analysis is the purpose of *Prairie Fire.* It is a bold attempt that paves the way for a re-opening of this long brushed over topic."

Maizie lived in the Bay Area and became a part of our Prairie Fire Organizing Committee. However, we wanted to reach more people and also take up this dialogue more directly with activists around the country. The next question for the WUO was how to make this happen.

ON THE ROAD

IT WAS TIME TO GET the word out, and groups of WUO supporters were simultaneously formed in New York and California—Prairie Fire Distributing Committees—to get the job done. In the Bay Area, the five members of our secret WUO collective called for a Bay Area Prairie Fire Distributing Committee (PFDC). About thirty people responded and attended the first meeting where it was decided to organize discussion groups and take on the task of distribution.

Our WUO collective continued to meet secretly as a group, at times with leaders of the WUO. We were among the thirty people at the first PFDC meeting. In a sense this was a part of the WUO peeking out of the shadows.

By now Howie and I were living behind a friend's house on Blake Street in Berkeley, in a garage with no heat except for a potbelly stove. There was no running water in the garage, so it was entertaining to run through the rain to go to the bathroom in the main house. But this idyll was not to last. The second stage of work around the reprinting of *Prairie Fire* was about to begin.

Howie and I had signed onto the task months before and now we were to leave within days for Eugene, Oregon, where Clayton Van Lydegraf was already at work with the radical Jackrabbit Press. The three of us, along with Jackrabbit Press, would produce another version of the book for more mass distribution. We packed a couple of small bags and off we went. Howie's college friend Robin worked for Planned Parenthood in the area and was gracious enough to put us up.

It was exhilarating to wake up each morning to the dense evergreen forest within a stone's throw. We finally got our wish to hike in and around the deep green mountains of the Northwest. Overall, however, the experience was miserable.

I had a difficult time working with Van (as everybody referred to him) but that didn't obscure my understanding that he was an amazing person. Born in 1915, Van was 60 years old at the time we met. With long gray hair and a full beard, he looked like Karl Marx's brother. Van was a serious Marxist-Leninist and one of the few members of the Old Left who grasped the significance and vibrancy of the movements of the 1960s. While others of his age and political background had made peace with capitalism, Van remained a relentless revolutionary. He had served as a pilot in the U.S. Air Force during World War II and was an important member of the Seattle, Washington, Communist Party until he broke with the CP sometime in the 1950s due to political differences. For a while he was a member of the pro-Chinese Progressive Labor Party, but parted ways with that organization as well.

In 1956 Van was an "unfriendly witness" during the HUAC hearings. His participation in progressive activities did not let up, and in 1973 he was subpoenaed to (and defied) a federal grand jury in San Francisco. Van had also written several pieces that influenced many of us in and around the WUO, particularly "The Movement and the Workers" and "The Object is to Win."

It is difficult to sort out in retrospect what occurred between Van and me. Working together was a jagged process. Our disagreements over the layout of the book were political in nature. The only one I recall specifically was about including a picture of Ethel and Julius Rosenberg in the book. Van was vehemently opposed. Perhaps he saw them as a symbol of the Communist Party. Van hated "the Party" and felt it had betrayed the people's movements. I, on the other hand, (the Red Diaper Baby) thought that the Rosenbergs had died for "the revolution" and ought to be acknowledged with a picture. I "won" that struggle since Howie and I could outvote Van, but it was perhaps an unfair and pyrrhic victory.

Van was part of the WUO and had helped write the book, but he also seemed to be in conflict with the leadership in some way that I wasn't really privy to. And now there was this tension between Van and myself as well. I thought male chauvinism was at the root of our skirmishes. He probably saw me as a disrespectful upstart with revisionist politics. At one point, things got so bad that Bill Ayers (aka Joe aka Bill) came up from the Bay Area to mediate. What's more, after frequent hikes in the woods, I was covered with a very nasty case of poison oak that had made the month-long experience even more unpleasant.

Eventually, however, we managed to produce a book, and Jackrabbit Press printed thousands of them, giving us much more to work with. About 35,000 such copies were distributed without assistance from a corporate publisher; yet another example of the strength of alternative institutions at that time.

In October of 1974 Howie and I traveled to New York to attend the huge Madison Square Rally for Puerto Rican Independence. Since the 1930s, the Nationalist Party under Pedro Albizu Campos had led the struggle for Puerto Rican Independence. Despite fierce repression by the U.S., including the imprisonment of their leader, assassinations, and the brutal suppression of the Jayuya uprising in 1950, the party soldiered on. In 1954, four Nationalists led by Lolita Lebron unfurled a Puerto Rican flag in the gallery of the U.S. Congress, shouted "Viva Puerto Rico Libre!" and began shooting. Four congressmen were wounded and the Nationalists were captured. Twenty years later, they were still in prison.

Now, in 1974, 20,000 people were jammed into "the Garden" and, under huge portraits of the Puerto Rican Nationalists, entertainers, and celebrities addressed the crowd, calling for independence for Puerto Rico and the release of the Nationalist political prisoners. Howie and I participated and left, fired up for our next adventure.

In the fall of 1974, a few months after the release of *Prairie Fire,* we were ready to embark on an unusual journey around the country, a trip by five PFDC members to discuss the book with supporters and other interested parties. All of us were "supporters" of the politics of *Prairie Fire* (and secretly WUO members). Our job was to engage in a dialogue about how we could continue building a revolutionary mass movement.

Depending on how you date it, there had been by then a decade or more of radical, New Left political history. There were many experiences, some victories and certainly some failures, to reflect upon. The anti-war movement was much diminished, and to some extent the counterculture as well. Yes, the '60s were over but, in the wake, there were literally thousands of people who believed, in one way or another, that a radical transformation of the United States was necessary if we were to pursue a genuinely human society. Some of these were small informal collectives with little ability to connect nationally. Others were much larger organizations of hundreds of people gathered around a well-defined political ideology. What they all had in common was the inability, and even an adamant refusal, to talk to each other in an effort to find common ground. The Left was becoming more sectarian as political views (lines) hardened; or, if not sectarian, at least unwilling to put themselves out in the world and subject their ideas to conflicting opinions.

The WUO saw itself as uniquely situated to move into this void. Thousands of people had great respect for the organization. Some had profound political differences with the WUO but nonetheless viewed the organization as a dedicated, skilled group of people with a real willingness to sacrifice. Political activists and leaders with years of experience agreed to meet with us because we were representatives of the WUO.

By the time the trip was being planned, I was more intensely studying and participating in discussions in both the WUO and in the PFDC. We were still reading works by contemporary revolutionaries around the world. But we were also more intensively reading classic Marxism-Leninism, and discussing the need for a communist party. Although born a Red Diaper Baby, the only Marx I had read was in college, and even then just *The Communist Manifesto* and a bit of his early writings. Now I was moving into a different phase. We were reading Lenin's *What Is to Be Done?* and *Imperialism, the Highest Stage of Capitalism.* My trip to Vietnam as well as my disappointment with the limits of the Yippie process left me open to embracing Marxism-Leninism.

In November of 1974 the five of us set out to travel first through the Midwest and then through the South. The itinerary was planned in advance, contacting people the WUO knew personally and pursuing others whose work was thought to be significant. Spending about five days in each place, we sent detailed reports back home to our friends and comrades after our experiences in each city.

For the trip as a whole, we set several inter-related tasks for ourselves. First of all, there was a recession going on with inflation and unemployment on the rise. We wanted to understand what conditions were like in different parts of the nation and how the Left might be able to participate in and enhance people's struggles.

Secondly, as I already mentioned, we wanted to be in dialogue with other activists. Part of such a process would have to be navigating and challenging the sectarianism of the Left.

Thirdly, we wanted to seek opportunities to go beyond political activists and to talk with "the man and the woman on the street" to test out our ideas with non-Movement people. We knew that this kind of "mass work" could not be successfully carried out by people in town for a couple of days or hours, but it was a direction we were committed to, a breaking out of the narrow confines of the Left.

Finally, we hoped to meet with individual women and women's groups wherever we went, in order to deepen our own practice around women's liberation and to help strengthen that aspect of the Movement. We felt that much of the organized Left was male-dominated, incorrectly dismissive of women's contributions as "bourgeois feminism," and threatened by women's self-organization. We wanted the Left to be something different.

We traveled by car, and sometimes bus, from city to city, occasionally dividing up and then reconvening. Our itinerary included a number of college towns or areas where there were substantial counter-cultural youth communities—Ann Arbor, Madison, the Twin Cities (Minneapolis and St. Paul)—where we were very positively received and even embraced. We also went to major cities such as Detroit and Chicago.

Many of the people we met with expressed general agreement with the politics of *Prairie Fire* and support for the WUO bombings because they were connected to mass struggle and to things people cared about. Some thought the actions were premature because most people couldn't relate to them. Others thought that because of the growing dissatisfaction with the economy and the government, more people might be in a place to understand them.

We were welcomed by activists in Chicago's growing Puerto Rican community, who were appreciative of *Prairie Fire*'s support for the Independence Movement. (Who could foresee that within seven years I would be living in Chicago and that very same Puerto Rican community would have a huge impact on just about every aspect of my life?) Activists in factories, concentrating on union and workplace issues, were more skeptical of us. Organized Left parties such as the Revolutionary Union (RU) were generally downright opposed to our ideas.

First after Chicago was Detroit, clearly already an industrial city in decline with a one-crop economy (the automobile industry). We took a guided tour of the Chrysler-Plymouth plant, a mammoth operation; we noted that a great percentage of the workers were either black or long-haired youth. We took this as confirmation of the "changing nature of the working class" as discussed in *Prairie Fire*: "The interpenetration of women's consciousness, youth consciousness, and Third World national identity are great channels through which [workers'] class consciousness— ... can be irrigated and made fertile."

Some of us, myself included, were enthusiastic about leafleting the auto plants with flyers about *Prairie Fire*, to see what kind of discussion we could stimulate. Others felt it would be meaningless and arrogant of us to pop in as outsiders, leaflet and then be gone. We gave it up completely when our hosts insisted it would hurt their work, particularly because there was already a real distrust of national groups based on past experience. Everywhere we went, in each of our travel destinations, we tried to organize women's meetings. In Detroit we got together with a group of six socialist women who expressed their deep estrangement from the feminist movement. We encouraged them not to write off "bourgeois student feminists" and expressed our belief in the need for a feminist force within the radical movement.

We were expected in Madison when the opportunity arose to meet with James and Grace Lee Boggs. This was too important to miss so we temporarily split up. Howie and I had roots in Madison so we took off while the three others remained to meet with the Boggses. James Boggs, an African-American Marxist intellectual and labor activist, had authored important political works such as *The American Revolution: Pages from a Negro Worker's Notebook* (1963). He had been an autoworker at the Chrysler plant from 1940 to 1968. Grace Lee Boggs was a Chinese-American activist. Together they had written *Racism and the Class Struggle*, a book that all of us in the WUO had studied. They had worked closely with the West Indian Marxist historian C.L.R. James, and were an important part of radical history. We were told that the Boggs viewed the WUO as a group of people who were seriously attempting to grapple with how to transform society and therefore they agreed to meet with us.

When our group reconnected, the others recounted to me and Howie that the Boggses had been quite critical of the politics of *Prairie Fire*. Their differences were many—and emphatic:

> *"You (the WUO) are "third worlders" who use an international perspective to avoid the task of making revolution here. Anti-imperialism as a strategy is starting from the wrong point. It is not national liberation that is needed or women's liberation. What people in the U.S. need, is "revolution," not "liberation." The WUO romanticizes workers, prisoners, people on welfare. The working class moves around selfishness and until that changes, nothing good can come. The rebellion at Attica was "adventurist," a battle against the state that couldn't possibly be won. Sectarianism is not the problem. It is liberalism that is the main pitfall."*

I didn't agree (mostly), but I certainly took it to heart and mulled it over respectfully, and it became part of our report back to the WUO leadership.

After the Midwest trip and a week for R&R, we headed south. As a group we were unfamiliar with the South and this was my first trip to this foreboding area of the country that I had heard so much about. I viewed it primarily as an investigative learning experience.

North Carolina is tobacco land. A friend in Durham took the five of us on a public tour of Liggett and Meyers, L&M. Whew! "Dedicated to the millions who smoke the cigarette that satisfies." That's what their plaque said. The factory workers, many of them women, were a lot older and whiter than the workers in the Detroit auto plant. The noise was overwhelming and people were wearing earplugs. The Black people who did work there seemed to have the lousiest jobs. But L&M "paid well." Once you quit, we were told, you could never come back, so most people never quit. We learned that more people were on death row in North Carolina than in all other states put together and that Durham was a city where there seemed to be two of everything—universities, hospitals—one for Blacks and one for whites, with the latter far more highly endowed.

The mass media in North Carolina was full of stories about important struggles around prisoners. We had never heard of the case of JoAnn Little—a 20-year-old Black woman facing first degree murder charges who would go on to become the first woman in U.S. history to be acquitted using the defense that she had employed deadly force to resist a rape, in her case by a prison guard. (Some of us would later join the work of defending her.)

We met with Owusu Sadaukai (previously and subsequently known as Howard Fuller), another iconic figure willing to engage in discussion with us. After visiting liberated zones in Mozambique, Owusu had founded the African Liberation Support Committee (ALSC) which had mobilized thousands in the U.S. to march against Portuguese colonialism in Africa and against white settler rule in South Africa. Owusu was now involved with labor organizing in the hospitals in Durham.

Owusu maintained that the central task of Black revolutionaries was to root themselves in the working class, to learn Marxism-Leninism toward building a multi-national communist party. He questioned *Prairie Fire*'s position on self-determination. He took issue with the following statement in the book: "Whatever decisions Black people and other oppressed peoples make in exercising this right to self-determination, white revolutionaries and anti-imperialists have a very clear-cut responsibility to support these decisions once they are arrived at." (*Prairie Fire*, p. 122)

Owusu argued that revolutionaries had a responsibility to struggle where there are differences. Yes, white revolutionaries were racist toward the Black movement in the past, but on the other hand, uncritical support is not helpful either. "We're trying to develop new people, new organizations," he argued, "and we don't want to compound the errors of the past by going too far in the other direction. What if secession of Black people in the south is what some revolutionaries are demanding, but it would put the whole struggle in jeopardy? What would that mean to you?"

Here he was criticizing *Prairie Fire*'s position that Black people had the right to form a separate nation in the South. He argued that "Stalin laid out the position that Black people were a nation in the South. But it's a mechanical application with no reality to it."

In parting, Owusu urged us to "go to the class—ideologically and physically ... And study. That's crucial. That's what you should be doing."

Duke University is known as the Harvard of the South. A compliment, I suppose. We had a meeting with about 30 people with one day's notice in the middle of exam period. Many of them were in the New American Movement (NAM). The discussion centered around the common issues that had been raised in other places—armed struggle and the class question. However, some of attendees were quite combative and we were less prepared than we would have liked to have been. At the end we criticized them for their sectarian attitudes, for not conducting themselves in a comradely manner. After the meeting the NAM people accepted the criticism and invited us to a party. We went, dutifully, but it wasn't all that much fun.

We took a short side trip to Greensboro where we met with the Youth Organization for Black Unity (YOBU), a primarily student organization that produced *African World*, the excellent newspaper that we all had been reading. The focus once more was on class and armed struggle.

They felt we all needed to be asking, "Where do you begin to entrench yourself in the working class?" They suggested that bombings avoid the real work within the class, and that the industrial proletariat rejects violence. We said the white working class in South Boston didn't seem to have much difficulty using violence in their fight against Black folks and busing. We reasserted the necessity for mass work and argued for the connection between mass work and armed activity.

Our Southern trip ended with brief stopovers in Atlanta and Lowndes County, Alabama. My most vivid memories are from Lowndes County, where 80 per cent of the Black people there lived below the poverty line, and not a single Black resident was registered to vote. I had never seen anything like it, and couldn't shake the feeling that we had traveled overseas to an extremely poor Third World nation. There was not a white person around for miles and miles and miles. It was a completely agrarian society with miles of small shacks, and chickens and other animals running around freely. Here we did not have long ideological discussions. We were there with eyes wide open to learn as we struggled to absorb the fact that such a place existed in these United States.

So concluded our trip around the country. Exhausted mentally and physically, we were all ready to go home. It was time to digest what we had learned and to mull it over with our friends and comrades.

When I think about that trip today, I am struck by the breadth and diversity of radical activity that existed throughout the country in the mid-70s, and the reservoir of support that there was for the WUO, as well as a willingness on the part of many others to engage in discussion with us. Thousands of people, influenced by the upheaval of the '60s, were active with the intention of radically transforming American society. They seemed willing to adjust their lives to make it happen.

The trip made it clear that if the Left were to advance in any meaningful way, both women and women's liberation would have to be more seriously incorporated. Radicals would need to support the independent organizing of women. The other issues that were raised over and over again were armed struggle and the necessity of organizing the working class. Everywhere we went we argued for the centrality of race and the importance of solidarity with the struggles of Third World people (what is now referred to as "people of color") both within the United States and globally. We also continued to argue for the necessity of building an armed movement to go hand in hand with the activity of a mass movement. The issues raised about "class," particularly coming from Black activists such as Sadaukai and the Boggses, were challenging. How could we integrate a class perspective and practice with a commitment to anti-racism and anti-imperialism? We thought we had begun to do so in the publication of *Prairie Fire*, but would we be able to deepen our understanding and put it into practice?

Interestingly enough, there was an important tendency in the struggle of Black people that we did not visit—Black Nationalism. Had we done so, we would have encountered different arguments that might have led to different consequences. At that time I didn't have a good grasp of the different currents among Black radicals. In any event, I had little to do with the planning of who we visited and was not privy to the decision making. I was still learning.

HARD TIMES CONFERENCE

The impact of the trip across the country reinforced what many people in the WUO had been thinking. There was an economic recession and people were suffering. As an organization composed largely of activists who had come from the campuses, we felt we needed to change our practice, to reach out and "broaden the class base" of our organization.

Our politics were significantly different from that of most other groups that were trying to organize among working people. Marx predicted that the industrial proletariat in the capitalist countries would lead in overthrowing the system; that was its historic mission. We felt that the old Left and many of the new Marxist-Leninist (M-L) groups that sprung up in the 1960s and '70s mechanically embraced traditional Marxism without taking into consideration contemporary reality. Since according to Marx only the industrial proletariat could overthrow capitalism and install socialism, these M-L groups often downplayed racism and argued that the demands of Black people had to be postponed or muted because they would "divide the class" by alienating white workers.

Our years of experience in the civil rights and anti-war movements pointed us in the WUO in a different direction. We intended to be part of organizing the working class without selling out the demands of people of color, by following the lead of Black and other third world workers who were now in strategic working-class positions within the steel, auto, chemical, and transportation industries. At the same time, we would continue to support the struggles of people of color outside the workplace—poor, unemployed and imprisoned people.

We wanted to be different from the other M-L groups in another major way. The women's liberation movement was burgeoning, breaking out all over, and we wanted to be a part of that motion as well. On our trip we had made it a point to have women's meetings wherever we went, and we intended to continue to support the struggle of women. We felt it was inadequate to define a woman's class solely by her role in the workforce since many women were engaged in unpaid labor—caring for children, elders, husband, and home.

The WUO was developing a strategy that could put us in a position to help lead, along with many others, a mass movement in response to the economic recession. We were determined to avoid the historical errors of the past that had swept the problems of racism and sexism under the rug; we intended rather to keep them up front and foremost. Nor did we want to ignore the role the U.S. played globally. We were eager to build an anti-imperialist movement based in the U.S. working class.

We would be different. We would become working class organizers without falling into the racism and sexism of the other M-L groups. We WOULD be different.

The next year was spent developing the PFDC as it evolved into the Prairie Fire Organizing Committee (PFOC). It seemed important to become a more permanent political group committed to organizing. But as time went on, tensions within the group developed. There was, as I previously explained, our secret collective of WUO members who were leaders of the PFOC. From the point of view of this WUO core, it was important to maintain control over the direction of the Prairie Fire Organizing Committee, a group that was really, in its origins, a public extension of the Weather Underground.

Van Lydegraf was no longer part of the WUO. Whatever differences existed, they had become too acute for him to remain a member.

However, he played an increasingly active leadership role in PFOC, and he had strong ideas about the direction we should take. One central difference was whether or not PFOC should become a communist cadre organization—with internal discipline and a unified "line." Van argued "yes." We argued "no." As far as we were concerned, we were already in a communist cadre organization, the WUO, and wanted PFOC to be its arm for mass organizing. Van, of course, knew all about this involvement with the WUO. He knew we were secret members of the WUO with allegiance to that organization above all. His strategy was to take PFOC in a different direction because he disagreed with the political direction the WUO was taking.

The WUO was developing a strategy to broaden the movement by calling for a national Hard Times Conference. The idea, in part generated by our trip around the Midwest and South, was to respond aggressively to the economic recession that was gripping the nation in the '70s, and to call for a massive conference in Chicago. We hoped that organizations, collectives and individuals around the country would join together, launch a national campaign to fight against the "Hard Times," and in the process, reinvigorate a mass movement that we would help lead. Most of 1974 and 1975 was spent organizing for this conference.

During this time, the WUO published and distributed a magazine entitled *Osawatomie.* The militant abolitionist John Brown was sometimes known as Osawatomie Brown, a name derived from the area in Kansas where he led a fierce battle against pro-slavery militias, and the magazine was named in his honor.

Right about that same time I became pregnant with my first child. Howie and I decided we needed to move from the garage with no heat and no bathroom. We found a new apartment in North Oakland along with our friend Miriam and her two daughters. Miriam and the girls had been living in a well-known Berkeley collective, the Derby Dump, but were also ready for a somewhat more conventional lifestyle. We rented side-by-side apartments on 41st Street in Oakland. It felt like the height of luxury. We had a shared washer/dryer and a lovely backyard that

Miriam planted with all kinds of flowers and veggies. We had dinner together several times a week and helped each other out.

My pregnancy was physically easy and wonderful. We had no money, but friends gave us hand-me-down maternity clothes. For a changing table we got a secondhand dresser, painted it light blue and white, and covered it with foam. A brightly colored Chinese painting hung above the changing table—a surreal picture of mango-colored fish leaping through the air. With the addition of a second-hand cradle, hand-me-down baby clothes and things, we were all set. Toward the end of my pregnancy Howie was briefly hospitalized with a collapsed lung. I was grateful to be living in a collective setting, and most particularly to have Miriam's support to help me get through that rough patch.

Meanwhile, the debate in PFOC intensified and became quite acrimonious. Van and those who supported him believed that the Hard Times strategy was wrong. He argued that we should be building a communist organization as opposed to our emphasis on mass organizing. Most importantly, he took issue with the "political line" of the Hard Times Conference. Van maintained that the literature we published as well as the talks we gave as we organized were an abandonment of our core politics, minimizing the different impact the economic recession was having on people of color and white people in the U.S. He argued that we were ignoring the fact that the U.S. is actually an oppressor nation that holds whole nations captive—the Black Nation, Native American Nations, Chicago/Mexicanos and the territory of Puerto Rico—and that we were abandoning support for those struggles.

Van asserted that these politics also sold out the independent struggle of women. Women in PFOC added weight to Van's argument by decrying a piece that appeared in *Osawatomie* titled "The Women's Question Is a Class Question," which emphasized economic issues. It did not address male supremacy, violence against women, reproductive rights, lesbianism, or the right of women to self-organize.

This "opportunist" line also involved a backing away from armed struggle as a necessity for revolution in the U.S. It was not stated publicly but there was an underlying suspicion that the WUO was intending to "invert," to surface the organization and try to cut the losses as much as possible in order to become primarily a public organization which would then lead mass struggle. In short, Van and others believed we were going the way of most white Left organizations, developing a racist and sexist ideology and practice, and abandoning people of color, women and all militancy.

As the debate intensified in PFOC, it also intensified within the Weather Underground Organization. I attended a cadre school that took place in a magnificent home right on the Pacific Ocean a few hours north of San Francisco. There were members of the WUO from around the country at the school. I had been to a cadre school once before and it was an interesting and inspiring experience, meeting other members of the WUO, some of whom I had never met and others known to me before but not as members of the organization. Studying and learning together with like-minded people was great.

This time, however, was different. I found myself sobbing to Bernardine, totally confused about what I thought or what was the correct way to move in the situation. I felt completely torn up about remaining true to our politics regarding women, third world liberation struggles inside the U.S., and armed struggle on the one hand, and on the other hand wanting to reach more people, to broaden out and foster the development of a real mass movement based among working people. It didn't help that I was in my last trimester of pregnancy.

By now I was employed as a secretarial temp for the Oakland Unified School District. I had had amniocentesis and learned that I would be having a baby girl. I wrote to my parents that some nights I didn't get much sleep: "Just as I settled down to bed, the baby woke up and really started moving around. I think she was playing kickball most of the night. If you have to lose sleep, that's the nicest way."

A new life can kick off old memories as well. I had broken with many of my old Yippie friends, and lost touch with others. The saddest loss for me was Phil Ochs, that gentle soul. I knew he had been badly shaken by the violence in Chicago. I knew he had gone to Chile during the Allende years and made friends with folk singer Victor Jara, who was tortured and killed during the coup. I had heard he was depressed and drinking heavily. So when he played a concert in Santa Cruz, Howie and I drove down to meet him. It was a brief, sad rendezvous. I was surprised to see him looking so old, bloated and blue. He wanted us to stay and hang out after the show, but uncomfortably pregnant, I didn't feel up to it, so we headed home. Phil took his own life a few months later. Wish I had stayed.

The Hard Times Conference was planned for January of 1976 in Chicago. The baby was due two weeks before the Hard Times Conference so Howie and I knew we wouldn't be attending. As it turned out, she had a mind of her own from the start and arrived two weeks late. At the exact time of the Conference I was recovering in Alta Bates Hospital. I had prepared myself for a completely natural childbirth but that was not in the stars because my rebellious baby was in a position that resulted in a long, arduous back labor that ended with a Cesarean section. Through the fog of dissipating anesthesia I heard the nurse practitioner say, "You have a beautiful baby girl," as she handed me my daughter. She was perfect with a big mop of dark hair. We named her Rosa Machel. "Rosa" for my beloved Aunt Roz who had died a few years earlier of breast cancer, and also for Bernardine whose clandestine name at that time was Rose, and finally, after Rosa Parks, who 20 years earlier had refused to move to the back of the bus. The "M" was for Howie's grandfather, Max, and for Josina Machel, a revolutionary from Mozambique who had been married to Samora Machel, the leader of the liberation movement that had won Mozambique's independence from Portugal.

An activist friend was an orderly at Alta Bates Hospital and he pushed me down the hall to my room, where I listened to the Hard Times Conference as it was broadcast over KPFA radio while recovering from the Cesarean. Hard Times indeed! Has any conference ever been such a numerical success and yet had such negative consequences? Two thousand activists attended who were involved in a broad array of activities around the country, just as we had planned—but the conference itself was completely wrought with dissension, just as Van and others predicted. Although unplanned for and perhaps discouraged by the conference organizers, a Black caucus as well as a women's caucus immediately began to meet. They felt they were being disregarded, disrespected, and excluded. The Black caucus proposed that Imari Obadele of the Republic of New Africa (RNA), a respected Black Nationalist group, speak at the plenary, but he was prevented from doing so by the organizers. "Racism" and "Betrayal!" cried many. The rest of the conference was dominated by these tensions and no future program was developed. I was actually glad to have missed that conference and to have my awesome baby girl in my arms. I was in love.

RECTIFICATION

The Dylanesque "Weather Bureau" had by now morphed into the five-member Central Committee of the WUO, reflecting the shift toward more traditional Marxism-Leninism. They looked on from underground in dismay as the Hard Times Conference collapsed. On the other hand, many others who were present, including most members of the Prairie Fire Organizing Committee, understood in a flash that we had all made a big mistake. For years we had fought for an understanding of racism that made it central to any U.S. organizing strategy. We had deep respect for the Republic of New Africa, which, in the spirit of Malcolm X, had signed a declaration stating that Black people were a separate nation with the right to independence in the Deep South.

After the debacle of the Hard Times Conference, there was an internal "rectification" process in PFOC. The word "rectification" was drawn from the language of the Chinese revolution where people went through an intense process of admitting their "errors" before being welcomed back into the struggle. I will not venture an opinion about how it played out in China, but I am sure our experience with "rectification" was not to be emulated. There was a lot of finger pointing and blaming. Led by the leadership of PFOC, people who had worked together closely for years were described as "betraying" the movement and in need of "rectification."

I had been wracked by indecision before the conference, but the Hard Times events appeared to bring some clarity, along with a deep sadness.

Alas, the criticisms of Van and others seemed confirmed. Most PFOC members felt similarly, although some left the organization at that point rather than go through "rectification." I chose to stay and attempt to "change my own views." I wrote a series of "self-criticisms," full of jargon and some insight, over the course of the next couple of years and eventually ended up back in good graces with the leadership, and over time, became a second tier leader of the group as well.

I was forbidden by the leadership of PFOC to have any contact whatsoever with the underground as a condition of my "probation." Some people were arbitrarily considered better than others. Friendships and relationships were torn asunder. Usually women were seen as having more potential for rectification than men. I suppose that was a nice inversion of the usual power relations, but still not so great. This caused a good deal of tension between people, including Howie and me. We both wanted to remain in PFOC, but his status was more tenuous. I was on probation. He was suspended. Honestly, I believe it was more a matter of who the new leadership had an affinity for. I could be "rectified" because one of the women leaders had taken a liking to me. Conducting business this way did not bode well for the future. It left a rancid taste and encouraged future splitting and a lack of solidarity among those left standing.

This "rectification" process that began in PFOC quickly became internal to the Weather Underground Organization as a whole and was reflected in the magazine *Osawatomie*. In June of 1976 the WUO issued a self-criticism, then a second in October. Soon something called the Revolutionary Committee (RC) announced that there was now a "split" in the WUO, acknowledging that there was no longer a unified organization. It seemed like "rectification" in fact meant not really a split, but the disintegration of the WUO.

In November, Bernardine Dohrn issued a statement of her own, embracing the criticisms and seemingly joining with the politics of the Prairie Fire Organizing Committee and the RC. She acknowledged that the "culmination of this strategy was to be inversion, the word we used to describe surfacing the entire organization.... Inversion sums up the total negation of the original principles which founded the WUO—support for national liberation movements and armed struggle."

I still felt great affection for Bernardine and was hopeful that she and I would once more be comrades. However, as a condition of my "rectification," I had agreed to sever all ties with the old leaders of the WUO, and did not see any of them until years later. Practically speaking I could not have found her even if I had wanted to. Even in the best of times I did not see the old leaders often, and could never just call them to say, "Hey, let's go for a cup of coffee and talk this through." It was always a convoluted process to safely meet with them and I had lost the thread. I have only glimpses of their personal political journey from 1976 until the time they surfaced in 1980. I'm sure it was a painful and difficult period for them. Personally, I missed the friendship of Bernardine and Bill, but I was committed to building a revolutionary organization and did whatever needed to be done to remain a part of the process.

With the WUO splintering and people jumping ship, it must have been a very dangerous and frightening time for all those living underground. Who to trust? Who to put faith in? After all those years of sustaining one another, each man and woman lived for themselves.

The same month that Bernardine's statement was issued, November of 1976, a national conference of the Prairie Fire Organizing Committee was held in Boston. We were now the people who had accepted the criticisms of the Hard Times Conference and were supposedly united in our thinking. However, this would be the last such conference. As it happened, the east and west coast divisions split, once more recalling the Monty Python movie, *The Life of Brian*, in which the Judean Liberation Front splits with the Front for the Liberation of Judea. All I remember from this meeting is the East Coast women screaming at us that we were bourgeois and that "working class women lead the revolution." I remember also believing that the split had to do with the East Coast viewing us as reformist, unwilling to really carry out armed struggle. Perhaps we shared in this feeding frenzy as well. In any event, and for whatever reasons, there were now two separate and distinct organizations, both of them considerably smaller. On the West Coast we kept the name of the Prairie Fire Organizing Committee. On the East Coast they called themselves the May 19th Communist Movement, named after Malcolm X and Ho Chi Minh, whose birthdays were May 19th.

By then the WUO had fractured in multiple directions, with some people falling entirely by the wayside and disappearing from political life. Others surfaced and then joined PFOC. Several remained underground and were later apprehended on the East Coast in a series of high profile arrests after working with May 19th and members of the Black Liberation Army.

There was of course a positive side of "rectification." One practical impact was that many of us reevaluated our political work and returned to the kind of work we had been doing before the Hard Times strategy. For me that was a return to prison work. I had been involved with the Ruchel Magee defense committee and now was part of a newly formed group to draw attention to racist conditions at San Quentin. We held demonstrations several hundred strong outside the gates of the prison. And I got to work with my friend China Brotsky which helped make it fun. China stood out among the PF women. With very dark brown hair, a swarthy complexion, and distinct high cheekbones, she was quite a saxophone-playing sight. Outspoken with a very quick mind, she thinks outside the box. China understood way before most of us the critical importance of environmental issues.

In a joint project with the prisoners, the group went on to publish and distribute a newspaper that gave the prisoners at San Quentin a voice—*Arm the Spirit.* Though short-lived for me, that was some of the best political work I had ever done and was a forerunner of much of my future political life.

Our politics and practice about women grew stronger. More women joined PFOC and women took on leadership roles. A women's caucus met regularly, studying together and writing about women's liberation. We published a pamphlet titled "Women's Liberation and Imperialism" that discussed the dual consciousness of white women (or "women of the oppressor nation" in our lingo), enjoying relative privilege vis-à-vis people of color and yet oppressed by a male supremacist society though economic, legal, political, psychological, physical, and sexual means. We saw white working-class women as the most progressive element in the oppressor nation and the most likely allies of national liberation. We put forward the concept of the double shift (one shift in the workplace and one shift at home) as a key element in the oppression of women.

The pamphlet also acknowledged the role that lesbians played in the struggle against male supremacy: "By demonstrating that women can live, work and make love with each other; break out of the passivity, dependence and competition among women that is fostered by male supremacy." In our organization lesbians were playing an increasingly important role, both ideologically and practically. Gay liberation was finally being addressed, although gay men were looked upon more skeptically since they were, after all, still men.

Our politics about women's liberation were reflected in another very significant arena. The Left in general seemed to have minimal participation from women, and even less from women with children. We were determined to be different.

My daughter Rosa was one of the first babies to be born in the organization, but she would be far from the last. Miriam made Rosa a simple patchwork quilt, initiating a tradition within the organization. As new babies were born, the women in Prairie Fire would each contribute a patch and these later quilts would become increasingly elaborate with tie-dies, batik, embroidery, etc. The patches reflected themes as diverse as Palestine and Big Bird. But I always was most touched by Miriam's simple quilt, by her connecting us to an old tradition among women and initiating it in our organization.

Although the organization welcomed Rosa and the other babies that were on their way, they did present us with a dilemma. We believed in women's leadership but with babies coming along, how could women find the time and space to lead? To think? To write?

Our response to that question was one of not just talking the talk, but walking the walk. I don't know of any other Left organization that did what we did. Our solution was to form childcare teams, groups of members that would share the work and the joy of helping to raise the kids. I speak from experience, since Rosa's team was one of the first. I would now have time to attend meetings, do political work, and even read! Each new baby that came along would have such a childcare team.

In theory it was wonderful. In practice it started off a bit rocky. On Rosa's team were a couple of men who had no experience with babies and were very unprepared to help. Their intentions were good but I was afraid to leave Rosa alone with them. Luckily at the same time I went to a political rally and met a young woman who was speaking. Not only did Meryl love kids, but she was interested in our political work. Ten years my junior, she joined the Prairie Fire Organizing Committee and we became the best of friends. Luckily for me, she and Rosa also became good friends. Meryl was the heart of Rosa's childcare team and saved my political life.

LOS ANGELES

When Rosa was a year old I was asked to leave the Bay Area and move to Los Angeles to help develop a new chapter of the Prairie Fire Organizing Committee. A few Angelenos had formed a PF study group, but the leadership of PFOC felt someone from the Bay Area was needed. Howie and I and the baby were the chosen ones. I didn't want to leave my friends and was somewhat concerned about starting all over anew, especially now that Rosa was along for the ride. But of course we agreed because it seemed important politically.

I have always been a terrible mover/packer. We rented a U-Haul and on the day of the move, at the moment of truth, it seemed like half our stuff was still strewn all over the apartment. Our friends helped us throw it all in the truck and we were on our way. So began our L.A. adventure.

Paulette D'auteuil was the most active member of the small study group. She was a tireless soul, with more energy in her little pinkie than I have in my whole body. She had a teenage son, Mark. Then there was Paulette's partner at the time, Paul, and two or three others. Paulette was an immense help and a very generous spirit, but L.A. was difficult for me. Neither Howie nor I had ever been there before. We had little money, not much in the way of jobs, and no real community of support as we did in the Bay Area.

I argued that more people needed to be sent to L.A. from the Bay Area. The leadership agreed but the process was sluggish until unexpected developments transformed the situation.

Stimulated by a United Nations initiative, the Carter administration in 1977 issued a call for an International Women's Year conference to be held in November in Houston, Texas. This set in motion and funded a process whereby official delegations would be elected in each state to be sent to the conference. The conference was charged with developing a National Plan of Action that would lead to the establishment of a Women's Department within the federal bureaucracy. From our point of view the conference was an attempt by the Carter administration to co-opt the energy of the women's movement and channel it into acceptable modes that would suit its own interests and strategies.

However, we felt the International Women's year Conference was extremely important for several different reasons. We wanted the women's movement to grow. We intended to participate in the activities and influence the conference in the direction of developing "a more conscious anti-imperialist politics and leadership" according to our journal *Breakthrough.* In preparation we spent long hours in women's meetings discussing our understanding of the situation of women and it was at this time that we produced the pamphlet titled "Women's Liberation and Imperialism."

Although I was living in L.A. much of this time, I did occasionally participate in the discussions in the Bay Area. They were led by the Women's Commission of Prairie Fire and took place in the Women's Caucus, a grouping that involved all the women in the organization.

As part of the National Committee of PFOC I had actively organized and prepared for the Hard Times Conference by supporting "bad" ideas about women's organizing. That is, I argued for the politics of the WUO which increasingly put forward ideas of women's organizing that focused on economic issues, on issues of the workplace, and minimized other critical dimensions of women's oppression and liberation, e.g., reproductive rights, lesbianism, violence against women and patriarchy. Therefore the Women's Caucus meetings were intimidating because I was unsure of myself and cautious about what I said for fear of being wrong or revealing myself as backward.

Additionally, many women in the organization were now coming out as lesbians and other lesbians were joining. Our most articulate and outspoken members were participants in the lesbian caucus and were leading this process of developing women's politics. I felt defensive about my monogamous heterosexual relationship and kept myself on the fringes of the discussion. More speechless and unsure than usual, I told myself that I needed to listen and learn, and be willing to leave my comfort zone in order to grow.

As the Houston conference neared, it became clear that a significant right-wing offensive was gaining momentum, fueled by Anita Bryant, a high-profile entertainer and conservative Baptist who led a national "Save Our Children" anti-gay campaign from her home in Miami, Florida. Houston was a magnet for members of the KKK, and other right-wing groups were getting involved as well. As delegations were forming around the country, it became increasingly obvious that the right wing was participating eagerly. In fact, they had taken over the official delegations in ten states, including Mississippi. A huge right-wing rally was planned at the Astro Arena, not far from the convention itself and a confrontation seemed likely, possibly even a physical confrontation.

We wanted to oppose this right-wing offensive and help to physically defend the women's movement, if necessary. About a dozen or more women from Prairie Fire traveled to Houston from the Bay Area and L.A. There were thousands of women who were going to Houston, many of them in non-official capacities, and we would be among them. We intended to distribute our literature and participate in non-delegate meetings and demonstrations.

Van was planning to infiltrate the right-wing rally to get a real sense of what was going on there. To do so, he would travel to Houston *incognito,* keeping his distance from us in order to avoid detection by any possible right-wing surveillance. I was the liaison charged with communicating between the larger group of Prairie Fire women and Van. He and I were to have various secret meetings and phone calls at pre-designated times and places.

Two thousand women attended the IWY Convention as official delegates, and the Carter administration put forward their resolutions and plans. Thousands more "unofficials" participated outside and attended the various caucuses including those of women of color, lesbians and Left feminists, that were composed of both delegate and non-delegates alike. They presented alternative resolutions that addressed specific concerns for each grouping and in some cases marked a real step forward.

Lesbian and gay rights were given strong support at the conference, a positive step in resisting right-wing attacks on lesbians, meant to weaken and divide the women's movement. A 600-strong Lesbian Caucus debated whether or not to accept the Justice Department's offer of protection against the right wing, and decided to turn it down after a heated debate about the role of the government and the trustworthiness of the police.

The situation with regard to women of color was much more problematic. On the one hand, a "minority" resolution called for support for Native sovereignty and treaty rights, bilingual education and affirmative action, an end to forced sterilization and limitations on deportations. It was supported by a majority of the white women present.

On the other hand, the lack of support for Black delegates was shameful. Black delegates from various states attempted to unseat the all-white KKK Mississippi delegation, but the majority of attendees did not support the initiative and the all-white delegation remained seated. That stand by the official delegates was most disturbing.

The Puerto Rican women at the conference sponsored a resolution calling for the freedom of political prisoner Lolita Lebron and the four other Nationalists, and that resolution was never allowed to reach the Convention floor. Meanwhile an official resolution asserted that Puerto Ricans were citizens of the U.S., which angered many Puerto Ricans, who felt it obscured the colonial nature of the relationship of Puerto Rico to the U.S. For instance, although Puerto Ricans could serve in the U.S. Army, they were not allowed to vote for President of the United States. (This is still the case today.)

Here we were in Texas, land that was stolen in the first place from Mexico, and outside the Convention there was a Chicana-led rally of about 200 people protesting the arrests of undocumented workers by La Migra (Immigration).

I slinked away from all activities at the IWY conference to perform my assigned duties as go-between, and met Van at a pre-determined restaurant before he went off to the right-wing rally at the Astro Arena. Over coffee we were cool but cordial. That would be the last time he and I would connect. Later that day I heard on the radio about the arrest of several individuals as they left the rally at the Arena. I was shocked beyond belief to learn that one of those people was our own Clayton Van Lydegraf! Just as shocking was the fact that there were two women arrested along with Van and I'd never even heard of them. In a related story, we heard that two men were simultaneously busted in Los Angeles, again with unfamiliar names.

All five were charged with conspiracy to possess explosives with intent to damage and injure. More particularly, they were accused of intending to place a small explosive device outside the office of California State Senator Briggs. Briggs was anathema to us all. He was a rabid reactionary, advocating vociferously for reinstating the death penalty and for prohibiting gay teachers in the schools.

To say that I was shocked by the accusations and arrests is an understatement. After all, I was supposed to be the liaison between Van and the other Prairie Fire women, and I had no clue that something like this might happen. What was going on? All of us in Prairie Fire dropped everything we were doing and met for hours in a hotel room trying to figure it out. What should we do? After all, a prominent leader of our organization was now behind bars and would be arraigned in court the next morning. We decided to hold a press conference and pack the courtroom if possible. Working hard in the few hours of the day that remained made it possible, but barely. The courtroom for the arraignment was filled with Prairie Fire members and many friends, some that we had just met through the IWY activities.

Shortly after the arrests, it became clear that not one of us recognized the names of any of those arrested with Van because those were fake, underground names. They were the members of the WUO who had become the Revolutionary Committee (RC) that led the "split," resulting in the demise of the WUO. They were comrades who, like Van, believed that white and male supremacy within the WUO had caused the abandonment of armed struggle and clandestinity.

I could now understand why moving us down to L.A. had been such a priority. It was in part to develop a support system for this clandestine group that was, in effect, a secret part of PFOC. Van and others had been furious at our collective of five for participating secretly in the WUO before the Hard Times Conference. Now here was Van in a secret collective of his own.

Looking back on all this, I don't blame the RC for any of this, at least not exclusively. Despite the charged language and high emotions of rectification, we were all still close politically. It was on all of us. We should have been able to work out our differences. And yet we weren't. And so we didn't.

Because of the Briggs charges, the defendants were soon hauled off to California and exorbitant bails were set, from $200,000 to $350,000. Since we couldn't afford their bail, it was likely they would be in the L.A. County Jail for the duration of their trial and, if convicted, possibly even for the remainder of their lives. We wanted to understand what had happened in order to prevent repeating those errors in the future.

We soon learned that the FBI had planted two agents in our midst. One of them had "befriended" Van for the past two and a half years, succeeded in becoming his roommate and part of this underground group, and eventually turned the whole bunch in. The more we learned, the more dismayed—and self-critical—we felt.

As Diana Block, a leader of PFOC at the time, wrote in her memoir, *Arm The Spirit*:

> *"While the majority of the leadership collective was women, we had allowed Van to shape and guide most of the decisions of the organization in classically dependent ways. We didn't just blame him. We blamed ourselves. And the women of the LA5 blamed themselves. However we women wanted to engage in a process of self-criticism and Van did not."*

After much discussion, we decided this was not the time for a trial, that the best outcome would be a plea bargain. We were still newcomers in L.A. and the political climate was such that we doubted there would be much support in the community. The defendants were facing potentially very long sentences. Also, a trial would drain our limited human and financial resources. Black comrades argued that it would be wrong to turn our organization into a defense committee for five white people and let all our other work go. We agreed.

Judith Mirkinson, a Bay Area leader of PFOC, came to L.A., charged with finding a lawyer. Together she and I met with attorney Leslie Abramson. We immediately felt "she's the one," probably because she reminded us of more flashy versions of ourselves. Leslie was short and New York Jewish with a big blond Jewfro. More importantly, she was tough as nails. With her chutzpah and her savvy ways she had excellent connections to the L.A. courts. Leslie was excited about taking on the case and working with us. She thought a plea bargain could be worked out. We certainly hoped so.

By now lots of people from the Bay Area Prairie Fire had moved down to L.A. to strengthen the work. I was excited that my good friend Meryl was among them. We all took turns visiting the defendants and discussing our limited options. We wanted to win them over to the idea of avoiding a trial.

Van did not agree with us at all, not at all. He wanted to defend himself, reject a plea agreement and conduct a political trial. But after many long and difficult discussions, he was overruled. Ultimately, but not necessarily with equanimity, the LA 5 decided to accept Leslie's hard-won plea bargain.

There would be no trial. The defendants agreed to plead guilty to lesser offenses and would each spend between two and four years in prison. Nonetheless we considered that a victory, given the other possibilities.

In April of 1978 FBI Director Patrick Gray and two other FBI agents were indicted for illegal activity in the pursuit of the Weather Underground. In the wake of the Watergate affair, it was revealed that they had illegally tapped telephones, broken into people's homes, and written a plan to kidnap Bernardine Dohrn's infant nephew. As a result of these revelations, federal conspiracy charges against Bernardine and

Bill Ayers were later dropped due to extreme government misconduct. I sometimes wonder whether something of this nature was at work in the plea bargain of the LA 5.

There was much political work to be done in L.A., but where to begin? In PFOC we began to examine everything we were doing once again. Our discussion centered in part on analyzing IWY and our relationship to it. At first we declared that IWY had laid the basis for "a new stage in the women's movement" based in international solidarity and "women's solidarity." Then, as the struggles that had begun with Rectification continued, we concluded that our analysis of IWY was "opportunist and wrong. We had distorted what happened at IWY to fit our political line on women's liberation...."

It seems that everything we did in those years required sharp self-criticism. According to *Breakthrough*, our own journal, we never got anything right. We were constantly berating ourselves. I think that's because we had a tendency to exaggerate the revolutionary, anti-imperialist nature of social developments. We were desperately searching for potential. First it was about working-class struggle during the Hard Times Conference. Now it was International Women's Year. It seems that whether it was the working class or women, we were skilled at wishful thinking that led us to various forms of opportunism and then *mea culpas.*

We wanted to build a revolutionary movement, but not in isolation from Black, Puerto Rican, Mexican, and Native American revolutionaries. After the bust of the LA 5, we intensified our work accordingly. Ever since my experience with the Chicago 8 Conspiracy Trial, prisons and political prisoners were on my mind. When I first arrived in California back in 1973, before I found the Weather Underground, I had been part of the campaign to free Ruchell Magee. Then after the Hard Times conference, in working with prisoners to expose racist conditions in San Quentin, I began to do educational work to free Black political prisoners Assata Shakir and Sundiata Acoli.

Now, in 1980 L.A., I joined the campaign to free Geronimo Pratt. Elmer "Geronimo" Pratt was a Vietnam Vet who had been attending

UCLA on the GI bill, joined the Black Panther Party and became the Minister of Defense. In 1968 he was charged with the robbery and murder of a young teacher on a Santa Monica tennis court. The primary witness against him was an informant for the FBI, although for years that fact was suppressed. Geronimo was convicted even though prosecutors knew for a fact that he was at a Black Panther meeting hundreds of miles away at the time of the murder. (Geronimo was clearly a victim of the FBI's Counterintelligence Program, and spent 27 years behind bars before he was finally vindicated in 1997.)

We also participated in coalitions against police brutality, bringing the kids along on all the demonstrations. I still have the clipping of Rosa's friend, little Maia Werner, standing in front of her mother, Nancy Werner, holding a sign bigger than she was, saying "Stop Killer Cops." *The Los Angeles Times* caption reads:

> *"Upset Over Boy's Death: Demonstrators, including a [young] girl, protest outside the Los Angeles County Sheriff's Department Monday after a rookie police officer in nearby Stanton shot and killed a 5-year-old boy. Police said the officer, Anthony Speri, 24, mistook a toy gun held by Patrick Mason for the real item."*

In September of 1980 a group of us attended a neighborhood watch meeting of several hundred people in Venice, California and interjected the issue of police brutality. *The Los Angeles Times* of September 29th described my role in the following way:

> *"Questioners shouted to be heard. A young woman who gave her name as Nancy Kurshan prevailed, prompting the evening's most intriguing exchange.*
>
> *Her complaint, she said, was about "killer cops." Smith [Commander of the Venice Police division] bristled. Her demand was for an explanation of the incidence of officer-involved shootings, particularly the February wounding of Cornelius Tatum, a 22-year-old gas station attendant in South Central Los Angeles.*
>
> *Fifteen years ago, Kurshan's question might have roused unity in such a crowd in Venice. Instead, in 1980, the crowd, as if with one voice, began to shout her down."*

Sound familiar? This was 1980. Eleven years later the repeated beating by Los Angeles police of Rodney King, an African-American man, would be caught on videotape. The subsequent acquittal of the cops in that case would ignite the 1992 Los Angeles rebellion.

Attorney Len Weinglass and I had become friends during the Chicago 8 trial, and when I moved to L.A. he offered me a part-time job as his legal secretary. Well, part legal secretary, part Gal Friday. Lenny traveled all the time and I kept the home fires burning. Len's downtown L.A. office was in the exquisite turn-of-the century Bradbury Building with its skylit atrium, ornate ironwork and birdcage elevators. Across the street was a huge Mexican market open on the sides to the warm L.A. streets. I answered phones and typed an occasional brief. I also picked up laundry and checked on Len's house while he was gone. I loved working in that office because Len was involved with so many important trials. I would read all the papers as I filed them. Meryl worked for another criminal attorney in the same building, and we were sometimes able to spend time together. Life was sweet and after May of 1979 I brought Michael, my new baby boy, to work so I could nurse him. I also brought him along on a San Quentin visit to see Geronimo and Sadauki, another prisoner in Southern California. I nursed him, as discreetly as possible, at a picnic table in a big yard filled with male prisoners, visitors and of course, guards.

Until I lived in L.A. I had no idea that Los Angeles County is home to the largest urban American Indian population in the United States. In the late 1970s it was a center of Native American activity and one of the most important events in the city was the trial of Skyhorse and Mohawk, for which Len Weinglass was the attorney.

Skyhorse and Mohawk had been falsely charged in the 1974 murder of a taxi driver in Ventura County, just north of L.A. Their indictment came in the midst of other FBI Counter Intelligence Program (*COINTELPRO*) assaults aimed at destroying the American Indian Movement. There had been the siege of Wounded Knee, the mysterious death of another young activist, Ana Mae Aquash, the imprisonment of Leonard Peltier (amazingly, released in 2025), and the death by fire of

John Trudell's wife and children. The Skyhorse-Mohawk trial lasted for three years, the longest trial in L.A. history to that date, and they were eventually acquitted. During that time we went to court, marched and picketed, attended many pow wows and ate our fair share of fry bread. Most of the time we took Rosa (and later her baby brother Michael) with us wherever we went.

When Rosa was two years old, she and I went on the Longest Walk. This long trek had begun on February 11, 1978, taking off from Alcatraz Island in the San Francisco Bay. Walking for five months clear across the continent, 3000 Native Americans and their supporters marched on Washington, D.C. with spiritual leaders and elders of over 80 Indian nations at the head of the line. The focus of the march was the anti-Indian legislation that was pending in Congress, legislation that would legitimize the continuing refusal of the U.S. government to honor the more than 300 treaties that were signed with the indigenous peoples.

To show our support and at least join in some part of the trip, I packed up a few things and my 2-year-old daughter, and headed back east along with Judy, another PFOC member. In Ohio we visited with my in-laws, the Emmers, who played and cuddled with their granddaughter and then drove us to meet up with the march, which was passing through Ohio. Judy and I camped out for several nights and walked in the day, carrying Rosa in a backpack as long as we could stand it … and sometimes resorted to accepting rides. After a few days we made our way back to a Greyhound station as planned and headed home.

A couple of hours up the coast from L.A. is Point Conception, a dramatically exquisite and yet intimately tranquil place. It seemed to occupy a magical space and also be occupied by magical spirits. Even my stoned atheist self could feel it. A breathtaking rocky headland that juts out into the Pacific Ocean, it is a remote spot surrounded by a huge private ranch and far from any public road. The Chumash people call it the "Western Gateway," a portal through which all new life arrives and the dead depart. It is also the site of ancient villages and burial sites.

Point Conception became the center of an intense controversy. In the wake of the 1970s energy crunch, it was the proposed location for a huge liquid natural gas plant. On one side of the fight was the Pacific Gas & Electric Company and the Southern California Gas Company. On the other side were the Chumash tribe and the American Indian Movement and a handful of supporters. The Chumash went to court to sue the power companies—and set up tents and kitchens and announced they would occupy the land for as long as it took to put an end to the madness. The Indians occupied Point Conception and called for all supporters to join them.

Paulette, a member of PFOC, was a strong supporter of the Native struggle and would stay at Point Conception for weeks at a time. Responding to her persistent advocacy, Ferd Eggan and I would often join her for weekends, heading out on Friday after work.

The Indians expected us to take part in the sweat lodge ceremonies and we tried to meet their expectations. The sweats were traditional ceremonies conducted by an elder spiritual leader. They built the sweat lodge out of tree branches covered with blankets and tarps. It was perhaps ten feet in diameter. Inside the lodge, big heated stones were splashed with water to create steam.

Ernie Peters, a Dakota Sioux, would often conduct the ceremony, leading the prayers and chants. Using the Sacred Pipe he would turn to each of the Four Directions and pay homage. In the beginning, burning sage would be passed around to each of the participants. We would have nothing but towels wrapped around us. Most often the prayers centered on bringing relief to Native people who were suffering under the pressure of poverty and racism, and all the associated evils such as alcoholism. Many people prayed for Native sovereignty and for land. There would always be prayers for Skyhorse and Mohawk and for political prisoner Leonard Peltier, a member of AIM who had been sentenced to two consecutive life terms in 1977 for the murder of two FBI agents at the Pine Ridge Indian Reservation in South Dakota (sentence commuted 2025). Every now and then, the fire tender would ladle water onto the hot rocks and the steam and heat would intensify. After about an hour, the blanket over the sweat lodge door would be pulled back and anyone who absolutely couldn't stand the heat could leave. Paulette,

Ferd and I would always try our hardest to stay, out of respect for our hosts. I sometimes got through it by thinking, "If Leonard Peltier can survive those hellhole prisons then I can make it through this sweat."

When the ceremony was over I was never sorry I had stuck it out. We would run immediately from the sweat lodge into the cool, cool stream that ran through the encampment. Sometimes the sweat lodge would be set up on the beach, and we would run straight into the Pacific. It was an incredible rush and when it was over, I did feel purified in both body and soul. Atheist or not.

In those days we took the kids most everywhere we went, and Rosa and Michael always enjoyed the Native functions. There were lots of children, friendly people, drumming, dancing and fry bread. We did not take children to Point Conception, however, since we knew it could come under attack by the authorities at any time. We were following the teaching of Che Guevara who said, "Only the children will be privileged." Imagine my delight when I learned that the Northern Chumash Tribal Council will soon be in a position to safeguard the entire central coast of California from offshore oil expansion and other threats. The Chumash Heritage Marine National Sanctuary was designated as such in October 2024, the first in the U.S. under the co-stewardship of a Tribal Council. I feel so lucky to have spent time in that magical space.

In 1979 there was a large community of Iranians in LA. Howie was going to school for his BA at Cal State LA and we became close friends with some of the Iranian students. They organized massive downtown demonstrations in support of the Iranian struggle against the US-installed Shah, and I would hear them outside my window in the Bradbury Building as they streamed by the office. Often I would join them. When the tear gas hit, it felt like being in a foreign land and I shouted *Mein Bah Shah* (Down With Shah) along with thousands of Iranians. In January the Shah fled Iran and went into exile. Our new baby boy, Michael, unknowingly in the oven at the Point Conception sweats, was born May 18, 1979. We gave him the middle name of Bijan in memory of Bijan Jazani, a communist leader of the Iranian resistance who was killed in 1975 by SAVAK, the Shah's intelligence goons. (The overthrow of the Shah did not, however, result in the triumph of the Left resistance. Many of them, including our friends, were killed, or forced into exile after Iran became the Islamic Republic.)

Although there were not very many Puerto Ricans in Los Angeles, as a national organization we were strengthening relations with the Puerto Rican independence movement.

By the late 1970s the Puerto Rican movement was going through changes. A clandestine Puerto Rican group, the *Fuerzas Armadas de Liberación* (FALN) was carrying out bombings and demanding the release of the four Puerto Rican Nationalists who had been in prison since the 1950s for attacking Congress. Federal grand juries were convened to investigate the Puerto Rican independence movement. Most of those called became grand jury resisters, and were sent to jail for refusing to cooperate.

Out of the resistance to the grand jury, the *Movimiento de Liberación Nacional* (MLN) was founded composed of Mexicans as well as Puerto Ricans. The Mexicans, from Colorado and California, had a vision of a socialist Mexico that would include the area of the Southwest that the United States had stolen from Mexico. Both the Mexican MLN and the Puerto Rican MLN were supporters of the FALN.

Puerto Rican resistance was deepening but so was repression in what seemed like a continuing spiral. On July 4, 1978, Nydia Cuevas and Pablo Marcano seized the Chilean consulate in San Juan to protest the July 4th celebrations, calling for independence for Puerto Rico and freedom for the Nationalists. July 25th, 1978 the Puerto Rican police under the direction of the FBI ambushed and assassinated two young *independentistas* on a mountain top in Cerro Maravilla, Puerto Rico.

On September 10, 1979, President Jimmy Carter commuted the sentences of the four Puerto Rican Nationalists. Not long after, PFOC brought Lolita Lebron to Los Angeles to speak at a large indoor rally. It was to be a very public forum and we feared for her safety. There were various right-wing groups in L.A. that might have planned to do her harm—disaffected Cubans possibly, good old American super-patriots, or even elements of law enforcement and the FBI. She was a national treasure of Puerto Rico and we felt a great responsibility to protect her.

Striving to be serious revolutionaries, we had made self-defense a part of our lifestyle. I was taking kung fu classes regularly and was also involved in weapons training.

I went along once or twice to gun shows and was amazed at my naivete about the easy accessibility of all these weapons. It was frightening to think of how many weapons were circulating in our society. The nonchalance at the gun shows, the rows and rows of people selling weapons, as if it were just another flea market, was chilling.

There were a few among us who knew how to shoot a gun and they took us to a range for target practice. The physical experience of shooting a gun was not that dramatic for me. Yes, at 120 pounds I had to brace myself for the recoil, but once I got the hang of that, the rest was not that difficult. I was pretty steady and not a bad shot.

However, I was nervous about it all. I realized that people were legally training all over the country and out in the open, but I felt that even if it was legal, we would be criminalized for doing so because of the thoughts in our heads. So for me it was a more furtive process. There was no macho swagger involved in my training. I was not in love with violence. If I associated guns with being macho before I went to Vietnam, I certainly left Vietnam believing it was rather a necessary element in revolutionary struggle.

I believed I would never use a gun to kill somebody unless it was in self-defense, but I needed to develop the skill to prepare for a possible future. And I doubted that outside of self-defense I would ever be able to pull the trigger against an animal. Would I ever really be able to aim a gun at a human being? And yet, given the level of violence directed against our movements, I wanted to be prepared. I had a chance to think about it more when we were asked to do security for Lolita Lebron. I decided that to protect Lolita, I would.

For her appearance, we placed ourselves in various parts of the building with good visibility of the goings-on. Some of our African-American comrades joined us in this effort so we had good coverage. I didn't actually hear Lolita speak, as I was out on a fire escape surveilling the scene. Lolita's appearance to a packed audience went off without a hitch. I sighed a huge sigh of relief.

During the 1970s I had a job with the Grand Jury Project of the SF National Lawyers Guild. Ten years later, the grand jury was still being used as a weapon against activists. José Lopez, a leader of the Puerto Rican independence movement in Chicago, was coming to San Francisco on a speaking tour and I traveled from L.A. to the Bay Area to hear him. José was a grand jury resister—when subpoenaed to testify before a federal grand jury investigating the independence movement, he took a stand of non-collaboration and refused to be interrogated about his politics, his friends, or his relatives. He was thrown into jail for seven months to coerce him to testify. He did not.

Accompanying José was Marta Rodriguez, an energetic woman lacking from birth in eyesight, but replete with vision and talent. Marta played guitar and sang songs she had written about the FALN, the Puerto Rican independence movement and revolutionary struggle worldwide. She was smart and quick as a whip, and she and José bantered back and forth in ways uncharacteristic of the movement people I knew. I reflected at that moment that these Puerto Ricans were gonna be fun.

By this time members of PFOC had attended several national conferences, building solidarity with the Puerto Rican independence movement. Those conferences took place in Chicago, a hub of support for the independence movement generally and the FALN in particular. In fact, several people from California PFOC had moved to Chicago at the request of the MLN.

Among those who moved were Edy Scripps and Ferd Eggan, both fluent in Spanish. After 4 years working with Cesar Chavez's Farmworkers, Edy came to Chicago and used her skills to start a childcare center in the Puerto Rican community. Young mothers who wanted to complete their high school education could leave their children at the center; and so too, could neighborhood families and activists. (Edy's compassion and care would later enrich my growing family as well.) Ferd would serve as the Principal of the alternative Puerto Rican High School for eleven years before moving on to become one of the founders of ACT-UP, the militant AIDS organization that changed how the world viewed the epidemic and, to a large extent, the gay community. Ferd was an original. Fierce and funny in turns, he was also a writer who would later become a key figure in the L.A. Health Department in the fight against AIDS.

The Nationalist prisoners had been released by Carter, but it didn't take long before a new generation of *independentistas* were imprisoned. On April 4, 1980, eleven Puerto Ricans were arrested in Evanston, Illinois. A shockwave ran through our organization. Five of the eleven were women and many of them were members of the Chicago Puerto Rican community with which we were familiar. The work of the small Chicago Prairie Fire chapter seemed more important than ever as PFOC joined the campaign to free the eleven political prisoners.

In California we devised ways to raise the issue of their release as well as Puerto Rican independence. During the 1980 Presidential campaign of Carter vs. Reagan, we occupied both the Republican and Democratic Party headquarters in L.A. and San Francisco. I was among those arrested in this action which the *Los Angeles Times* apparently thought was the work of two separate groups, and the paper was also puzzled as to why neither of these groups had any Puerto Rican members.

The Movement of the '60s was over, the war in Vietnam ended, and some strides had been made in terms of overthrowing overt segregation, but much of the oppressive structure remained both in the U.S. and around the world. When 5-year-old Patrick Mason was shot by the LAPD, it was as if our son had been shot. When Assata Shakur was freed by her comrades, liberated from a prison back east, we rejoiced as if she were our blood sister. We identified with the militant groups of revolutionaries arising from Black, Puerto Rican, and Mexican communities in the U.S.— the FALN 11, the Grand Jury Resistors, Assata Shakur, Sundiata Acoli, and the Black Liberation Army (BLA). These were our peers, and their militancy and courage caused us to reevaluate our relationship (once again) to armed struggle.

After much discussion, our PFOC leadership group decided that building a clandestine organization was still a priority. We continued to believe that the U.S. would not reform itself, that someday it would be necessary to take up arms. Though we were nowhere near strong enough to do anything like that at that present time, we wanted to build such a capacity so that when the conditions ripened, we would be ready. Additionally, after Houston, we understood more than ever that whatever we built would have to be very separate from our organization (PFOC), so that if we were infiltrated, it would not destroy the clandestine capacity that was being built. That understanding was a gift from Van.

It was decided that a small group of people would go off and begin to build a separate, clandestine organization. Except for very secret occasional meetings between PFOC leadership, that group would attempt to build clandestinely among new people in new places with the goal of independence from our organization. They would take their time, prepare carefully and patiently, and not yet engage in armed action.

The rest of us would remain part of PFOC, publicly continuing to support armed struggle in our propaganda, and steeling ourselves for future militant struggle by learning self-defense and engaging in weapons training. Some of us would later join the people in clandestinity and we would also funnel new people toward that clandestine work.

Although I was by now part of the L.A. leadership and therefore aware of the process, I didn't live in the Bay Area where the decisions were made regarding who would go underground. This was a wrenching and difficult process. In all cases it involved cutting ties with friends, family, and loved ones. In some cases, it involved leaving a beloved partner or a child. One at a time, friends disappeared from my life with invented cover stories about where they were going. Donna was "going to China to study acupuncture." Claude was going to "work at the border." I felt very fond of both of them and was really sad to see them go. I agreed to store a box of Claude's more cherished items for safekeeping. I had no idea that Donna and Claude would surprisingly reappear in my life a decade and a half later, but I took good care of Claude's box nonetheless.

I like to think that had I been chosen to go underground, I would have agreed to it. However, I know for sure that I was relieved to hear that that would not be my fate. What I was asked to do seemed much easier. My assignment was to visit with our chapter in Chicago. They were having difficulties and my task was to help bring cohesion to the group and build our practice there. This would require leaving my two little children for weeks at a time, which I was not happy to do, but it seemed like a small sacrifice compared to others. Although we would miss each other, the children would be well taken care of, I knew. We had become a close group in L.A., living collectively in various combinations in five or six houses with a fair degree of shuffling around. So Howie and the kids were in good hands.

However, after several trips to the Windy City, it was decided that Howie and I should move there permanently. The Chicago chapter of Prairie Fire was very small and we wanted it to grow more than ever since the arrest of the FALN 11. I returned to L.A. and began to prepare for the move while Edy looked for an apartment for us to move into. Another round of Chicago adventures was about to begin. My destiny seemed to be tied to that city.

CHICAGO PUERTO RICAN STYLE

WHILE MY EARLIER YEARS MAY have played out more visibly on the stage of history, the last four decades, although a more intimate tableau, have been deeply satisfying. My trip to the Bay Area to hear José Lopez speak changed my life forever. I was fascinated by José. At a few inches over 5 feet, José was a short guy with a huge presence. He was, of course, fully bilingual and spoke with only the slightest hint of a Puerto Rican accent (perhaps cadence is a better word). His appearance was conservative—short hair, clean shaven, sporting a traditional Puerto Rican guayabera, worn outside the trousers with two vertical rows of closely sewn pleats, running the length of the front and back of the shirt. When he spoke, he combined history, analysis, and personal reflection that connected to everyday experience. It struck me that he was probably a nerd in his earlier school days. A passionate, courageous revolutionary masquerading as a conservative gentleman. I would later realize that he is a renaissance man who, around the dinner table or from a podium, might refer to maroon societies, Bosnia/Herzegovina, Greece or ancient Egypt, DuBois' *The Soul of Black Folk*, or the Irish struggle against British colonialism. Or to the history of some food or another. I would always come away with my mind blown and often, my heart touched.

In 1981 the leadership of Prairie Fire asked me to move to Chicago to work with José and his organization in support of the Puerto Rican Independence movement. If it had been anyone else, perhaps I would not have uprooted my family again and moved from sunny California to the freezing city where in 1968 my friends and I had been treated like criminals. But it was José. And Howie and I felt it would be good to live closer to our families in Cleveland and New York. So we packed up and moved with our two kids to the Windy City. My connection to José and the Puerto Rican community around Division Street has long outlived the Prairie Fire Organizing Committee, but I have PFOC to thank for sending me there.

Immediately upon our arrival, we were welcomed by José, his family and other members of the community with a barbecue in his backyard. It was the first of many amazing meals he cooked for us. The food was great but the warm embrace was even better.

All future meals would be Puerto Rican. Chef José, with a twinkle in his eye, would always insist that Puerto Rican food is the best in the world. As is Puerto Rican music and dance and poetry, and you name it—Puerto Rican everything is the best. With a laugh. And always with respect and appreciation for other cultures.

Under his leadership as the director of the Puerto Rican Cultural Center (PRCC), the community has developed a number of initiatives in the Humboldt Park neighborhood, including an alternative high school, a parent-child learning center and day care, the only Puerto Rican museum in the country, a youth drop-in center, and an HIV education and advocacy organization. Two huge metallic flags announce a strip on Division Street as a Puerto Rican Zone, as they struggle to stave off the forces of gentrification. Murals abound and small mosaics representing Puerto Rican towns adorn the trash cans. On that strip of Division Street they have managed to develop a small-town feeling in the midst of a metropolis. Even as a non-Puerto Rican, I don't think I will ever feel that deep sense of community again.

When I enter Nelly's restaurant, it's like walking into Cheers where everybody knows your name. And everybody else's name. You can also get the most delicious Puerto Rican breakfast of avena (PR oatmeal), an omelet with *maduros* (sweet plantains), and strong black Puerto Rican coffee. Thinking about it now makes me yearn to be there, both for the *avena* and the special camaraderie.

Although a couple of years my junior, José has for 40 years now been a mentor to me (and to so many others). I also consider him a close friend and love him dearly. His brother, Puerto Rican *independentista* and national hero Oscar Lopez Rivera, was a political prisoner for 35 years. Decades before activism around prisons exploded, José articulated paradigm-shifting explanations of the role prisons play, not just in the lives of political prisoners. He connected the dots between political prisoners, all prisoners, and the social control of people of color more generally. For 15 years we organized many educational events and protests at prison gates around the Midwest and far beyond. It's hard to imagine it could have happened without José's extraordinary combination of intellect and practical organizing skills.

José felt that the popular American slogan "Live and Let Live" was unsatisfactory. And so he adopted the phrase, "Live and Help Live," a phrase coined by the Puerto Rican Nationalist Dona Consuelo Lee de Corretjer. With all that is already on his plate, José is able to pay attention to people's individual lives. He has always been there for me and my family through hard times and good. And for so many others as well. After Hurricane Maria, while he was helping organize airlifts to the island and services for the masses of folks arriving in Chicago, I'd get phone calls from him personally:

"There's a woman who has just come from the island and needs immediate chemotherapy for her breast cancer. Can you help her find a doctor?" or "[So and so] has just come from the island. We're looking for furniture for an apartment. Can you help?"

Although I am in it for the long haul, I sometimes become cynical or feel defeated. José always sees possibilities, solutions to problems, and can imagine a better world. That spirit of his, that imagination, has had a great impact on me. José lifts me up in conversation and by modeling unflagging determination and creativity in face of challenges.

I have watched José and the Puerto Rican Culture Center evolve and adapt to changing times. They have built lasting institutions, including Albizu Campos High School, named for the first leader of the Puerto Rican Nationalist Party. For decades I was on the Board of the school, as well as part of the Campaign to free the Puerto Rican political prisoners. I learned what real loyalty looks like, what it means to look out for the people you travel with in life, to really look out for them, when decade after decade José and the community organized to free the Puerto Rican political prisoners. They never gave up hope. They never stopped fighting for the freedom of the prisoners. It was never even a question. Their protracted but ultimately successful struggle deserves a book of its own, and it's their story to tell.

For my part I came to internalize other lessons more deeply in this journey to become a better *companera.* I became more aware that in the spirit of solidarity, white folks can have a role to play but we can't drive the train. The work has to be driven by those most affected. I needed to recognize the strength of their community and be helpful in ways that they thought were helpful. Now when I think I know best (which happens less and less), I check myself.

That is not to say we can't have opinions or express them. But the first step to a good relationship is trust, and our commitment needs to be demonstrated through practice, with boots on the ground. When my friends and I moved to Chicago to work with the Puerto Rican community, Ferd became the Principal of the alternative high school and over the years, helped a Puerto Rican to take over the helm. Edy developed a preschool in the community and similarly transferred it to others. My husband Steve brought many health and medical resources to the community. All of us in Prairie Fire did regular shifts of typesetting, childcare, and security, and organized demonstrations and protests for the political prisoners. We visited them in prison and raised funds.

But first we went slowly. We observed. We followed. Sometimes we wondered, is that the best way? But we did it anyway. We had many shared experiences and deep conversations, and eventually we were seen as *compañeras* and *compañeros.*

I also learned to sit with discomfort more easily. Self-talk: "Oh, I've been invited to something and it's likely I'll be the only white person there. I'll feel self-conscious and perhaps say or do the wrong thing. So I'll make an excuse and just not go." And then I would tell myself: "You

WILL go! This is an opportunity for growth. Now get up off it!" So I go. And immediately and over time, my life is enriched beyond words as we become friends across what are usually boundaries or even barriers.

I love the terms—*compañeras* and *compañeros.* An "ally" sounds like a temporary, military relationship based on opportunistic needs. These days "comrades" sounds rigid and compulsory. I think of a *compañera* as someone I feel deep affection for, and together we are traveling through life while trying to make a better world for all. Maybe I just love the Spanish language. It sounds so much more soulful.

GRIEVING LEAVING

I LEFT PRAIRIE FIRE ORGANIZING Committee sometime in the mid 1990s. I had had some political as well as personal disagreements with the leadership in San Francisco. I was no longer growing within their framework and was doubting its efficacy. My work with the Committee to End the Marion Lockdown was very time-consuming and they viewed it as competitive with Prairie Fire. Maybe they were right. But Prairie Fire was slowly declining and a few years later as an organization it would be gone. Nevertheless, I went through a grieving period because for two decades the WUO and its offshoot Prairie Fire had been such an important part of my life.

The WUO and its offshoots made mistakes. Early on, the process suffered from macho bravado. Throughout much of its history, the organization struggled with sexism and homophobia. Often we were arrogant; too much calling people out and not enough calling people in. Sigmund Freud's "narcissism of small differences" comes to mind when I think of how we suffered from a sectarianism that made us less attractive to people outside of the organization and led to splitting within the organization. There were also important currents that we were slow to understand and were dismissive of, such as early environmental issues.

For an organization aspiring to be revolutionary, our biggest failure may have been our inability to develop an anti-racist class perspective and practice that appealed to the white working class, young or otherwise. The Weather-initiated Hard Times Conference had held such promise but had collapsed right out of the gate.

In my experience the counter-cultural hippie phenomenon came closer to involving large numbers of disaffected white working-class youth. I suspect that the intersection between the anti-war movement and counter-cultural hippies was probably the most successful melding. I can't prove it, but I doubt anyone can disprove it. My family was solidly middle class by the 1960s, but in my experience there were working-class youth in Kent, Ohio as well as in Berkeley, California, the Lower East Side of New York, and in Manchester, New Hampshire. They were not that different than people I knew as a young child in Brooklyn. I met with deserters from the U.S. Army in Sweden and worked with Vietnam Veterans Against the War. In fact, resistance to the war inside the military, organizing on the outside at coffee houses set up near military bases, was essential to ending the war and most of the participants were working-class, albeit not just white.

It's also worth noting that despite some valiant attempts, no other Left organization succeeded in organizing white working-class people in any significant, sustained way either.

However, we in the WUO and its offshoots helped create a pole in the movement in opposition to white supremacy. We insisted that racism is a determining element in all aspects of U.S. society, as well as in international foreign policy. We called on white people to support the demands of people of color, especially Black Americans. We insisted that we needed to both fight the institutions of white supremacy and also challenge ourselves to understand our own privilege, while acting in solidarity with liberation movements at home and abroad. We built an organization of people who were committed to fighting white supremacy and who saw that as a prerequisite for building a movement for social justice. Decades, perhaps a half century before this became popular. That is a legacy we can be proud of.

FAMILY LIFE

My own personal Chicago story begins and ends with several more intimate love affairs. The first of these was with my children—Rosa and Michael. Rosa was six and Michael had just turned three when we moved to Chicago. Therefore most of our lives together, and most of their formative years, were spent in the City of Big Shoulders.

About six months after our arrival, Howie and I separated. I didn't know what the outcome would be but I knew we had to move apart. Relocating to Chicago had shaken up our relationship; perhaps it had just accentuated the fault lines. For the first time we were living alone as a nuclear family. We had two kids and twelve years behind us, but we were bickering or distant, it seemed to me, constantly. There were no others in the household to cushion the shocks or absorb any of the work or the tensions between us.

It was shortly after the new year of 1982 when we separated. One night my mother called to say that my sister Louise's wedding might be off (it wasn't) and I let her know that my marriage might be as well (it was).

Howie moved in with Edy and Melinda, another PFOC member. Melinda's twin sister, Margaret, swapped places with Howie and moved in with me and the kids. The kids would live half the time with me and half the time with Howie. I had no doubt he would take good care of the children. I was sad, nervous, and worried about the future. But I was also relieved. As time went by, the relief became stronger than the sadness and I realized that what might have been a temporary separation would now be permanent.

Of course they might speak differently, but I don't think the separation was too traumatic for the kids. Howie and I lived within a few blocks of each other and we remained political comrades with lives still very intertwined. However, between L.A. and Chicago, the kids lived with as many as 20 adults in the course of their growing up. Sometimes I feel guilty about that, but much of the time I believe those experiences contributed to their able and resilient personalities.

Besides moving back and forth from one apartment to the other in the middle of the week, there was also a childcare team to contend with. Members of the Chicago team came and went over the years and most of them had little to no experience dealing with kids. That is, apart from Edy, who had begun a childcare center of the United Farm Workers in California and now the Puerto Rican Cultural Center and was currently going for her master's degree in Early Childhood Education. Edy was much more than a babysitter. When the kids were at Howie's, Edy became an aunt or second mother to them. She went the extra mile. On freezing Chicago days she would take the kids, often walking, to the Y for swimming lessons; something I would have been reluctant to do.

At Howie's house the kids' bedroom was a corner of the living room where Edy hung a curtain as a separator. Often they would go to sleep on the one side of the curtain while adults were meeting on the other side. At my apartment, they slept in bunk beds in the tiny bedroom they shared. I slept on foam on top of plywood on top of bricks, and they often joined me in the wee hours.

As a group we were constantly going to meetings, writing propaganda, demonstrating, getting arrested for civil disobedience, going to court, and visiting prisoners. The kids' lives just melded into those activities. They went everywhere with us, including many demonstrations, and seemed to thrive. The reader may remember that when Rosa was six months old we took her to Philadelphia for the Bicentennial Without Colonies demonstration. At two I had carried her along on the Native American Walk.

SUN-TIMES / Al Podgorski

South Africans (from left) Rosa Kursham, 9; Sarah Zeller, 8½, and Michael Kursham, 5, join Operation PUSH, Free South Africa Movement and April Action Committee at the South African Consulate here yesterday to protest apartheid on the anniversary of the slaying of the Rev. Martin Luther King Jr.

4/5/85 Chi Trib p. 15

Above: *Chicago Tribune* mistakenly labels the kids—Rosa, Michael & Sarah Zeller—as South Africans, April 1985. **Below:** Ready to protest; Lexington, KY; April 19, 1987. Nancy and her 11 year old daughter Rosa, center right, with others.

Nancy, Rosa and Michael, Chicago, mid-1990s.

Several years after the arrest of the FALN 11, the kids lived through their own direct experience with the powers that be. When Michael was in preschool and Rosa in first grade, the FBI raided the Puerto Rican Cultural Center that housed *Centro Infantil,* the childcare center that Michael attended and Rosa went to for after-school care. In order to protect the children from future frightening incursions, *Centro Infantil* was moved to a secret location in a church. Edy and the other teachers at *Centro Infantil* talked with the children about what was going on and why.

By 1985 our family included Steve, the other love of my life. But that story calls for a little background. By the time I moved to Chicago, the mass movement/counterculture of the '60s and early '70s had faded to gray. The Weather Underground was gone and Prairie Fire had fractured further, no longer a national force. In Chicago, our small Prairie Fire chapter was still united and supporting each other's efforts, but we were meeting and working with lots of different people. We found ourselves part of a modest (perhaps several hundred) but vibrant community of activists. As I explored the political scene, I quickly bumped into people in motion around a variety of issues: newly energized anti-war activists trying to stop the U.S.-sponsored carnage in Central America; radical "liberation theology" nuns and priests; radical lawyers and activists taking on the torture of Black men by Chicago police, the freeing of Puerto Rican political prisoners, as well as the lockdown at Marion Federal Penitentiary; feminists fighting to defend the abortion clinics from right-wing attacks; and anti-racists concerned about the recently energized Klan/Nazi activity in the area.

All of us Prairie Fire members came to Chicago to develop support for the Puerto Rican independence struggle. But we were branching out in various ways. While Ferd and Melinda worked in a Puerto Rican solidarity group, Edy worked on abortion rights with ECDC (Emergency Committee to Defend the Clinics). Howie and Arawn helped start the John Brown Anti-Klan Committee. We were decompressing, breathing more freely and happy to give up the idea that we were these "exceptional white people." We joined with other like-minded folks and it was a healthy process. We even made new friendships outside of our small circle.

Margaret and I were drawn to Chicago's Disarm Now Action Group (affectionately called DNA), working to shut down the Rock Island Arsenal, a key weapons manufacturing plant for the U.S. military. It sat on an island in the Mississippi, accessed by four bridges from Iowa and Illinois. All we had to do was stop traffic on those bridges, and business as usual would be halted. Piece of cake!

Steve and I were acquainted because we had participated in various Rock Island planning meetings. In fact, years later I was cleaning out a box of papers and came across a bail slip that indicated that I, Nancy Kurshan, had bailed out one Steve Whitman in Rock Island, Illinois.

Steve had been arrested sitting down in the street with a group blocking a bridge. I had the job of bailing them all out. How strange that I had saved that particular bail slip, which now resides in our scrapbook along with pictures of us when we were babies, since lo and behold, we were born on the same street in the Flatbush section of Brooklyn! How strange, but true! Steve liked to claim he remembered me and that we played "doctor" together. Less true.

Although already slightly acquainted, our paths became intertwined when in 1985 the leader of the *Contras* in Nicaragua came to speak at Northwestern University in Evanston.

Between the war in Vietnam and the war in Iraq, the U.S. was not really at peace. What seemed like peace to citizens of the U.S. was experienced as war by millions around the globe. One such area of conflict was Central America. The U.S. had been interfering in the region long before the 1980s, overthrowing governments, supporting dictators, and funding military death squads.

When the Nicaraguan dictator Somoza was overthrown by the Left revolutionary Sandinistas, the U.S. began funding and training right-wing paramilitary forces known as the *Contras (contrarevolucionarios)*, who immediately went to work, sabotaging the new regime. When the U.S. Congress cut off funding "for the purpose of overthrowing the government of Nicaragua," the *Contras* by 1985 were searching for private American funding for their murderous efforts.

Our small but determined Chicago movement in the 1980s included activists of many stripes: "New Left" communists such as myself who had been active since the '60s, nuns, priests and lay people, liberation theologians who had lived and worked in Central America, others who had visited Latin America and were angry about the U.S. role. About a hundred such folks formed the Pledge of Resistance. Although we had a good deal of unity, we also had our differences, especially regarding tactics, which generated much discussion.

Often we would demonstrate outside the federal building in downtown Chicago to expose the U.S. role in the wars in Central America. Several of us formed *No Pasaran,* a women's affinity group, and we became one of the most active groups in "The Pledge." We sat down not just in front of the doors but in the middle of the streets, thereby disrupting rush hour traffic. On International Women's Day we dipped our hands in red paint and left our "bloody" prints on the federal building. We chained ourselves to the doors of the South African consulate and sat-in at Marine headquarters. Along with other affinity groups, we went out in canoes and dyed the Chicago River red, representing the blood of the Central American people. (Of course we made sure the dye was biodegradable.)

About now you might be wondering what does this have to do with the love of my life? But hang in there, cause I'm getting there.

In the spring of 1985 Adolfo Calero, primary leader of the *Contras,* was invited to speak by the Young Republican Club at Northwestern University. He was coming to Illinois seeking support for Reagan's current proposal to revive aid to the *Contras* and also to seek $14 million in military aid from the Illinois Republican Assembly. Everybody in the peace movement in Chicago began brainstorming about how to confront him. Some people were going to try to shout him down. Others were going to attempt a citizens' arrest. My friends and I decided to bathe him in blood.

Real blood—from a butcher shop. We practiced filling balloons with blood and throwing them so that they would splatter upon impact. Once we perfected our technique, we went to Northwestern to "case the joint."

It was rumored that the University (fearing trouble) would close the event to people outside the academic community. We asked all our friends if they knew anyone at Northwestern, and several mentioned a certain Steve Whitman who worked there as a researcher. The name rang a bell.

Sure enough, it was "Rock Island Steve" who gave us a tour of the campus and lecture hall, and loaned me his university ID so that at least one of us would be able to get in if only university people were admitted.

On Calero's big night, I dressed up in stockings, heels, and a skirt. Arriving early with my friends to discover that no ID was required, we sat in the very front row. Soon the auditorium filled completely with hundreds of students, faculty, and anti-war troublemakers. The room was abuzz. Some of our Pledge pals were planning a citizen's arrest of Calero. We had agreed to wait a few minutes to allow them to attempt to carry it out, although we were skeptical that it would be possible.

Calero was introduced by the Young Republicans amidst shouts and boos. He came out to speak and a feisty young professor, Barbara Foley, jumped onto the stage and began to list the crimes he was guilty of. It was a long list. Calero was surrounded by security and Foley was roughly hustled out. Some people started chanting slogans, others were yelling at Calero, while still others were yelling at the people who were yelling. Chaos reigned for ten or fifteen minutes. There were no signs of the citizens' arrest; we were afraid to lose the momentum, and so we decided to act. I felt like my pounding heart would give us away. We hurled the blood and dashed out the side door, having scoped out the place for the fastest retreat. I lost a high heel shoe somewhere along the way. We split up and reconvened, out of breath and excited, at a prearranged Burger King.

We later found out that the meeting effectively ended at that moment. The news media was full of images of Adolfo Calero covered with blood, fleeing from the scene. There were lots of editorials and letters to the editors. *The Chicago Tribune* of April 19th ran an editorial titled "Splattering Free Speech." Although many of the editorials focused on the free speech issue, I felt satisfied with our efforts. We knew that

Calero's relationship to free speech was to shut people up by cutting their throats—which was revealed in subsequent UPI and *Newsweek* photos.

After the Calero episode, my relationship with Steve developed quickly. One day shortly thereafter, Rosa, Michael, and I walked over to his place, which was just a few blocks away from our home, in order to return his ID. I couldn't stay long because the kids' bikes were unlocked outside but I was there long enough to be introduced to a woman who I figured must be his girlfriend. He thought I was a lesbian. We both found out otherwise.

A few days later I invited him to a political meeting. He turned me down. The very next day he called to ask me if I'd "like to get together, for dinner, no agenda." I agreed. I liked him immediately. He was smart and funny and I was attracted to him, but I was nervous and cautious. In the last two or three years I had had one very brief yet complicated relationship. I didn't want to subject myself or the kids to another tenuous relationship. I wondered, could I trust Steve?

So I vetted him. I asked José what he thought of Steve and he told me he was "a good and very honest" person. Both Edy and Ferd knew him and liked him but Edy cautioned me to go slowly just in case. So I leapt.

It was romantic. One evening we walked along the path by Lake Michigan, then sat by the rocks at Belmont Harbor. That weekend we went on a picnic in the park and had our first kiss. Steve told me he wanted to see me as much as possible in the next few weeks because he had some obligations that would make it difficult to spend time with me later that summer. I went back home and thought about it.

Then thought about it some more.

I then called to ask him to meet me in front of the Bread Store on Halsted Street, sat him down at their sidewalk picnic table, and told him that if we were to proceed with this relationship, we had to get a few things straight. The way Steve tells the story, I presented him with a contract and asked him to sign. I told him that I was 41 years old with two kids and wasn't interested in fooling around or wasting time. I needed to know if a) he would agree to see me exclusively, and b) he was planning

Nancy and Steve; Chicago, circa mid–1990s.

on living in Chicago indefinitely. For some crazy reason, he agreed to my demands and more. He even seemed to welcome them. Steve was certain that we were going to be good together, and that would be that. I liked his certainty. It took me a while to believe it, but he was right.

One evening soon after this, I invited him to have dinner at my place and he accepted. As soon as we sat down to dinner—Steve, Rosa, Michael, my roommate Margaret, and me—the kids began to fight, probably about who got to sit in the "big chair," a funky stepstool I'd picked up at the Salvation Army that raised you a bit higher than the other chairs. They wouldn't stop bickering. I was embarrassed and dragged them into the bedroom to settle them down. Steve says Margaret sat there calmly, beginning to eat, so he did the same. I thought after that performance he wouldn't stick around but I was wrong. Ever the activist-scientist, he soon solved the "big chair" problem by drawing up a schedule.

Our next get-together was a trip to the movies to see *Back to the Future.* It was a hot night and Rosa at nine years of age got all dressed up in an outfit that was actually a pajama set. She wore pink and purple plastic beads and bangles. Walking in front of us, we heard her inform her brother that, "You know, they're more than friends. He's Mom's boyfriend." Michael nodded approvingly and Steve shot me a smile: You see? It seems that the kids had sealed the deal. He later "admitted" that the only woman he "might prefer" was Tina Turner. I eagerly forgave him that compliment.

From then on, Steve fit right in to the family and when it came to the kids, we had similar approaches. If we disagreed, we agreed I had the last word. Michael went to preschool, *Centro Infantil,* at the Puerto Rican Cultural Center, and the school bus would drop Rosa off there at the end of the school day where she'd stay until I picked them up after work. One day Michael came home from school with an important question. His friend Alexi, who was Puerto Rican, claimed that Michael was Puerto Rican, but their Mexican pal Urajuyuan insisted Michael was Mexican. So Michael came home looking for clarification about who was right. I had to explain to him that there were actually other possibilities and, in fact, that we were "none of the above."

We didn't raise the children with religion. Though I am (some would say) distinctively Jewish, most of my life I have not believed in God or organized religion. I was disillusioned with Israel and American Judaism's uncritical support. After the kids were born, different people would ask me how I would deal with religion now that I had had children. I never saw any reason to be other than honest with them. We lived our lives oriented not around a particular religion, but rather around the pursuit of a just world. Again, I don't believe they have suffered. However, that philosophy generated some interesting and comic moments.

One September day, Michael came home from school and reported that his new teacher had asked if anyone knew what Jewish holiday was coming up. Michael, who had some dim idea that he was Jewish, raised his hand high, sure that he knew the answer. "It's Hare Krishna Day," he announced. Not only did he miss by a mile, but he came home requesting to have the day off. Steve told him that he couldn't have the day off for a holiday whose name he couldn't pronounce (Rosh Hashanah). Seriously, I have no regrets about how we raised the children in this regard. They have both proved to be adults with a strong moral compass, in the sense that they recognize the common humanity of all people and see themselves as world citizens, not Americans first or Jews first. I completely trust their choices.

Between work and political activity, there were times when the children's needs went unmet. One night Michael came into a meeting in our living room that was going on much too long and said, "I'm hungry. Where's dinner?" Someone told him to go and make himself a peanut butter and jelly sandwich. He obligingly went off to do so, returning momentarily to report that there was no peanut butter. "How about cereal?" was the response. Again, he went off only to return to say there was no cereal. Humorous in the retelling, perhaps, but as a mother I am not proud of those moments. I like to think they were exceptions.

We were clearly intensely passionate about what we thought, enough to center our entire lives around our political beliefs. The children came to agree with much of what we thought and felt because it made sense to them. Our explanations helped them understand the world as they experienced it.

The kids also understood there were only certain things we really cared about, and the rest could go lots of ways. But those things we really cared about were non-negotiable. We decided early on that there would be no war toys in our house. Although we supported people fighting against colonialism with weapons in hand, and women defending themselves against male violence, these distinctions seemed too subtle to explain to the kids. We underestimated them. One day when Michael was seven, he came home with a plastic model helicopter. He had applied a revolutionary Puerto Rican FALN sticker to the plane and was quite proud of himself, certain that he had a freedom-fighting plane that would be acceptable in our household. We made it so.

When the kids were little, I did what I thought was right and hoped for the best. In later years, Rosa captured some of their growing up when she wrote:

But where is home? Where you find it? Where you make it?

Small children cuddling in bed with mommy,

By choice,

Then later less by choice as we grew older and

Slept 4 squeezed on floor and bed in the only tiny bedroom that had an air conditioner in the window

Meetings, Arguments

The Cosby show and brushing your teeth before going to bed

Science projects

and

lots of

Friends. Always friends.

The swing-set in the back yard that pulled

halfway out of the ground when you swang

Because the grownups put it up for us themselves

During the first Gulf War, Michael and his friends left elementary school and marched around the neighborhood holding signs and chanting anti-war slogans, while Rosa and her friends joined the takeover of the streets.

The kids went everywhere with us. We visited Puerto Rican political prisoners Alicia and Lucy Rodriguez at a federal women's prison until they were moved to California. They are the aunts of Michael's friend Alexi, and were always excited to see the kids. The children, in turn, picked up immediately that they were very warm and caring people.

For years the four of us visited our friend Yaki. He hadn't entered prison as a political prisoner, but he emerged after 40 years as a Black Nationalist (a self-described New Afrikan) revolutionary; a writer, a deep thinker and editor of several publications, with friends and colleagues on the inside and out. Steve and I and Rosa and Michael were proud to be among them.

Yaki was a nationalist in the spirit of Malcolm X, and stated that "The stand of Malcolm, the stand that We must take up and creatively develop, is the stand of the nation for independence." But he was also an internationalist and felt connected to oppressed people everywhere, writing articles about South Africa, Italy, and more. From within his prison cell, removed from the direct influences of women, he struggled to understand the condition of women, and particularly Black women in the U.S. At a time when many nationalists were resistant to accepting gay liberation, Yaki understood that homophobia needed to be defeated as part of the struggle of the human family.

When I moved to Chicago, I was assigned by the leadership of PFOC to visit Yaki. After I left the organization, I went to see him and explained to him that I still intended to visit if it was okay with him.

"Why do you want to visit someone like me?" he asked in his deep voice.

"I don't want to visit someone *like* you. I want to visit you. Because you're my friend," I responded without hesitation.

"Oh," he said with a quizzical look on his face. And then as a slight smile crept up the corners of his mouth, he said, "Okay then." And with that, an assignment really did turn into a friendship.

Above: Nancy, daughter Rosa; Jericho March, Washington DC; March 1998. **Below:** Nancy, son Michael, daughter Rosa; Jericho March, Washington DC; March 1998.

We proceeded to see each other for years to come. Sometimes alone but increasingly with Steve and the kids.

Visiting Yaki at various state prisons around Illinois was an integral part of Rosa and Michael's childhood. They were eight and ten when they began visiting; young adults when he was finally released after 40 years (off and on) and came to live in our home.

We used to joke that the only thing we did together as a family was visit prisoners. In truth, these visits taught the children some invaluable lessons. They noticed that the majority of the prisoners and their visitors were Black and Latino, even in prisons far away in downstate Illinois communities.

We had to drive for hours to get there and then hang out in the waiting room. After we showed our IDs to the guards, we locked our possessions in a locker and waited. When the time came (it was never clear quite when) our hands were stamped, we were pat-searched and then walked through a series of loudly slamming metal doors. We then checked in with the guard in the visiting room who examined our hand stamps. We took seats at an assigned table and waited for Yaki.

After a while we saw his tall frame behind a glass door. Yaki was over six feet tall and handsome, although he had a few missing teeth. I think he was self-conscious about that and smiled less often than he might have. When they were later fixed, you could see his great big beautiful smile, although still not often enough.

Our visits were under constant observation. We could get food from vending machines, but Yaki was not allowed to work the machines himself.

The kids loved Yaki, who was always really glad to see them. He would ask them their opinions on everything and treated them as young adults. The visits were hours long but the children never seemed to mind. Yaki and Michael enjoyed playing chess together. These get-togethers were usually joyful, almost carefree affairs, at least until it came time to leave. Then we would hug Yaki and he'd walk out a separate door for prisoners. We could see him waiting for the next set of bars to open before he disappeared into the prison. It was always an intensely somber moment, and when we'd get back into our car we'd be quiet, lost in our own sadness, for some time.

All adults had to get approval in advance to visit, but for young children that was not necessary. Sometimes the kids went to prisons without me, accompanying friends who were visiting other political prisoners.

Rosa and Michael came away from these visits feeling that these prisoners were wonderful people. In fact, they were among their favorite adults. They wondered why these people were behind bars and serving such long, harsh sentences. The visits helped them put our objections to American justice in context.

The older they got, the more they understood. The more they understood, the more they generously put up with our rather unusual family life. Rosa was off at college and Michael was a senior in high school when several of my comrades surprised us all, suddenly emerging from clandestinity and back into our lives. On New Years Eve 1998, Claude's birthday, we had a big party at our home and I was able to present him with his box that I had saved all those years. Shortly thereafter he and Donna were in the Metropolitan Corrections Center. They had turned themselves in on charges related to the Puerto Rican independence movement. Claude would eventually spend four years in prison, and Donna a year and half. Diana, Claude's wife and their two kids, Tony and Leila, came to stay with us while awaiting sentencing, a good portion of a year. Michael shared his space with them when he was at my house. When at his dad's house he lived with Donna's husband Rob and baby Zoe.

In college, Rosa joined us at the gates of various prisons, bringing along other students from Antioch College. We met Michael and his Hampshire College friends at a Free Mumia demonstration in Philadelphia. And the whole family marched in DC to free all political prisoners.

Rosa also wrote an essay called "Inspiration" which began: "The blood streamed across my mother's aging face."

It was the story of my 1985 confrontation with white supremacists—KKK, Neo-Nazis, and a group called Romantic Violence—who had been spray-painting racist graffiti in our neighborhood. We organized a Stamp

Out Racism campaign and went out to cover over their graffiti and replace it with our own. The Klansmen and neo-Nazis asserted their free speech rights with clubs and tire irons, bashing the heads of Bob, Russell, and me with their "shields." While a friend scooted the kids away, and the Klan shouted "White Power!" we three bloodied anti-racists were rushed to the hospital. I came home with a black eye and three stitches just above it. A few days later I started social work graduate school with a patch over my right eye.

Rosa's college essay concluded that the attack bolstered her "already-formed admiration for the work my parents and people around me do to try to change the world. That admiration continues to grow." How happy it made me to read that. When she and Michael were little I would often sing "*Die Gedanken Sind Frei*", a beautiful song about freedom of thought from as far back as the 1400 Peasant Wars in Germany. In his adult years, Michael's band performed a rocked-out version and every time I heard it, my heart took flight.

I am incredibly proud of Rosa and Michael. They are both teachers in the public schools of Oakland and Brooklyn, working with newcomers at a time when immigrants are severely stigmatized by many. They both walk through life very aware of the inequities and very conscious of their own place.

In 2004 a small group of persistent people were able to gain Yaki's release. As a condition of his parole, he came to live with Steve and me. The kids had already left the nest. We had been sick of living in an apartment where the heat broke down regularly in frigid Chicago winters, and the skylight that flew off the roof was finally replaced with a board. And we had known Yaki might be getting out, although we had thought it a long shot.

So, each of us now being 60 years old, we had bought a house and had a mortgage. A few weeks after Steve and I moved in, Yaki did come home. We were all amazed and I was also a bit nervous. It's always one thing to have a friendship and another quite different thing to live with that friend. And this was someone who had been incarcerated for so long. But I was also eager and excited.

Yaki was not permitted to leave our house for the first 90 days, and he arrived wearing an ankle monitor which would catch him in any violation. He also had to be at his phone for a daily phone check-in, and any time his parole officer (PO) arrived, we'd have to give him access. As it happened, his PO was a young Haitian man who carefully checked out our hundreds of books, including several about the Haitian revolution. I could see from the quizzical look on his face that he wondered what the hell these two old white folks were doing with this black felon!

So at first Yaki couldn't leave, but at least he had a whole floor to himself with his own bathroom, TV, computer, and jazz library, thanks to a group of his friends who helped us with all this.

The first thing Yaki wanted was food. Per request we brought him shrimp fried rice from the corner Chinese restaurant. And when he could leave home, we took him to our favorite Mexican restaurant and he ate everything in sight, including two desserts. But more often than not he made his prison concoction of sardines and tuna and ate standing up at the island counter.

For the most part, we got along fabulously. When I had decided he could live with us, I worried only about the kids, where they'd stay when they came to visit and how to spend some time alone with them. But I just figured we'd cross that bridge when we got to it. And then it happened. I had prepared Yaki for such a possibility but when I suggested that he stay for a couple of nights with his good friend David Saxner, the person who led the campaign to get him out, he got pretty bent out of shape. He didn't want to talk about it, but he did do it. I still don't know if it was right of me to ask that of him. I can't imagine the thoughts and feelings that those decades of imprisonment left him with. But by his choice we never discussed it again.

Yaki stayed with us for most of a year. The world had changed dramatically but Yaki was eager to embrace it, and I was amazed at how fast he adapted. He found a job with a non-profit organization that did work around prisons; he reconnected with his family and married the woman he was with before he went in; he developed a project to get other prisoners out and applied for a Soros grant.

After a while, Yaki was allowed to live on his own, but finding an apartment for a felon with no work history and no assets is not an easy task. Luckily, José Lopez helped find an apartment in the Puerto Rican community for Yaki and his wife, Akreeba.

Yaki smoked like a chimney and after a few years of freedom he died of lung cancer in 2008. I cried quiet tears through his memorial upon hearing especially the testimony from other African-American men who had been inside with Yaki. Their love for him came shining through as they thanked him for throwing them a lifeline. I love Yaki too, and I miss him.

But I need to circle back to my late husband Steve and explain what an amazing person he was long before I met him. Born into a working-class Jewish family in Brooklyn, he went to City College, which was completely free back then, and eventually got a PhD from Yale in biostatistics. Steve used to say PhD stood for "piled higher and deeper," but that he was committed to putting it to some real use. When he told his mother that he was going to join the Peace Corps, she announced that she would take to her bed and never get up again if he did. So he took a job as a math instructor at the historically black Miles College in Birmingham, Alabama. He spent the next ten years in Birmingham, where he became deeply involved in fighting racism, and increasingly spent time engaged in prison work that centered on Atmore's Holman prison. After ten years in Birmingham, Steve was offered a job at the Center for Urban Affairs of Northwestern University in Chicago. A wealthy woman had died and left an endowment for someone to research possible non-medical interventions for epilepsy. Steve worked for a number of years studying the social dimensions of epilepsy, which included work with prisoners. This resulted in a protocol utilizing progressive relaxation as a tool for dealing with epilepsy (described in his book, *Psychopathology in Epilepsy: Social Factors*; Oxford Press, 1986). It was during his time at Northwestern that I first met Steve.

When Steve outgrew his job at Northwestern, I supported his decision to take up an offer to become the chief epidemiologist at the Chicago Health Department. In that position he was able to advocate for needle exchanges and condom distribution in the fight against HIV. And when the heatwave of 1995 hit, he accurately counted the dead bodies as they piled up, over 700, and confronted Mayor Daley with the outrageous facts. Steve used his position to publicly explain that the deaths were not a result of natural disaster, but were a preventable result of racism and poverty. It was clear that people died or lived according to what zip code they lived in, and that those who died were disproportionately Black and poor. (See *Heat Wave: A Social Autopsy of Disaster in Chicago* by Eric Klinenberg, 2002; Steve appears also in the 2018 documentary *Cooked: Survival by Zip Code*, streaming on Prime Video.)

He eventually left the Health Department and set up his own shop at the poor safety net hospital of Mt. Sinai. He ended up with a dedicated staff that took on studying racial disparities in health with the aim of doing something about it. Huge door-to-door studies were done in a number of communities, really groundbreaking research was conducted, and successful (some yes, some no) interventions were put in place around diabetes, pediatric asthma, breast cancer, and more. Steve and his colleagues produced *Urban Health: Combating Disparities with Local Data* (Oxford University Press, 2011), used throughout the country by students of public health.

Always, Steve was an activist, organizing town hall meetings at Black, Mexican, and Puerto Rican churches and other community centers, culminating in large rallies and marches demanding more resources from the State for breast cancer interventions. A speech he gave at the time reflects, I think, his essence. After speaking about racial health disparities, Steve said, “We have to regard these problems as if it’s a problem in ***our*** family, as if what we’re discussing is ***our*** mothers, and ***our*** daughters and fathers … and we have to fight like hell to change it.” And then, slyly shifting gears, he promised the audience that if they joined him in taking action, not only would they become taller, but they would also be able to eat as much chocolate as they wanted without gaining any weight. Steve was very funny. As a friend put it, “Steve wore his many achievements so lightly that one remembers him for his playfulness and not for the eminent personality he was.”

In his spare time Steve played an important role in exposing police brutality. At one of the memorial services for Steve, Flint Taylor of the Peoples Law Office had this to say: "Steve's lifelong commitment to fighting racism and inequality brought him to play a key role in exposing the systemic nature of police torture and brutality in Chicago. His work was cited in studies and editorials condemning police brutality. The lawyers for the police unsuccessfully challenged Steve in court, and he wore their unprincipled attacks as a red badge of courage." Steve's adversaries, and many of his allies, had had no way of knowing that he was exhausted and in pain from his kidney cancer at the time.

Steve also developed groundbreaking statistics about race and imprisonment long before it became popular knowledge. Along with others, he and I worked in support of political prisoners. Over the years we published six editions of *Can't Jail the Spirit*, a collection of biographies and photographs of political prisoners (mostly, but not all, Black, Puerto Rican, and Native American) in the U.S.

Steve's scientific outlook helped me to put facts on my radical perspective and gain a deeper understanding. We both saw mass imprisonment as a response to the social uprisings of the '60s, and American prisons not as simply cruel or racist, but as successful institutions that meet the repressive goals of the rulers.

Perhaps the most substantial work we did together was the work of the Committee to End the Marion Lockdown (CEML). At a time when hardly anybody gave a shit about prisoners, we threw our hearts and souls into 15 years of uphill struggle to end long-term solitary confinement, first in the downstate Illinois federal prison of Marion. When those supermax prisons began proliferating in most other states, we began running around the country trying to stick our thumbs in the holes of all the dykes. But I have written a whole book about that, titled *Out of Control.* If you read it, you can eat as much chocolate as you like without gaining weight.

We organized caravans of hundreds of people to go to the gates of numerous prisons, wrote thousands of leaflets, stalked politicians to get their ear, and confronted the head of the Bureau of Prisons to his face.

Friday, February 2, 1990

Group protests lockdown

by John B. Henao

After driving from Chicago through pouring rain Thursday night, two women came to Champaign to denounce living conditions of inmates at the Marion, Ill., federal prison, about 20 miles east of Carbondale.

Nancy Kurshan and Kimberly Fitzgerald of the Chicago-based Committee to End the Marion Lockdown, told about 15 people gathered at the Illinois Disciples Foundation, 403 S. Wright St., Champaign, that Marion inmates are confined to their cells 22 hours a day and the prison's water source is contaminated by low-level toxic waste.

Marion, the only supermaximum-security prison, handles inmates considered the most dangerous or highest risk to security in the federal prison system. The prison was ostensibly created to replace Alcatraz Penitentiary in San Francisco Bay, which closed in 1963.

According to information provided by the committee, Marion has been on a lockdown status in October 1983 after two prison guards were killed by inmates in separate instances. But an article in the Jan. 15 issue of Newsweek magazine states that the two guards were killed on the same day in October 1983 and that nine inmates had been killed from February 1980 to October 1983.

Since then, inmates have been confined 22 hours a day to their seven-foot by nine-foot cells.

The main thrust of the speakers' presentation is best described by the words of Garnett Leacock, one of Marion's inmates: "There is no medium that can be utilized in order to project the oppressive, repressive, regressive and depressive feeling that someone incarcerated at Marion must survive with daily."

The level-six maximum security rating was created specifically for Marion, which holds about 350 men, said Kurshan. According to the video, a congressional report has shown that 80 percent of the men do not deserve to be in a level-six penitentiary.

However, Kurshan said that although the committee's plans are to eventually put an end to the lockdown status, its more immediate plans involve putting an end to the prisoners' consumption of water contaminated with toxic waste.

Kurshan said that the Marion-area Crab Orchard Lake is so contaminated that the town of Marion purchases water from surrounding towns rather than use the water from its own lake. However, the Environmental Protection Agency says the water meets federal standards for drinking water, according to Newsweek.

Kurshan

The only ones who do use the water—to drink, bathe and launder with—are the Marion prisoners, she said.

Below: Nancy, Chicago, 1986.

All in addition to our day jobs and raising kids. It exhausted us but it was also wonderful. We knew, just like on the steps of the Pentagon or Chicago '68, that we were doing the right thing.

I'm often asked what kept us going for 15 years. A big part of the answer is all the people we met along the way. Let me tell you about one—Sundiata Acoli.

Most of the earliest information and analysis about Marion Federal Penitentiary came to me from political prisoners at Marion. One of those was Sundiata Acoli, who, the reader may recall, had been a member of the Panther 21 (p. 174) To support his parole effort I worked on producing and distributing "Sundiata's Freedom Is Your Freedom," a pamphlet about his case. I was not permitted to visit Sundiata at Marion. If I had, it would have been a non-contact visit, sitting on either side of a plexiglass wall, talking on a telephone, with a guard behind my shoulder.

Most of our communication was through the telephone or snail mail, then in later years through the federal email system. As Sundiata has said, "At some point, Nancy and I began corresponding and struck up an instant friendship that morphed into an easy camaraderie." Over many years we collaborated on two larger projects as well. "*A Brief History of the New Afrikan Prison Struggle*" can be found online at Freedom Archives.

Then I assisted Sundiata with the completion of his autobiography and learned that in 1964, while working as a computer programmer, he read an article about the murder of the three civil rights workers—Goodman, Cheney and Schwerner—that implied the murders would deter volunteers from going south to register voters. So Sundiata stepped up and volunteered, paying his own way to spend the summer working with the Student Nonviolent Coordinating Committee. Sundiata felt that "too many of my brothers and sisters hadn't survived ... I was aware of the subtle pressures working to force upon me the acceptance of white values, to give up more and more of being Black.... I loved being Black—the Black mentality, mores, habits, and associations. I looked around for an organization that was dedicated to alleviating the suffering of Black people."

Sundiata joined the Harlem Chapter of the Black Panther Party. The organization was targeted by the FBI's Counterintelligence Program and that's when in 1969 Sundiata was arrested in the Panther 21 case. Denied bond, he spent two years in jail, waiting for a trial that lasted eight months, when all defendants were acquitted in a 56-minute jury deliberation!!!

Upon his release Sundiata was constantly followed and harassed before joining a clandestine organization. An ambush by state troopers on the New Jersey turnpike resulted in the murder of Zayd Malik Shakur and the serious wounding of Assata Shakur, as well as the death of Trooper Werner Foerster, killed by bullets of a state trooper's gun. Sundiata was convicted in an atmosphere of mass hysteria. The judge stated that Sundiata was an avowed revolutionary and gave him a life sentence, with no possibility of parole for 25 years.

Over the years I loved working with Sundiata. He was demanding. No, never demanding but yes, exacting. It took a long time for a project to be completed because the inside/outside prison dynamics slow everything down. How ironic that Sundiata, who used to be a professional computer programmer, had to write out by hand each and every word on paper and then send it to me. Sometimes I would do some research for him or make a few suggestions. I would then type and retype many, many more times, each time mailing him the new version. And then I'd wait for the yoyo to come back to me. I quickly came to understand that Sundiata is a meticulous perfectionist. But I didn't mind. I respected his work style and thoroughly enjoyed getting to know him.

We fell into a comfortable collaboration on his projects, and Sundiata generously wrote the Foreword to *Out of Control*, my book about prison work. In it he attributed his 1987 transfer from Marion (to Leavenworth Prison) to our organizing efforts, and explained: "At Leavenworth's contact visit I hugged my baby daughter, then a sophomore in college, for the first time since she was a toddler, and hugged my oldest daughter, a registered nurse, for the first time ever! The same held true for Nancy's visit and the joy of meeting her in person, thanking her for all she and CEML had done, and then celebrating our decampment from Marion

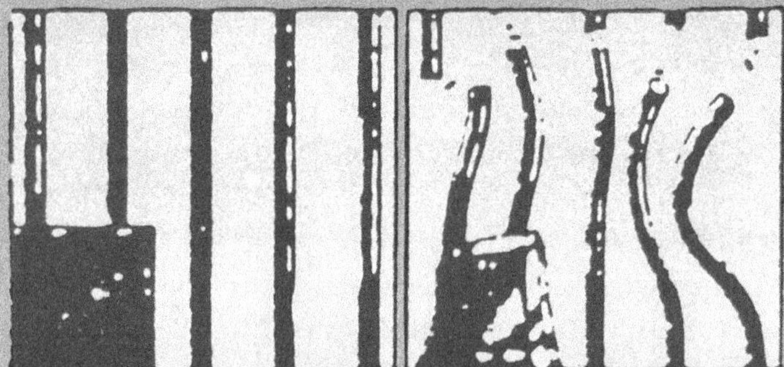

OUT OF CONTROL

A FIFTEEN YEAR BATTLE AGAINST CONTROL UNIT PRISONS

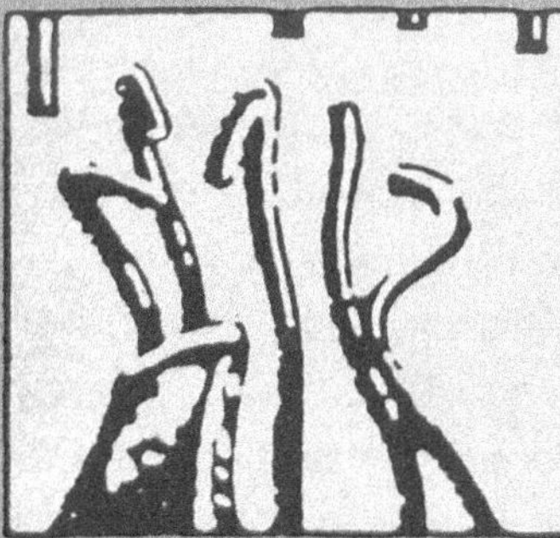

NANCY KURSHAN

Foreword by Sundiata Acoli

with a joyous feast on everything the vending machine had to offer." When I finally got to meet Sundiata face to face, he seemed both shorter and stronger in person than I had imagined. He was very muscular, and I knew for a fact he worked out regularly. Despite the oppressive life he's been forced to live, he always seems to have a great big smile the width of his face (Google his photos)—so broad you could actually hear it over the telephone—and a magnanimous spirit that is contagious. Sometimes he'd send me gifts of his artwork. Often, I am ashamed to say, I forget his birthday—January 14th. He never forgets mine! On Valentine's Day and Mother's Day cards often arrive right on time and, as the years tick on, they're addressed to the Silver Fox. Despite it all, he is also playful.

Sundiata has been eligible for parole since 1992. Yet he's been denied parole six times as a "risk to public safety." If he is a risk, why is it that the Bureau of Prisons tapped him to teach "Avoiding Criminal Thinking," a course designed to help incarcerated men avoid recidivism when they return to society? Sundiata is 84 years old and been inside for a half-century. He has had Covid and now, early stage dementia. His huge community of family and friends wants to welcome him home. It kills me that he can't come. [Update: In 2022 at age 85, Sundiata was finally granted parole and released from prison. I had the great fortune to sit with him at his favorite Thai restaurant and celebrate his freedom.]

Yup, it's the people I have met and traveled with along the way that sustain me. I feel such love and respect for so many. Susceptible to cynicism and frustration, it is people who have invariably lifted my spirit.

I recall picketing at USP Terre Haute (Indiana) in the rain. I was soaked to the core, my feet hurt, and I just wanted to get the hell home and rest. Just then, the legendary Puerto Rican *independentista* Rafael Cancel Miranda, one of the Five Nationalists, caught up to me and put his hand on my shoulder. "Thanks for making this happen, Nancy," he said. "It's great to be here, isn't it?" And I knew for sure that it was indeed great to be there—soggy socks and all.

Steve was always my biggest supporter, or maybe cheerleader is more accurate, encouraging me to do things I was reluctant to do. In 2010 I learned of the movie about the Chicago 8 in which Mayim Bialik played me. I wrote and told her that Steve and I were big fans of her (then) new show, *The Big Bang Theory*. She invited us to come see a taping. I told Steve about the offer but added that I didn't want to spend the money. His reaction: "Hell yes, we're going!". And we did. It was so much fun. We had coffee with Mayim and her parents, and then went to a live audience taping of the show and were treated like VIPs.

January 2013, another offer presented itself when the Vietnamese government invited peace activists who had visited North Vietnam during the American War (as they call it) to return for the 40th anniversary of the signing of the Paris Peace Accords. When I first heard about it from my old pal Judy Gumbo, I thought how great it would be to return to Vietnam with my old traveling companion. But then I thought, "Nah, I won't go. Too expensive, too this, too that." I told Steve and, in his repetitive pattern, he said, "Hell yes, we're going! This will be the trip of a lifetime!" And so we went. And so it was.

In terms of the trajectory of my life, I had come full circle. For someone who had been placed in handcuffs many times by my own government, I felt exonerated and more than that, affirmed. We were given the red carpet treatment, literally and figuratively. The President of Vietnam thanked us and shook our hands. But the ultimate was when I was actually embraced by Madame Binh (a huge hug from Madame Binh!), whose strength had caused Henry Kissinger to complain about her when he faced her across the negotiations table. It was an unequivocal affirmation of our work to stop the war.

I have always maintained that we helped to end the war, but on some level even I internalized the U.S. government's propaganda about our efforts, which either marginalized our impact or accused us of being the single cause for the U.S. defeat. It wasn't until this trip that I fully embraced and celebrated our contribution, my contribution. I was one of the 25,000 people at the first SDS DC demonstration, and kept organizing until the debate reached dinner tables across the nation and into the highest echelons of power. I persisted until we reached the hearts and minds of a significant number of Americans. We helped bring the war to an end, may have saved many lives, and perhaps evaded the

Above: Nancy with Madame Binh; 40th anniversary of the signing of the Peace Accords; Hanoi, 2013. **Below:** Nancy meets Mayim Bialik who played Nancy in a 2012 movie, *The Chicago 8*; 2012.

Below: Nancy and Sundiata celebrating his release: Brooklyn, New York, 2022.

nuclear option. We definitely demonstrated the possibility of a successful mass opposition to unjust war.

However, my return trip to Vietnam was also filled with many moments of pain, the dark side of the legacy of Vietnam. Once again, I heard the stories people shared about the torture they underwent in the Tiger Cages of the south. I visited schools filled with children who are disfigured from the effects of the Agent Orange that is still in their ecosystem today. The government of Vietnam estimates that 500,000 children have been born with such birth defects.

We learned that other children have died as a result of unexploded ordnance from the war. While playing outside in their village, they accidentally come across buried unexploded ordnance and within an instant it erupts and shatters their poor bodies forever. Since the end of the war, 100,000 such civilian deaths have been reported.

There were also awkward moments—as when Steve confronted the U.S. Ambassador and told him that 50 million dollars was "peanuts" for the U.S. to give to Vietnam to clean up the damage of Agent Orange. "Billions short and decades late." I could tell that our fellow travelers wished that Steve had kept his mouth shut. I squeezed his hand as we both got up and left.

That mouth, that hand, that man. I miss him every hour of every day. Steve was diagnosed with kidney cancer in the fall of that year, and died in July of 2014.

I'll spare you the shock, the grief, the pain of Steve's death. I was helped through it by the many relatives and friends who had loved and respected him, and most of all by my kids who had welcomed him into their lives. But in private, in the dark, the dreams persist for years. I write them down—

I dreamt Steve came back but he had a big gash across the top of his head. All I remember.

I had a previous dream where Steve and I got separated. He got on a train. I didn't. And then I kept calling his cell phone, his cell phone that has always been so reliable, and I could not reach him. I could never reach him. And I felt despair. Then I awoke.

I dreamt I was on a train and suddenly realized that Steve was on the same train. But he was getting off the train. I dashed out of the train and tried to find him but he had entered a train going in the opposite direction and I lost him. I awoke sad and yearning to see him.

I dreamt I was at a big women's rally and there were several scantily dressed feminists up on a small stage singing and dancing. Suddenly Steve showed up and said, "Hi, how are you?" "Okay," says I, "but can't you please stay a little while?" "I'm so sorry," he says, "I really can't. But I love you." And so I awoke.

Last night for the first time in my dreams about Steve, it was not about separation. Steve and I were together, talking, and touching. I even filled him in on certain mundane events that have gone on in his "absence." I woke up feeling grateful.

Well, my love affair with Steve lasted close to 30 years. I can't imagine a better man for me. At 41 years of age I found a man who not only made me laugh every day, but loved and supported me fully, was not in any way ambivalent about our relationship, and who was as devoted to the fight for justice as I was. He gave of himself freely and fully. How lucky is that! As my religious friends say, I am truly blessed.

THROUGH THE REARVIEW MIRROR

Of course, my old life was still there, reappearing at times, for good or ill, reawakening old memories. Twenty years after 1968, there was a Conspiracy Trial commemoration in Chicago, where I found myself on a stage with my old Yippie comrades Abbie Hoffman, Stew Albert, and several other men of the era. Twenty years later, long after the flowering of the women's liberation movement, and yet I was still the only woman on the platform! We all talked about the power of the movements of the 1960s, how the black liberation movement had shaped our consciousness. I defended the militancy of the '60s and argued that moderation was not what was called for, that we needed more righteous indignation and militancy. Then I crossed the line:

> *"I am the token woman on this panel. In fact, one of two women in this entire weekendlong affair. In some sense, it shows you just how far we really have NOT come. Our movement was extremely male-dominated as were our personal relationships. As women, we did a great deal of the work but were invisible or seen as the helpmates of men. One of the most profound and transforming outgrowths of the '60s was the movement for women's liberation, and it grew as a reaction to the dominant and rampant male supremacy. And it was really a movement for liberation, not just for a larger slice of the American pie. It reached into the lives of millions of Americans."*

My remarks were well-received by the audience. However, only one of my old "comrades" had anything to say to me, and that was to complain that I had read my presentation instead of speaking "off-the cuff." (Yippie style?). No word of praise or encouragement, only criticism. No one had treated me that way in a long while, and all the old feelings came flooding back. I first felt humiliated as if it were my fault, as if I were back at Sproul Plaza being berated by Jerry. After some effort and a lot of help from Steve and other friends I let righteous anger wipe away the humiliation. I am so thankful for the women's liberation movement!

Abbie died in 1989, reportedly a suicide by overdose. He was barely fifty. In spite of our differences, I still admired his humor and commitment to justice. I had lost touch with him and had known little of the melancholy that had dogged him for years.

Jerry died in 1994, hit by a car while jaywalking on Los Angeles's Wilshire Boulevard. We hadn't spoken in years, but I still remember his generosity, his bright intelligence, his affection and need (if not always regard) for me.

Jerry and I did not remain friends and never renewed our friendship. The very rare times we saw each other, it had been tense and disagreeable. He chastised me for continuing to do the same thing over and over, even if it wasn't going to go anywhere, and he never apologized to me for his part in the unequal relationship we had had. I never apologized to him for what must have seemed to be a very abrupt departure. But when people criticize him for "betraying the movement," I come to his defense, protective of him as if he were my brother.

After my time with Jerry, he began searching for a different path, investigating various elements of the self-actualization movement, a short stint on Wall Street and entrepreneurial pursuits. I understand his seeking an alternative journey. Even when he turned to Wall Street, I never felt he was a traitor, a Benedict Arnold, as some people opined. I was disappointed and would have preferred him to do it quietly. But that wasn't in his character.

I understand his search. I ask you to wonder what if: What if you had been called to HUAC three times? What if you had served several criminal sentences for nonviolently protesting the war, sometimes in uncomfortable places like Cook County Jail? What if you had been kidnapped by prison guards, and then withstood a harrowing trip across country? What if you were indicted on conspiracy felony charges, spent ten months on trial as well as some time in jail before it was reversed on appeal? What if you had been knocked around by the cops in your own apartment and had your coccyx messed up? What if your finances were being investigated by the IRS? Your phone tapped regularly? Undercover agents tracking you? Do you think your anxiety might drive you to consider a different path? I think Jerry's core beliefs had not changed, but he was looking for a safer, calmer, and yes, more lucrative harbor.

I didn't like his turn toward the self-actualization movement because it seemed so either/or. It could have been an attempt to combine the two worlds, take the best of each. Much as today's activists often try to include self-care. But it came across like a repudiation of those who continued in our activism. Over time I have come to see it in a somewhat different light. Jerry had some serious personal work to do that needed to take precedence. He had individual and interpersonal issues to deal with. I have never fully understood if he found some peace, but I hope so.

In the 1980s, Abbie and Jerry traveled the country with a Yippie vs Yuppie debate that left me with a sour taste. I didn't like Jerry's embrace of that label. I didn't like the playing out of their differences on a public stage and I wish they hadn't done that. I thought it was a result of both their desires for continued fame, which seemed shabby. But I later learned that Jerry may have agreed to it in order to help Abbie out, because he needed the fees they were paid from the speakers bureau.

Jerry wanted to see an infusion of capital into the depressed areas of our economy. When he died crossing Wilshire Boulevard, he was reportedly on his way to a meeting about marketing a health product, the proceeds of which would go toward the Black community of Watts. I like to think he was trying to combine his entrepreneurial spirit with a spirit of reparations for the destruction that racist capitalism had wrought in poor Black neighborhoods in L.A.

I greatly admire the Jerry I keep in my head. He is sharply critical of U.S. society and especially the U.S. government, and passionately identifies with people around the world who are struggling for a better existence. He is an activist intellectual, inspired by C. Wright Mills, Che Guevara and Bertrand Russell; a brilliant organizer who is able to imagine a better future for all and is willing to turn his life over to get there. He is very brave, not physically, but is willing to take unpopular positions and actions because that is often necessary to challenge the existing order. He speaks truth to power. We need more people like that.

Despite the obstacles, there had always been real unexpressed affection between Anita Hoffman and me. We kept in touch although we lived thousands of miles apart; she on the West Coast and I in Chicago.

When I got her email in the fall of 1998 informing me that she was dying of cancer, I was shocked. I picked up the phone and called her immediately. Her voice was strong and clear. She told me she was now in hospice; that new drugs were keeping the pain at bay, but she was paralyzed from the waist down and didn't have long to live. "Why don't you come see me?" she asked calmly. My heart was beating rapidly as I hopped on a plane to California.

The house address I had been given was in the extremely upscale Pacific Heights neighborhood of San Francisco. I found Anita in an upstairs bedroom, her hospital bed facing a full wall of windows that offered a sweeping view of the Bay and the Golden Gate Bridge. Just outside her window was a bird feeder where several exquisite yellow finches were feeding. In the two days that we spent together, it was clear that she still enjoyed many of life's offerings. We shared ice cream and chocolate, watched TV and swapped stories, talking about old times and new.

Although the physical surroundings were beautiful, what moved me most deeply and warmed my heart most thoroughly, was the way Anita was being looked after by her women friends. In her final hours, her women's group turned over their lives to take care of her. Rosemary, another "'60s wife," had been married to Timothy Leary. Cindy Horowitz had come to know Anita and Rosemary while putting together a chronicle of Leary's activities. In recent years, the three had become good friends. This beautiful house belonged to Cindy's daughter, the actress Winona Ryder.

A day after I arrived to see Anita, Stew and Judy Gumbo arrived as well. As the three of us sat around Anita's bed, Judy presented Anita with presents from their recent trip to Israel. Anita was touched by their first gift of a menorah. Although she no longer practiced Judaism, she said she appreciated it very much as a reminder of her childhood. I knew that Anita meant what she said since she rarely minced words. I, on the other hand, winced when I saw the menorah. I too have removed myself from Judaism, in no small part due to the occupation of Palestine and the support that world Jewry has given to that apartheid system.

Then Judy Gumbo took out a very beautiful tallit (Jewish prayer shawl) and told Anita, "This is for you to be draped in after your death." Not skipping a beat, Anita said, "Give it to someone else, Judy. I won't drape myself in a symbol of that patriarchal religion."

Anita was an original item. She was smart and quick, quirky and compassionate, opinionated, and often brutally honest. Always more glamorous than the rest of us, slender with striking sculpted features, dark dark hair and olive skin, she looked beautiful even on her deathbed. Before I left (and she left) she thanked me for coming and told me: "You are such a clear cogent thinker and writer, Nancy. I'm impressed. I don't agree always but usually I do." Okay, so maybe it was an overstatement. However, that was the nicest thing any Yippie had ever said to me, and I was grateful. Still am.

Stew Albert died in 2006. His next to last words were "My politics haven't changed." I never doubted it. I will always remember his speech on the steps of the Pentagon, his uncanny ability to put things in words that people could relate to.

Fortunately for me, Judy Gumbo is still with us and going strong, my most constant of Yippie friends. Not only did we travel back to Vietnam together, but Judy was one of my greatest supports during my early, desperate grieving for Steve. Her kindness in opening up her home to me acted as a protective balm. As the years go by, we look more and more like doppelgängers. Still short, of course, but now both with similar heads of white hair. She is still a spunky spark plug, and has written a memoir called *Yippie Girl.*

But perhaps the greatest surprise from that era is to have Bernardine and Bill back in my life. In Chicago I finally reconnected with my old friends, after a long time apart. The second Iraq war of 2003 was threatening, and a large national anti-war demonstration was called for Washington, D.C. Unusual as it may sound, some airlines steeply cut fares to D.C. Still working full-time, Steve and I decided to fly in and out for the demonstration. Who do we meet in the airport doing the same thing? Yup, yet another serendipitous meeting with Bernardine. And Billy. With time on our hands, we head to an airport café and talk until the flight.

They had surfaced many years before and I had seen them once or twice years ago when they first moved to Chicago. But with the crush of life—working, raising kids, as well as political activism—we hadn't renewed our friendship. Now all our kids had left the nest and I was close to retirement. From then on I would continue to see Bill and Bernardine, but especially Bernardine.

Bernardine was an associate clinical professor at the Northwestern University Law School and the director of its Children and Family Justice Center. She and I would meet at a small food concession in the lobby of a university building. We would sit together, drinking coffee and shooting the breeze. It was as if we had never had a break in our friendship. Sometimes we'd talk about the past but mostly we lived in the present. Other times I'd sit on the beautiful back deck of their Hyde Park home or she'd come north and we'd walk the 606 trail, old elevated rail tracks converted into an elongated 3-mile park. Bernardine was always encouraging me to write this memoir.

After I returned from Vietnam in 2013, I later joined my fellow travelers in writing a chapter for a book—*The People Make the Peace.* Bill organized a book reading for myself and editor Frank Joyce. On a freezing, snowy Chicago night, my son Michael and I drove to the 57th Street bookstore in Hyde Park. I was nervous as usual when faced with public speaking. Michael lovingly assured me, "You'll be great, Mom. You always are. And lots of your friends are here." I wore the black pajamas and conical hat of the Vietnamese resistance that I had been given in 1970, and while we waited for folks to get seated, I played '60s anti-war rock 'n' roll—"(Four Dead in) Ohio" (CSNY); "Chicago" (Graham Nash); "Gotta Revolution" (Jefferson Airplane), etc. But I was somewhat reticent, especially during the Q&A, letting mostly Frank respond. Then suddenly Bill persisted in drawing me out. I was resistant and yet appreciative. After the reading, Bill and Bernardine opened up their home, along with snacks and drinks, to those who wanted to join.

Pulling Bernardine aside I said, "Wow, I so appreciate Bill for drawing me out. I know it's not always easy. So I'm really impressed with his sensitivity."

"Yes," she said. "He's certainly evolved. But the truth is, I passed him a note asking him to do that."

I had to laugh but am grateful all the time for the feminist movement. However, I still struggle with public speaking.

A few weeks before I left Chicago to move to Oakland in August 2018, I went to see Bill and Bernardine.

"I understand your reasons for leaving but I'll be sad to see you go," Bernardine said, "and we'll have a goodbye party for you. You invite twenty of your favorite people."

"No, no," I objected. "I don't like having parties for myself."

"Well, you're not having it for yourself. We are. Just give us the names and we'll do all the rest. Food and drink on our back porch in this beautiful summer weather. You've lived, worked and played here for thirty years. You can't just sneak out."

And so, I agreed. And so, they did throw me a party and I had a great time. I had no trouble speaking, telling a short story about each and every person there. It was easy because I love them all.

Interestingly enough, in 2021 my phone rang here in California and it was Bernardine: "We're in the Bay Area, waiting for Chesa and Valerie's baby to arrive." (Chesa, the wonderfully progressive District Attorney of San Francisco, was raised by Bill and Bernardine, since his biological parents were serving draconian prison terms as political prisoners.)

I was very glad to hear Bernardine's voice, and we got together later that day. I hadn't been able to return to Chicago because of the pandemic, so I was especially delighted to sit on a park bench with Bernardine. This time in Oakland's lovely Dracena Park amidst the tall walls of an old quarry surrounded by a small redwood forest. Hours flew by as we talked about everything, from our families, what was happening in Nicaragua and Cuba, the recall campaign of the Governor but also of course of Chesa. Bernardine has lots more wrinkles (that's what happens when we age naturally), and her hair is now a lovely gray. Her tan skin reflects her love of nature, and she is quite tatted up. About to turn 80, Bernardine is as beautiful as ever. It's an inside-outside sort of thing.

I really appreciate Bernardine and Bill as individuals, but I tell the story also as an example of the resolution of the rifts that existed within the movement of our youth. In my experience, when we sit down together decades later, even if we haven't seen each other for years, there is so much commonality of ideas, so much shared history. It's just old friends who haven't missed a beat.

I have had other, more personal losses as well as personal gifts. My mother and father were two of my greatest supports in life. The older I get, the more I understand how fortunate I was to have had such incredible, loving parents. Through all my changes, we never lost touch. In between visits, we wrote old-fashioned letters, many I've saved to this day, and stayed in phone contact as well. They embraced me and protected me. When Rosa and then Michael were born, they were on a plane and there in what seemed like minutes. My younger sister Louise is part of this loving circle and the gift that stays with me. We were both with my parents when they died. And when Steve passed away, Louise and her husband John wrapped me in their arms and pulled me back into this world, which I no longer wanted.

Hey, I'm now a gray-haired, wrinkled old lady who sometimes thinks she's a 20-year-old inhabitant of someone else's body. Born a Red Diaper Baby who morphed into a Yippie and joined the Weather Underground, I love the life I've led. Along with the many others I have traveled with on this journey, we have given it our all. At times, we were at the epicenter of the historic moment. At other times we were marginalized. But at all times, we did what we thought was right and we did it with full-throttle passion and commitment. Did we make mistakes? You bet we did. Were we headstrong at times? Of course. But I am grateful to have been a part of all this and have no regrets.

The same can be said for my personal life. I have given it my all as well and been surrounded with people who have loved me in a full and mutual way. As Steve liked to say when we were sitting in the car, stuck in hellacious Chicago traffic jams, "Well, here we are together, Nancy. It doesn't get any better than this, does it?"

No, Steve, it doesn't. It has really been a great ride!

CHANGE

A FRIEND RECENTLY ASKED ME these provocative questions: "Lots of people think there's been a hard turn to the right in this country, and many leftists are discouraged. Do you think we can have a society free of white privilege and white supremacist institutions? Do you still have hope for revolutionary action?" To that I have to answer, "I have more questions than answers. But I have some thoughts."

Today after purchasing *The Ministry of the Future,* I sat in my car and while listening to the Rolling Stones' "You Got the Silver," I found myself sobbing—I was crying because there is ice in the hearts of too many Americans and looming existential doom in my grandson's future and that of the planet. Also, because it's been seven years, yet I still yearn for my husband Steve every single day.

The Italian Marxist Antonio Gramsci used the phrase "Pessimism of the intellect, optimism of the will." I take that as a caution against wishful thinking on the one hand, and a warning against resignation on the other. Gramsci is proposing a determined, yet open-eyed engagement and I try to embrace that.

So with open eyes, my thinking today is different than that of my youth. The world has changed. Back then successful anti-colonial struggles were sweeping the globe and it was not uncommon for the leadership of those struggles to declare themselves as socialists as well. In the U.S., much of the Black, Puerto Rican, American Indian, and Mexicano/

Chicano movements viewed themselves in that context. That was the backdrop for the activist work that I pursued.

That was then. This is now. Many of those anti-colonial struggles succeeded, although at a great price. Those were incredible victories, yet on my 2013 trip to Vietnam, many people I spoke with were reluctant to say that they had "won the war." "How can we talk of 'winning' when millions died?" was a refrain heard over and over.

As hard as it was to win their independence, the building of socialism has proven to be an even more stubbornly difficult process. Something I did not foresee. Reinforced by my 1970 trip to Moscow, I understood many of the problems of the Soviet Union and was not at all surprised when it fell. However, I realized that it would have negative consequences for many anti-colonial struggles and newly independent countries who relied on Soviet aid. However, I underestimated both the internal challenges and problems that would arise in the newly independent nations and especially the strength of Western capitalism's ability to spread throughout the world.

The Trump phenomenon and the insurgent right wing is not confined to the United States.

Today, authoritarianism is on the rise around the world—from Modi in India to Bolsonaro in Brazil (no longer in power, but you get my point), just to name a couple of America's allies. That makes the situation here even more important and fraught with danger.

However, we are faced with a more complicated set of factors than just a "hard turn to the right." I believe much of the U.S. population has moved significantly to the Left, embracing many of the understandings my friends and I espoused for years. Every day I see evidence of it.

It is heartening to see so many white folks, especially youth, continue the struggle while embracing ideas similar to those we fought for. The language has even penetrated the mainstream media. If you listened to CNN in the wake of George Floyd, you heard terms such as "white supremacy," "white privilege," "institutional racism," "patriarchy," "LGBTQ," "reparations," and more. Even "socialism," apparently no longer a dirty word to many young white people. In 2021 it was announced that the U.S. Postal Service will produce a stamp with an image of Pete Seeger! The same Pete Seeger I had seen and heard sing at Camp Woodland just before he was due to appear before the House Un-American Activities Committee (HUAC). The "traitor" has become the "patriot."

A big thank you goes out to Occupy, the Bernie campaign, the Me Too movement, the LGBTQ fight, the movement to combat climate change led by indigenous people, the anti-gun violence movement, the campaign of Medicare for All, the movement against food insecurity and housing uncertainty, the disability rights movement. And especially, the Black Lives Matter movement. However, while consciousness of many has changed, we have not succeeded in changing power relationships or transforming institutions.

The Covid pandemic revealed so much to so many; can that consciousness help change the course of our society and planet? The writer Arundhati Roy from the subcontinent of India has said that the pandemic is a portal through which we can walk, leaving our baggage behind, and come out with transformed societies. While that is a possibility, in the spirit of Gramsci I would say it is far from a given, and I am impatient with those who fail to acknowledge the minefield we are currently walking through. Yet I also take issue with friends who see no reason for action and are resigned to accept the status quo as a permanent state of affairs.

The persistence and profound depth of white supremacy challenges my thinking about what's probable. In America there are twin pandemics—the Covid virus and racism. The one first appeared in 2020. The other has been here since the founding of this country and has once again been dramatically revealed during the pandemic. When understanding of the deeply racist nature of American life has come to the fore in the past, at best it has been a flash in the pan with lots of handwringing and even government investigations, but then as quickly as the conversation arrives, it disappears. Will this time be different?

In my corner of the movement, we exaggerated the importance of our own willingness to make change. That is, we thought if we really wanted it enough and we worked hard enough, we could transform society. We put less stock into understanding the actual conditions of society and the limits of our objective reality. The upside was that we threw ourselves wholeheartedly into the struggle. Perhaps that exaggeration of our own ability to make change was also a function of the arrogance of youth. But vibrant movements are those where youth are central actors. Much of the time our movement was impressive, and I believe we had a huge impact, one that we didn't always recognize. But …

In my lifetime the Left has never been able to successfully wed the struggle against a white supremacist system, against racialized capitalism, with the righteous (as opposed to racist) grievances of the white working class. There were valiant attempts by various Left organizations, but their fruits were not wide, deep, or lasting. Had we been able to do so, Trumpism would not be the problem that it is.

Today as the Trump forces regroup and regain momentum, we are faced with a similar dilemma. Can we reach white working-class folks with an anti-racist, anti-capitalist practice? Is it simply a weakness on our part? Are we too middle class? Too arrogant to those who don't agree with us? Or is white supremacy so deeply ingrained in our society that there is no way for an anti-racist left to successfully appeal to a large segment of the white working class? Can we, through electoral politics, make incremental changes and move toward a social democracy similar to European countries? If they were to be enacted, would policies like "Medicare for All" lift all boats and improve the lives of people of color as well as white folks? Most past reforms have not done so. Will it really be sufficient to rely on changing demographics, the relative decline of the white population, to bring about a fully just and democratic society? Or will we then be faced with an armed white population that will make the January 2021 attempted coup look like a picnic?

Much remains to be seen.

REVOLUTION AND ABOLITION

Will I see revolution in my lifetime? Although I've learned from history there can be some pretty great surprises, I don't think so. However, revolution is still something I aspire to. I love to imagine a just, equitable and peaceful world. One that is in harmony with nature. Meanwhile, I want to continue to be a part of the fight to move in that direction.

I feel similarly about the abolition of prisons and police. Have we been pretending for decades that reforming these institutions is a possibility? There's been lots of episodic outrage and some small steps in the right direction, while these institutions remain barbaric, destructive, and widespread. But, like revolution, abolition is aspirational for me as well. It's important for us to imagine alternative systems and solutions, and where and when possible, to implement pieces of a more enlightened way to deal with problems. But I don't see that we can abolish police or prisons completely, as long as we have such terrible inequities. So we have to fight like hell for a more just system overall, one that does not have such disparities in wealth that are reflected in every other aspect of society. That would be a revolution. Then perhaps we could abolish prisons and police. Meanwhile, let's fight like hell to raise the vision of abolition, reduce the footprint of the criminal "injustice'" system, provide some relief for those ensnared in it, and put resources into developing alternative restorative justice solutions. One trip to Mars might cover all that.

My thinking now is less "either/or" than it was in my youth. I can see that in many instances there is more than one right way, and the best approach is to try things, honestly evaluate, and learn from them. For example, my views on elections have changed. I have seen that when there is an engaged community, an electorate engaged in advancing the whole community, elected officials can be an important element, especially on the local level.

In the early 1960s I campaigned for Robert Kastenmeier, the Congressman from Wisconsin. He won. In the mid-'60s I did not campaign to get Robert Scheer to Congress (Jerry Rubin chastised me for that). I did vote for Scheer. He lost. Then I campaigned for Jerry's run for Mayor of Berkeley. (I was living with him. How could I not?) He lost. It would then be about twenty more years before I'd vote again, that time for Harold Washington who became the first Black Mayor of Chicago. (The leaders in Prairie Fire didn't approve.) I campaigned in Indiana and Michigan for Obama during his first run for President, with eyes wide open about what to expect from his presidency. (I had some very interesting conversations with the people who answered their doors.) I sat out the second round. I worked hard for Bernie in 2020 and let others do the work in the general election. It may be that Rep. Clybourn is one of the sharpest tacks. He knew Bernie couldn't win; enough white people weren't ready. But Biden could win while Bernie's platform might possibly prevail, at least among Democrats. I think to myself, "Can this new flock of Congressional progressives, the Squad and others, make a difference? Or am I just drinking the Kool-Aid?" Time will tell.

In any case, I have not altered my opinion that the motor for change comes from mass collective action at the grassroots. The truth is that none of those progressives would be in Congress without that wind beneath their sails. Although the electoral arena can be important terrain for struggle, our two-party system has ensured that progressives have not gained power in a way that comes close to the European social democracies, even in terms of any significant domestic social safety net, i.e., healthcare, childcare, etc. So I suggest—have realistic expectations and stay in the streets for the hope of progress. On days that I can walk okay, I'll be with you.

WHAT WE LEAVE BEHIND

WHILE CONSCIOUSNESS ISN'T SUFFICIENT, it is a necessary component of change. I believe that we, collectively, the movements and activities of the last half century, planted seeds in yesterday's gardens that have blossomed. Movements open up conversations and create spaces. But change can happen only when actual people move into those spaces with energy and actions that can take many different forms.

I hope I have planted some of those seeds. I spent decades of time and money fighting the criminal justice system after my school social worker day job. Freedom Archives published my narrative *Out of Control: A Fifteen Year Battle Against Control Unit Prisons*, which can also be found on their website along with many related documents. Sundiata Acoli has referred to it as "Nancy's legacy to a movement in the midst of a renaissance, rising this time from a wider more popular base." My piece about "Women & Imprisonment in the U.S.: History & Current Reality" has been in multiple editions of a popular women's studies textbook titled *Women's Lives: Multicultural Perspectives.* A lot of what I have said here about Aaron Sorkin's movie *The Trial of the Chicago 7* is from a piece I wrote that got thousands of hits. That and other articles remain online at *Counterpunch. The People Make the Peace* has a chapter I wrote. These are tangible artifacts that can be considered a legacy.

My husband Steve would have been so excited to see the vibrant and massive Black Lives Matter movement, the breadth and depth of activity

Nancy, circa 2016.

around the abolition of police and prisons, including the response of many white people. In addition to his work around prisons and police violence, Steve spent his whole professional life fighting all aspects of racism that lead to disparities in healthcare. In 2021 a book arrived in my mailbox hot off the Johns Hopkins presses. *Unequal: Structural Racism and the Death Gap in America's Largest Cities* is edited by Maureen Benjamins & Fernando De Maio. The book is dedicated "To a Visionary Advocate Steve Whitman, Ph.D., in memoriam." Steve would have been proud of this book, and particularly proud of its point of view. Maureen, a wonderful younger epidemiologist, acknowledges that "I am forever grateful for having had Steve [Whitman] as my mentor. His work and passion for social justice inspired me and so many others. He taught us that 'if our data just sit on a shelf, we have failed' and that we always need to call out racism as a cause of health inequities."

When Steve was very conscious of his waning time, he hoped his epidemiological work would be carried on with that particular lens. He never got to see the documentary *Cooked,* in which he appears (streaming on Prime Video). It tells the story of the Chicago Heat Wave when Steve was Chief Epidemiologist for the Health Department and foreshadows the racial dynamics of Hurricane Katrina and the Covid pandemic, while suggesting insights into the global climate crisis.

However, beyond books and movies, it is the people I have touched and that have touched me that move me most to believe this country has changed. This year I was honored to be an invited panelist in a Zoom conversation about the history of prison work in Illinois. But what really got me was that the invitation came from the Mass Incarceration Working Group of the University of Chicago! I am just so excited that such a group even exists. Nothing like that would have been possible at U of C back in the day. We had to fight tooth and nail for any kind of exposure or even discussion of prisons.

Often I am contacted on Facebook by high school and college students who want to interview me about the Yippies, the Chicago 8, or WITCH. Young people are still intrigued by the way we incorporated imaginative, humorous elements into our Yippie and WITCH protests.

In 2020 I mentored 20 young volunteers in the Bernie campaign who live in Southern California and Texas. By telephone I got to swap stories with each of them. I loved hearing why they were in the campaign. All their districts went for Bernie, and then he lost. They were heartbroken although many went on to continue working in different ways. I also had the pleasure of "onboarding" (a new word for me) several young people who were drawn to SURJ (Showing Up for Racial Justice), a national organization that has grown substantially since Black Lives Matter.

I've come to understand that we move individuals we encounter in life without even realizing. In recent years I've developed a friendship with a high school acquaintance and was surprised to learn it was life-changing for her when I organized a bus to attend a demonstration in D.C. and she came along. Another friend was very shy in high school and I barely knew her. She is now fully chatty and has been active in the movement to stop gun violence. I love spending time with both those women. When I went to see Mayim Bialik in a taping of *The Big Bang Theory*, I was treated like a VIP, and during an intermission, one of the Assistant Directors approached me to thank me for the Yippie years. He was in high school at the time and we were his heroes! At a recent commemoration of the Kent State murders, one participant shared that he had heard me speak in 1971 and it dramatically changed his thinking. These stories remind me that what we do, what we say, matters, even when we ourselves are unable to see it.

I am not exceptional. Most of the activists I know from the movements of the last four decades of the 20th century have not disappeared into the woodwork. On the contrary, many of them are also engaged in political activity, some of them much more substantially than I am. Claude is the director of the Freedom Archives https://freedomarchives.org. Diana is a founding member of the California Coalition for Women Prisoners https://womenprisoners.org. Donna is a central member of Catalyst and has mentored people all around the country in anti-racist activism https://collectiveliberation.org. Lynn and Karin have been active for years in SURJ (Showing Up for Racial Justice) https://surj.org. China is on the Board of the international https://350.org. In their day jobs, some are/were secretaries, social workers, librarians, teachers, nurses, archivists, doctors, professors, people's lawyers, legal workers, private eyes, therapists, accountants, engineers, public health workers, writers, copy editors, technicians, landscapers, carpenters, and more. Many use their skills working for non-profits that deal with housing issues, prison issues, climate change, and other social problems. Some are artists, musicians, actors, martial artists, poets, and photographers.

When I moved back to California after thirty or so years, I was amazed at the warm welcome I received from a whole community of graying activists. I have had such a meaningful, interesting life and am so appreciative to have wonderful friends who remain engaged in one way or another. We shared years of rich experiences and those friendships are very enduring. Maybe struggling for justice and peace has become our culture? When my grandchildren were born—Julian in 2020 and Santi in 2024— my friends and family contributed quilt squares that Edy then assembled. Miriam, my friend who created the first quilt for my baby daughter Rosa, now created squares for each of my grandchildren. The quilts are filled with unicorns and birds but also "say no to racism" and "bread and roses." I would not have lived my life in any other way. Now it is the birthright of Julian and Santi.

AFTERWORD

I FIRST ENCOUNTERED NANCY KURSHAN in 2013, when I was researching my book *Did It! Jerry Rubin: An American Revolutionary.* After several phone calls, Nancy realized I was sincere in my pursuit of chronicling the life of Jerry Rubin—who until then had been ignored or unfairly maligned in any recounting of the Yippie Movement and their anti-Vietnam War protests. She invited me to visit her in Chicago for several days—we spent hours talking on and off about that era—and then her husband Steve Whitman filled in the blanks on her later activism, as Nancy was too modest to put herself 'in front' of the narrative. While you (the reader) have just read an entire book by Nancy—her modesty prevails throughout her memoir and I wanted the chance to share some of our conversations with you.

In 1965, Vietnam was heating up, with increased media coverage and burgeoning student revolt. Nancy was attracted to the Free Speech Movement protests on the UC Berkeley campus. Arriving in Berkeley that autumn to pursue her PhD in Child Psychology, she immediately encountered a political activist sporting "a handlebar mustache . . . that gave him the look of a classic Italian anarchist." Jerry and Nancy began spending time at the Mediterranean Café on Telegraph Avenue, "eating and drinking coffee, and arguing about politics."

Nancy Kurshan: Jerry introduced me to those kinds of places in Berkeley, because he liked to just schmooze around, and bump into various people. He wrote me a letter about how when you meet someone and you just gel, just sync, he said that was happening with us, and he wanted me to meet Moe Hirsch and Steve Smale who were also on the steering committee for the Vietnam Day Committee, or VDC, as we called it. I thought Jerry was kind and giving to his friends, the people that he really cared about. I liked him.

When Nancy arrived in Berkeley she was an active member of Students for a Democratic Society (SDS) along with her high school pal David Kotz, Michael James and others. SDS was often at odds with Jerry's political approach. She felt pulled toward their model of grassroots organizing, going door-to-door, speaking one on one and trying to build organization in a slow, deliberate process. Yet she recognized the success of Jerry Rubin's VDC (Vietnam Day Committee) in utilizing the mass media to educate huge numbers of people and providing outlets for action.

With the decline of the VDC, in the fall of 1966 Jerry joined forces with SDS (and Nancy) to promote a huge event in support of Black Power.

In June of that year James Meredith started his "March Against Fear," a one-man walk from Memphis to Jackson when a sniper wounded him. After the shooting, Stokely Carmichael, Martin Luther King Jr., and others continued to march and they were arrested. Upon his release from jail, Carmichael gave this historic speech to a crowd of supporters: "This is the twenty-seventh time I have been arrested and I ain't going to jail no more! The only way we gonna stop them white men from whuppun' us is to take over. What we gonna start sayin' now is Black Power!"

There's a two-page letter signed by Jerry Rubin (as the Berkeley Students for a Democratic Society a.k.a. "Campus SDS") despite the fact that he was not a student. Jerry, the "outside agitator", outlines why it's important to support the concept of Black Power, how the mass media deliberately distorts the idea of Black Power, and how the event would be a strong follow up to earlier UC Berkeley student/political events.

There's a memorandum from the Assistant Dean of Students from October 12, 1966, outlining the rules and regulations of the event and the responsibilities that SDS must take on for the "proposed conference on Black Power" to be endorsed by UC Berkeley. Apparently SDS disagreed, as there's a memo boldly titled "NO AGREEMENT!" which reads, in part, "The 'guidelines' by the Administration for their granting of facilities for Black Power Day are neither within the framework of the traditions of free speech on this campus, nor are they compatible with the implementation of an effective conference on Black Power."

Also, in Kurshan's archives is a flyer that cries out *Black Power Day Crisis!* telling the public that "we need $2700 by October 19th" to present the event. All expenses are listed, including flying Stokely Carmichael from Atlanta for $300, Floyd McKissick from New York for $300, Rennie Davis from Chicago for $200, and "four from Watts" for $100 total. Make checks payable to "S.D.S. Black Power Day," and send them to N. Kurshan at 2632 Regent Street in Berkeley. Another flyer says, "Come off it baby, ain't no white folks around, let's tell it like it is."

These earnest documents are naively charming—and the timing is significant. The phrase *Black Power* was just starting to emerge on the West Coast—as was the Black Panther Party, which coincidentally was founded just down the road (in West Oakland) during the exact same week these memos were going back and forth across the Berkeley campus. On October 15, 1966 (just two weeks before *Black Power Day*), they established the Black Panther Party for Self Defense by writing the "Ten Point Program" detailing and demanding, "What We Want, What We Believe."

Nancy, Jerry and SDS were ahead of the curve by organizing this event. Two years later, cries of "Black Power!" would be commonplace amongst white radicals, but not in 1966.

Next up was Jerry's run for Mayor of Berkeley, Nancy helped organized his campaign, initially just to educate the public on issues.

> **Nancy Kurshan:** Stew Albert and I were really active in Jerry's campaign for mayor. And in the beginning, we said to ourselves, "There's no way we're going to win this, but we're going to use it to educate." We spent a long time putting together a campaign platform, which had

> opinions from everything to the kitchen sink to what our opinion on China was. *So very important for a mayor!*
>
> But I soon realized that Jerry was serious about winning and he insisted that I should be burning both ends of the candle to accomplishment that. So, I started to pull back and turn towards my PhD studies. But then not long after Jerry lost the election, Dave Dellinger invited us to come east and help organize a national march on Washington, DC on behalf of the National Mobilization to End the War in Vietnam (the MOBE). I had just completed two years of my graduate program and was in good standing. But Dave had made us an offer I couldn't refuse. So, I quit school right then and there.
>
> Some people liked Jerry, and some people didn't. They really didn't like his theatrical, politically confrontational style of things. Especially SDS, which was very "you have to go door to door in the neighborhoods," kind of thing. Jerry was skipping over the door-to-door, going right for the front page. Too bad they couldn't figure out how to work both ends, because it would have been effective. But the incredible Dave Dellinger, for some reason, he got it. And he wanted that energy. He sensed it could be transformative.
>
> For the next five years Jerry and I were inseparable and went through extraordinary times. Sometimes it felt like we were in control, changing the world according to our dreams. At other times, we were on a speeding train, way beyond our control.

Jerry went to New York first while Nancy stayed in Berkeley closing up shop. Not long after he got there, she received an excited late night call. Jerry had met a dozen freaks that convinced him to join their prank of dropping hundreds of dollar bills onto the floor of the Stock Exchange. When Nancy asked who this new friend was, Jerry replied, "Abbie Hoffman." Years later, Nancy wrote, "From that moment on, life changed."

When Nancy arrived in Manhattan, she fell into a social circle with Abbie and Anita Hoffman, along with Paul Krassner and Phil Ochs. She remembers that everyone would "smoke some weed and talk, talk, talk." In 2013, Nancy told me that whenever Jerry and Abbie weren't getting along, "Anita and I would never talk candidly, because we each had to stand by our man. Later in life, we did talk. But not back then."

I asked Nancy to detail her daily activities in the Yippies:

> **Nancy Kurshan:** Once I dropped out of the MOBE, I started working with Abbie on the Lower East Side. There was a free store and a free clinic. Really, I didn't know what I was doing, there was a doctor that saw people for free, and he would call me. One time somebody was having a bad trip, and I had to take her to the hospital, which was on the other end of the city. I did a lot of random things. We also had a Yippie office. I was in charge of the literature, the buttons, and all the nuts and bolts of it. When the YIP-In happened, and everyone was arrested, I was in charge of bailing everyone out. You know, I think in some ways I wasn't . . . although I agreed with all the Yippie stuff, I don't think I was a natural Yippie, performer kind of person. So, I did everything else that wasn't flashy.

Despite minor political squabbles, Jerry Rubin and Phil Ochs remained tight, and on the weekend of July 26, 1968, Jerry invited Phil to accompany him and Nancy Kurshan to the Newport Folk Festival to see Joan Baez, Tim Buckley, and Joni Mitchell. Phil resisted, because he hadn't been invited to perform. Jerry quickly crushed Phil's insecurity by saying, "I'm inviting you!" Phil quickly capitulated and joined the couple. In classic Yippie fashion, the trio entered the grounds by displaying phony press credentials. Jerry and Nancy handed out a pamphlet that included this charming pronouncement:

> *Who says that rich White America can tell the Chinese what is best? How dare you tell the poor that their poverty is deserved?*
>
> *Laugh at professors: disobey your parents: burn your money: you know life is a dream and all of our institutions are man-made illusions effective because YOU take the dream for reality.*

According to Ochs biographer Marc Eliot, "Someone recognized Rubin and he was immediately ejected from the festival grounds." Eliot goes on to describe encountering Phil, Jerry, and Nancy later that evening, drinking in a local bar, when Phil spotted William F. Buckley. Phil engaged Buckley in a conversation about Gene McCarthy's bid for president now that Robert Kennedy was dead. The trio was later kicked out of a party hosted by Newport Festival organizer George Wein. With the Chicago protests exactly a month away, Rubin declared, "Don't worry, Phil—the real party is just beginning."

Nancy and Jerry's relationship peaked in the late '60s. Although nonviolent, they shared "the feelings of extremist revolutionaries" (although neither had fired a gun or planted a bomb). They were committed to being "morally right." In their youth, they "had been taught that the Good Germans who did nothing to stop Hitler were also morally responsible for his crimes. They felt anger at the gap between America's ideals and the cold reality of its power system." Nancy says, "during those years Jerry and I beat with the same heart, politically at least." Yet, the media attention surrounding the Chicago Trial was part of their undoing as a couple.

> **Nancy Kurshan:** I think when Jerry and Abbie went to jail after they were convicted, that freed me up again in a lot of ways. When I was with Jerry, I had a lot to do, honestly. I cooked, I shopped, I cleaned, and I worked a day job. I was the only one who brought in an income. Then when he wasn't around, Anita and I did the burning of the robes together. And then she and I organized a big demonstration in response to the convictions. I also got a chance to travel around the country with Bill Kunstler and speak about the trial. Later Judy and I traveled to Stockholm, Algeria, and Vietnam. We were organizing this conference of fifty musicians and artists across the globe. But it wasn't a festival, it was a meeting, and it was going to be in Cuba, and we were organizing lists of who we were going to have go. Unfortunately, it got called off, but the planning enabled Judy and I to go to both Vietnam and Cuba.
>
> Well, I think the further we got into all this, and the further Jerry's fame grew, the crazier it got. I don't know what fame is like for other people, but I don't think it did him any good. He was nervous about his speaking abilities, even though he was a good speaker, and regularly taking Ritalin didn't help. He probably tried too hard . . . For a long time, it was not the greatest situation, and he was getting more and

Phil Ochs with Jerry, Nancy and unknown person, circa 1970.

more famous, more and more crazed about being famous. And I wasn't having such a good time. But, at the same time, he kept going to jail. I felt like I couldn't just leave. And I didn't really have anybody to talk to about it, hardly at all.

Like you said, it wasn't like you were going to go to Anita, or somebody else, and say, "This is what I'm mulling over. What do you think?"

Nancy Kurshan: Nope, because the lines of communication were not open between us. So that was what was so nice later about the women's movement. Then, being in Vietnam, just us three women [Nancy, Judy Gumbo, and Genie Plamondon of the White Panthers, visited North Vietnam in 1970] was pretty liberating, seeing women in Vietnam in all walks of life—mayors of villages, women doctors, woman in the military. I was really ready for a change.

LOOKING BACK

Nancy Kurshan: It's funny, because they ended up differently, but initially Jerry was more serious politically. And Abbie was more of a comedian. In the beginning, Jerry thought more about building a movement—while Abbie was more of a brilliant individualist. They were both really smart; Jerry was great at figuring out how to work with mass actions, setting them up in ways that would be effective and dramatic. I don't think Abbie was particularly good at that.

The Jerry I know was sharply critical of US society and the government, and passionately identified with people who were struggling for a better existence. When I say passionately, I mean passionately. And was willing to turn one hundred percent of his life over to try to help transform the world. He was willing to take unpopular positions, and do unpopular things, and really challenge the existing order. And I think he wasn't brave physically. But he was very brave. There needs to be more people like that.

So here I am, telling you I never was *done* with the movement. But I also wasn't in the crosshairs in the same way that Jerry was. I didn't have to travel cross-country in prison shackles. I didn't have to stay in Cook County Jail, which is pretty awful. I didn't have my coccyx broken by the police when they threw me around. There were a lot of things that were different. I don't know if that would have stopped me or not. I'm not saying that would have, but I can't say. I wonder if there wasn't a third way, though. Did Jerry have to go on that Yippie vs. Yuppie tour with Abbie, because that was oppositional to those us who continued to struggle, and saying that—I don't know exactly what Jerry said in those debates.

One legacy of the Yippies is that you can participate in social movements, using culture, humor, multimedia, and reach people in all those different ways, not just through the written or spoken word. The Yippies said, "Be creative. You don't have to just follow these molds. That you could think and be outside the box and do all kinds of things." Today, a lot of people are trying Yippie-type things. But, I think it's now much harder to break through the media. People think of the Yippies as theater and costumes. But there's another level of the Yippies, and that was figuring out all kinds of creative ways to really confront the powers that be and bring it to the TV and front page. Nobody could design that better than Jerry did. We could use more of that. But that's also more challenging now.

I spent three days at Nancy's home in 2013 with Nancy and her husband Steve Whitman. Both are committed activists. When I ask how they met some years ago, they said they met when one bailed the other out of jail after attempting to shut down the Rock Island arsenal by blockading the 4 bridges. Although Whitman didn't know Nancy during her Yippie years, he is eager to fill in the past few decades for me.

Steve Whitman: I would say that the thing that characterizes Nancy most is a constant overarching pursuit of social justice. It's really burned into her heart and soul. As we get older, the number of people who were politically active, but who have stopped, some of whom have even stopped believing what they used to believe, is painfully large. And the number who have continued on, are few.

Nancy is one of the most remarkable people I've ever encountered in that way. Nowadays, it's complicated to figure out what's an optimal

Nancy and Steve; Chicago, circa early 2000s.

> thing to do, what's a good strategy. Or whether we should drag our seventy-year-old bones out to a demonstration when it's zero degrees out. But the notion of the value of the demonstration, our desire to see the demonstration succeed, is unquestioned to Nancy. And I've never seen anyone persevere that much, in pursuit of social justice. She just truly and sincerely and passionately believes in the rights of the oppressed, and puts her body and her mind on the line for that, everyday.
>
> Nancy now is about seventy-years-old [82 as of 2025], and I would say she's been doing this since she's ten. So, for sixty years, in different ways, she's been fighting like this. Robin Morgan wrote this famous essay in the '60s, called "Goodbye to All That." And at the end of the essay, there's a paragraph that says, "Free Robin Morgan." And the "All That" was sexism in the movement. "Free Kathleen Cleaver," and so on. And one of the names is "Free Nancy Kurshan." Several years ago, we saw that Robin was going to be keynoting a NOW convention at a Hyatt in the suburbs.
>
> So, I said to Nancy, "Why don't you go and say hello to Robin?" Because they were good friends back in the day, and Nancy said, "I don't want to bother her." And so, I said, "Nancy, it's just the most ridiculous thing in the world, why don't you just take the train, it's a buck-fifty, and if it's not good, come back." So, she did. Halfway through her talk, Robin looked up and saw Nancy in the room, and she said, "I just have to stop for a minute, and introduce you to somebody. Because if you really want to know what we all need to do in order to succeed, it's that we need to be like Nancy Kurshan."
>
> Robin said, "Nancy's really a long-distance runner, and that's what we all need to learn how to be." She just stopped her entire keynote address to introduce Nancy. I don't know anybody who knows Nancy, politically, who doesn't feel that way about her.

Nancy and Steve dragged her children along to every political function. Prison reform became Nancy's strongest passion, and in 2013, she wrote a book, *Out of Control: A Fifteen Year Battle Against Control Unit Prisons,* that chronicles her work of organizing hundreds of educational programs and demonstrations fighting against the prison industrial complex. Nancy, Steve, and the children spent innumerable hours visiting prisoners. Because the drive could take hours, they would often stay from noon till eight at night. Whenever they could, they'd share a sandwich with an inmate. One time, the four of them were driving home after a long day of visitation, and her son Michael blurted, "the only time we ever sit down and eat dinner together as a family is when we're in a prison."

Minutes before I'm due to leave, they dig out videotape from the 1980s. It has that warped look of being recorded "off the air" from the local news. Uniformed Neo-Nazis and skinheads are marching through the Chicago streets. Nancy and others are leading a "Stamp Out Racist Graffiti" counter-demonstration. Both sides are yelling back and forth when a huge fight breaks out. Nancy gets hit in the face, just below her eye. Bleeding profusely, the first thing she does (before seeking safety or medical attention) was to find the television crew covering the riot, and yell into the camera, "We must get these Fascists out of Chicago!"

In a 2013 email to me, Robin Morgan agreed that Nancy was a vital part of the movement. "More so than any of the guys, for that matter, in intelligence, quiet accomplishment, and getting things done . . . You can quote me on that."

LOOKING FORWARD

In 2025, I approached Nancy for another conversation.

Let's talk about today. The Palestine/Israel conflict is a hot issue for many people right now. Did the Yippies have a position on the Palestinian/Israeli conflict?

> **Nancy Kurshan:** The Yippies were not exactly the kind of organization that had huge debates about ideology and then came to a unified position. But I can say with absolute certainty that Jerry and I were both totally in support of the Palestinian struggle, as was Abbie. You can see it in their writings at that time. I didn't write back then for all the same reasons that I didn't speak much at that

time— lack of confidence and lack of support, lack of a welcoming cohort. But I did have many conversations with Jerry about the time each of us had spent in Israel.

What we had seen with our own eyes ultimately led each of us to reach similar conclusions of support for the Palestinian struggle. We viewed it in many ways similar to the Vietnamese national liberation struggle and in other ways similar to the Native American fight for sovereignty. We didn't have a full "settler colonial" analysis. But, for instance, Jerry did write that "If Moses were alive today, he'd be an Arab guerrilla." I think that's a pretty clear statement of support for the Palestinian resistance.

Do you see the spirit of the Yippies in today's movements?

Nancy Kurshan: Oh yes definitely. Well first of all some of us Yippies are still here and we're in the streets. We just happen to now be feminists, fighting for reproductive rights and against misogyny. We push for the abolition of prisons and an end to immoral disparities of wealth. We're present at ceasefire protests around the country and pilgrimages for the right of return of Palestinians. We're insisting on a swift and just transition away from fossil fuels. We believe that there are no illegal aliens on stolen lands and we act to protect our neighbors. Along with millions of others we are pushing back against the rise of authoritarianism. And we are imagining a better, more loving, more generous world for all; one that is in harmony with Mother Nature.

I myself am so fortunate to have found, in the San Francisco Bay Area, a fabulous organization of elder women planet protectors — 1,000 Grandmothers for Future Generations. It began in 2016 in response to the protests of the Dakota Access Pipeline struggle at Standing Rock. A group of older women, inspired especially by the Lakota grandmothers, decided to create a climate justice organization in the Bay Area.

What kind of things do you do?

Nancy Kurshan: Well, if you go to our website you will see, that first of all WE SHOW UP. At international, national and local climate justice actions and demonstrations. At legislative and electional campaigns

Above: Nancy Kurshan (far right) with Nancy Feinstein (to the left) and others of 1,000 Grandmothers for Future Generations when tens of thousands joined the NY Climate March to End Fossil Fuels, September 17, 2023.
Below: Nancy (far left) with Susan Segal in 1000 Grandmothers sweat shirts, along with others protesting planned reopening of prison as an ICE detention center; Dublin, CA, March 1, 2025.

that confront the power of the fossil fuel industry. We show up to support indigenous and front line struggles, to protests called for by youth leaders, to hearings and boycotts and campaigns to stop the fossil fuel industry from destroying our only planet.

As Grandmothers we have a lot to say but we want to do more than bring our wisdom. We know that those who will lead us into the future, need us to have their backs. They are counting on us to show up. And when we show up, we show up with art and music. Our Art Team is wonderful and they have created unforgettable giant puppets whose presence is always appreciated. And we often participate in Art Builds where we create signs, banners, silkscreened pin-on squares, and posters which are creative and colorful. And we have singing Grandmothers who bring their great group singing to our actions. And then there are times when we are called upon to wear our orange vests and stand between the police and the activists when they engage in nonviolent direct action while some of us participate in the direct actions as well.

One of the first actions I helped organize was on Valentine's Day when a couple hundred of us set up a picket line outside of our local Wells Fargo and let them know that if they didn't break up with the fossil fuel industry, we'd break up with them. And while we marched and sang and asked people on the busy shopping street to sign petitions, a group went in to present the petitions to the bank manager and let them all know why we were there.

So, you are focused on climate justice. But do you connect with those who are working on different issues?

Nancy Kurshan: Well during this era—of virulent authoritarianism, the genocide of Palestinians, the expelling/deporting/imprisoning many of our neighbors, the demonizing of trans people, the dangerous state of reproductive care, the continuing mass incarceration of people of color, the attack on the safety net for the most vulnerable people, the dismantling of public health, and the list really does go on and on —during this time we also see a vital and growing resistance. And as that resistance develops, the silos are collapsing and we are all out there together. So, you will see many of us Grandmothers show up not only at strictly climate justice actions but in all these different places, whether we're wearing our official Grandmother shirts and hoodies, or not. Because we need to be all in this together, all have each other's backs, and together is how we can grow this resistance and help create a better world for all on this miraculous planet.

Pat Thomas
Author of *Did It! Jerry Rubin: An American Revolutionary* and *Listen Whitey! The Sounds of Black Power 1965–75*

ACKNOWLEDGMENTS

THIS IS THE HARDEST PART OF writing my memoir because I feel so connected to so many people. It's often hard to tell where I begin and end, and where you begin and end. I feel so very grateful for all the interesting and wonderful people I have met along this journey. Every one of them is a part of this story whether they're named or not. It is what has kept me going on this road and I really feel they're all a part of me. I thank all who eagerly asked me if and when they can read my memoir—my extended family; Camp Woodland friends; Wheatley high school pals; college friends; comrades from Weather and Prairie Fire; all the wonderful people I worked and played with for 30 years in Chicago; and now all my running mates in the Bay Area, old and new, especially the 1,000 Grandmothers For Future Generations.

Initially, I intended this memoir to be a gift primarily for my children, in part to get them to stop asking, "How come you never told us that?" It was my husband, Steve Whitman, who first encouraged me to take it beyond our family. He's no longer with me but he is a constant part of me and sustains me still. I thank you, Steve, and I love you always, as you know because despite your physical absence, I still talk with you.

I want to thank my friend Jose Lopez who has always supported my development. In his Preface to this memoir, he stated that "Without succumbing to protagonism Nancy tells us about her activism, her commitment to radical change for the liberation of humanity, to the building of a world where there are no oppressors and no oppressed and where the people themselves are the leaders of their own freedom." That was music to my ears and fortified me in my resistance to the mantra coming to me from the publishing industry—"You must be more the hero of your own story."

Yet I had already tweaked the memoir, changing a few "we" to "I" and tried in other ways to center myself a bit more. But in truth it took a village of encouragement for me to even complete this project. I am so grateful to all who were part of that effort. Bernardine Dohrn was an early supporter as we walked together on Chicago's 606. My first drafts were read first and foremost by my children, Michael Kurshan Emmer and Rosa Kurshan-Emmer, both of whom gave me great constructive criticism. My sister and brother-in-law, Louise Kurshan and John DeWind, avid readers both, were encouraging and helpful as well. My pal Jade Dell, a Raging Granny, proofread the early manuscript on the margins of her very busy life. When my resolve lagged, I took heart from the words of my college roommate Susan Dalsimer, an experienced editor who understands the publishing world. Most recently the very generous support of my powerful sister Robin Morgan has meant so much to me. I love you all.

As time went by, I found that I had written a large chunk of my memoir about our 15-year active campaign to abolish long-term solitary confinement in U.S. prisons. Then along came Claude Marks and Nathaniel Moore of Freedom Archives who, with Lincoln Bergman as editor, published *Out of Control: A Fifteen Year Battle Against Control Unit Prisons.* I thank all of them for believing I had something to say which emboldened me to complete my memoir.

Just when I was exhausted with "living in the past" with no way to pass it on to those who will be here in the future, I was gifted the incredible writer Terry Bisson who helped me restructure and improve what was becoming an over lengthy tome. He then gifted me Lisa Goldstein who I thank for bringing a talented, needed feminine lens. But most importantly Terry renewed my confidence because he liked *Levitating.* He also added the yippie play on words to the title. I came to cherish Terry as a dear friend and now that he's gone, I miss his presence in my life. I have Terry to thank, however, for introducing me to his wife Judy Jensen as she and I continue our journeys.

And very importantly, this memoir would never have seen the light of day if not for the indomitable Pat Thomas. When a couple of left presses said, "this deserves to be published, but the bottom line is the bottom line, and no one is interested in the '60s anymore," I was ready to throw in the towel. Then Pat stepped up to the plate and found me Three Rooms Press and has been shepherding me and "Levitating" through this process. He also added the talented designer Darryl Norsen to the mix whose great work is evident. I'd like to give a big shout out to Darryl for his ability to work quickly, collaboratively and creatively. I also appreciate the invisible but important work of Kari Pearson in proofreading/editing my manuscript.

And finally, a big thank you goes out to Kat Georges and Peter Carlaftes at Three Rooms Press for taking a chance on me and for providing me with a wider opportunity to travel the country encouraging people not to give up, but to continue to create ever enlarging circles of loving community and Resist! Resist! Resist! The time is now. The place is here. Together perhaps we can make it through a portal to a better world for all.

RECENT AND FORTHCOMING BOOKS FROM THREE ROOMS PRESS

FICTION

Lucy Jane Bledsoe
No Stopping Us Now

Rishab Borah
The Door to Inferna

Meagan Brothers
Weird Girl and What's His Name

Christopher Chambers
Scavenger
Standalone
StreetWhys

Ebele Chizea
Aquarian Dawn

Heather Colley
The Gilded Butterfly Effect

Ron Dakron
Hello Devilfish!

Ron Dakron
Hello Devilfish!

Robert Duncan
Loudmouth

Amanda Eisenberg
People Are Talking

Michael T. Fournier
Hidden Wheel
Swing State

Kate Gale
Under a Neon Sun

Aaron Hamburger
Nirvana Is Here

William Least Heat-Moon
Celestial Mechanics

Aimee Herman
Everything Grows

Kelly Ann Jacobson
Tink and Wendy
Robin and Her Misfits
Lies of the Toymaker

Jethro K. Lieberman
Everything Is Jake

Eamon Loingsigh
Light of the Diddicoy
Exile on Bridge Street

John Marshall
The Greenfather

Alvin Orloff
Vulgarian Rhapsody

Micki Janae
Of Blood and Lightning

Aram Saroyan
Still Night in L.A.

Robert Silverberg
The Face of the Waters

Stephen Spotte
Animal Wrongs

Max Talley
Peace, Love and Haight

Richard Vetere
The Writers Afterlife
Champagne and Cocaine

Jessamyn Violet
Secret Rules to Being a Rockstar

Julia Watts
Quiver
Needlework
Lovesick Blossoms

Gina Yates
Narcissus Nobody

MEMOIR & BIOGRAPHY

Nassrine Azimi and Michel Wasserman
Last Boat to Yokohama: The Life and Legacy of Beate Sirota Gordon

William S. Burroughs & Allen Ginsberg
Don't Hide the Madness
edited by Steven Taylor

James Carr
BAD: The Autobiography of James Carr

Judy Gumbo
Yippie Girl: Exploits in Protest and Defeating the FBI

Nancy Kurshan
Levitating the Pentagon and Other Uplifting Stories

Hédi A. Jaouad
The Immortal Journeys of Isabelle Eberhardt

Judith Malina
Full Moon Stages: Personal Notes from 50 Years of The Living Theatre

Phil Marcade
Punk Avenue: Inside the New York City Underground, 1972–1982

Jillian Marshall
Japanthem: Counter-Cultural Experiences; Cross-Cultural Remixes

Alvin Orloff
Disasterama! Adventures in the Queer Underground 1977–1997

Angelica Page
A Delicious Life: Growing Up with Geraldine Page

Ray by Ray: A Daughter's Take on the Legend of Nicholas Ray

Nicca Ray
Ray by Ray: A Daughter's Take on the Legend of Nicholas Ray

Aram Saroyan
Before I Forget: A Memoir

Stephen Spotte
My Watery Self: Memoirs of a Marine Scientist

Christina Vo & Nghia M. Vo
My Vietnam, Your Vietnam
Vietnamese translation: *Việt Nam Của Con, Việt Nam Của Cha*

PHOTOGRAPHY-MEMOIR

Mike Watt
On & Off Bass

DADA

Maintenant: A Journal of Contemporary Dada Writing & Art (annual, since 2008)

MIXED MEDIA

John S. Paul
Sign Language: A Painter's Notebook (photography, poetry and prose)

HUMOR

Peter Carlaftes
A Year on Facebook

FILM & PLAYS

Israel Horovitz
My Old Lady: Complete Stage Play and Screenplay with an Essay on Adaptation

Peter Carlaftes
Triumph For Rent (3 Plays)
Teatrophy (3 More Plays)

Kat Georges
Three Somebodies: Plays

TRANSLATIONS

Thomas Bernhard
On Earth and in Hell
(poems; German and English)

Patrizia Gattaceca
Isula d'Anima (Corsican & English)

César Vallejo | Gerard Malanga
Malanga Chasing Vallejo (Spanish & English)

George Wallace
EOS: Abductor of Men (Greek & English)

ESSAYS

Richard Katrovas
Raising Girls in Bohemia

Vanessa Baden Kelly
Far Away From Close to Home

Erin Wildermuth
Womentality

SHORT STORY ANTHOLOGIES

SINGLE AUTHOR

Alien Archives: Stories
by Robert Silverberg

First-Person Singularities: Stories
by Robert Silverberg

Tales from the Eternal Café: Stories
by Janet Hamill, intro by Patti Smith

Time and Time Again: Sixteen Trips in Time
by Robert Silverberg

The Unvarnished Gary Phillips: A Mondo Pulp Collection
by Gary Phillips

Voyagers: Twelve Journeys in Space and Time
by Robert Silverberg

MULTI-AUTHOR

The Colors of April
edited by Quan Manh Ha & Cab Tran

Crime + Music: Nineteen Stories of Music-Themed Noir
edited by Jim Fusilli

Dark City Lights: New York Stories
edited by Lawrence Block

The Faking of the President: Twenty Stories of White House Noir
edited by Peter Carlaftes

Florida Happens:
edited by Greg Herren

Have a NYC I, II & III: New York Stories;
edited by Peter Carlaftes & Kat Georges

Songs of My Selfie
edited by Constance Renfrow

The Obama Inheritance: 15 Stories of Conspiracy Noir
edited by Gary Phillips

This Way to the End Times: Classic & New Stories of the Apocalypse
edited by Robert Silverberg

POETRY COLLECTIONS

Hala Alyan
Atrium

Peter Carlaftes
DrunkYard Dog
I Fold with the Hand I Was Dealt
Life in the Past Lane

Thomas Fucaloro
It Starts from the Belly and Blooms

Kat Georges
Our Lady of the Hunger
Awe and Other Words Like Wow

Robert Gibbons
Close to the Tree

Israel Horovitz
Heaven and Other Poems

David Lawton
Sharp Blue Stream

Jane LeCroy
Signature Play

Philip Meersman
This Is Belgian Chocolate

Jane Ormerod
Recreational Vehicles on Fire
Welcome to the Museum of Cattle

Lisa Panepinto
On This Borrowed Bike

George Wallace
Poppin' Johnny

Three Rooms Press | New York, NY | Current Catalog: www.threeroomspress.com
Three Rooms Press books are distributed by Publishers Group West: www.pgw.com

www.ingramcontent.com/pod-product-compliance
Lightning Source LLC
Jackson TN
JSHW020722070326
98766JS00001B/1